The Scene Before You:

A New Approach
to American Culture

THE SCENE BEFORE YOU

Edited and with a Preface by CHANDLER BROSSARD

A NEW APPROACH

TO AMERICAN CULTURE

Rinehart and Company, Incorporated

NEW YORK   TORONTO

PUBLISHED SIMULTANEOUSLY IN CANADA BY
CLARKE, IRWIN & COMPANY, LTD., TORONTO
COPYRIGHT © 1955 BY CHANDLER BROSSARD
PRINTED IN THE UNITED STATES OF AMERICA
ALL RIGHTS RESERVED

LIBRARY OF CONGRESS CATALOG CARD NUMBER: 55-8733

Acknowledgments

Grateful acknowledgment is expressed to the following who have so generously granted permission for the use of the essays which appear in this volume:

AMERICAN JEWISH CONGRESS, for permission to reprint *The Rhetoric of Intergroup Liberalism,* by Don J. Hager, Copyright, 1954, by the American Jewish Congress Weekly.

AMERICAN MERCURY and WILLIAM S. POSTER, for permission to reprint *Sense and Nonsense,* by William S. Poster, Copyright, 1951, by American Mercury.

WILLIAM BARRETT, for permission to reprint *New Innocents Abroad,* by William Barrett, Copyright, 1950, by Partisan Review.

JAMES BROWN ASSOCIATES and PARTISAN REVIEW, for permission to reprint *Popular Taste and "The Caine Mutiny,"* by Harvey Swados, Copyright, 1953, by Partisan Review.

COMMENTARY, for permission to reprint *Dashiell Hammett's "Private Eye,"* by David T. Bazelon, Copyright, 1949, by the American Jewish Committee; *Plaint of a Gentile Intellectual,* by Chandler Brossard, Copyright, 1950, by the American Jewish Committee; *Hail, Meeters! Greeters, Farewell!,* by Reuel Denney, Copyright, 1951, by the American Jewish Committee; *Movies Aren't Movies Any More,* by Manny Farber, Copyright, 1952, by the American Jewish Committee; *Why Americans Feel Insecure,* by Arnold Green, Copyright, 1948, by the American Jewish Committee; *The American Woman as Snow-Queen,* by Elizabeth Hardwick, Copyright, 1951, by the American Jewish Committee; *Greenwich Village: Decline and Fall,* by Milton Klonsky, Copyright, 1948, by the American Jewish Committee; *Our Middle-Aged "Young Writers,"* by Seymour Krim, Copyright, 1952, by the American Jewish Committee; *Our Changing Ideals, as Seen on TV,* by Norman Podhoretz, Copyright, 1953, by the American Jewish Committee; *From Little Nemo to Li'l Abner*, by Heinz Politzer, Copyright, 1949, by the American Jewish Committee; *The Psychoanalysts and the Writer*, by Harold Rosenberg, Copyright, 1950, by the American Jewish Committee; *The Liberal Conscience in "The Crucible,"* by Robert Warshow, Copyright, 1953, by the American Jewish Committee; and *Ecstatic in Blackface: The Negro as Song-and-Dance Man*, by Bernard Wolfe, Copyright, 1949, by the American Jewish Committee.

CLEMENT GREENBERG, for permission to reprint *American Type Painting*, by Clement Greenberg, Copyright, 1955, by the American Jewish Committee.

MARSHALL McLUHAN, for permission to reprint *The Psychopathology of Time and Life*, Copyright, 1949, by Neurotica.

PARTISAN REVIEW, for permission to reprint *A Portrait of the Hipster*, by Anatole Broyard, Copyright, 1948, by Partisan Review; *American Painting Since 1940*, by Clement Greenberg, Copyright, 1955, by Partisan Review; *Muskrat Ramble: Popular and Unpopular Music*, by Weldon Kees, Copyright, 1948, by Partisan Review; and *The Highbrow in American Politics*, by Arthur Schlesinger, Jr., Copyright, 1953, by Partisan Review.

THE VIKING PRESS, for permission to reprint *Sex and Science: The Kinsey Report* from THE LIBERAL IMAGINATION, by Lionel Trilling, Copyright, 1948, 1950, by Lionel Trilling.

SUE S. WOLPERT and PARTISAN REVIEW, for permission to reprint *The American Intelligentsia*, by J. F. Wolpert, Copyright, 1947, by Partisan Review.

Contents

To Guy Hottel

To Our Hotel

Preface

The purpose of this book is to give the reader a kaleidoscopic view of the contemporary American cultural scene. A view that cuts through the sentimentality, wrongness, clichés and myths that have, through the years, settled on our subject like radioactive sludge. The people who wrote these pieces—or critical studies, if you prefer—are perceptive, serious, sensitive people. They are not journalistic or academic hacks or professional "commentators" whose livelihood depends on their constantly commenting even though they do it in a vacuum. They are not trying to kid anybody or be cute or set up between themselves and the reader any false cameraderie. They have spent a good many years trying honestly to comprehend, with as few preconceptions as possible, that astonishing phenomenon, the American experience. I am grateful to them for deciding to put down their observations for others to read, for each piece has added something to my own understanding, sharpened it, clarified it, or even in some cases totally changed it. I hope that after reading the book, a lot of other people say the same thing.

I would like to thank the editors of *Partisan Review*, *Commentary*, *Neurotica*, and *The American Mercury* for permission to reprint work from their pages. A great deal of this work (which has been published over the last ten years) originally appeared in *Commentary*, whose editors have been almost uniquely aware of the need to define American culture, in the broadest sense, and who have pursued this awareness with diligence and originality. Because of this their magazine remains one of the very few current publications one can scan without feeling disappointed or embarrassed. The man who pioneered a great deal of this work on *Commentary*, Robert Warshow, died suddenly while this book was in preparation. His death deprived America of one of her finest editors and intellectuals.

My particular thanks on this whole undertaking are due

David T. Bazelon and Herbert Poster and William Poster. Men of vision, they helped spring the mote from my eye.

CHANDLER BROSSARD

New York City, 1955

The Scene Before You:

A New Approach
to American Culture

Movies Aren't Movies

Any More
by Manny Farber

SOMEBODY once told me, no doubt inaccurately, that lady golfers in the Victorian era used a certain gimmick that went by the name of "Gimp." It was a cord running from hem of skirt to waistband; when preparing to hit the ball, you flicked it with your little finger and up came the hem. Thus suddenly, for a brief instant, it revealed Kro-Flite, high-button shoes, and greensward, but left everything else carefully concealed behind yards of eyeleted cambric. Something like this device has now been developed in Hollywood. Whenever the modern film-maker feels that his movie has taken too conventional a direction and is neglecting "art," he need only jerk the Gimp-string, and behold!— curious and exotic but "psychic" images are flashed before the audience, pepping things up at the crucial moment, making you think such thoughts as "The hero has a mother complex," or "He slapped that girl out of ambivalent rage at his father image which he says he carries around in his stomach," or "He chomps angrily on unlit cigarettes to show he comes from a Puritan environment and has a will of iron."

Over the past couple of years one movie after another has been filled with low-key photography, shallow perspectives, screwy pantomime, ominously timed action, hollow-sounding voices. All this pseudo-undershot stuff, swiped from any and every "highbrow" work of films, painting, literature, has gone into ultra-serious movies that express enough discontent with capitalist society to please any progressive. In these beautifully controlled Freud-Marx epics, the only things that really move are the tricks and symbols designed to make you think, "God, this is sensitive!"

Somehow the nature of this new mannerist flicker has been misinterpreted by critics, by the good ones as well as the merely earnest publicists. With their preconceptions, their ennui, and their formularized responses to stimuli, the critics go their complacent (or disgruntled) ways, finding movies better (or worse) than ever, but never noticing that movies *aren't* movies any more. Not so long ago, the movies, whatever their over-simplifications and distortions, still rested on the assumption that their function was to present some intelligible, structured image of reality—on the simplest level, to tell a story and to entertain, but, more generally, to extend the spectator's meaningful experience, to offer him a window on the real world. What are they now?

Well, icebergs of a sort, one-tenth image, action, plot, nine-tenths submerged popular "insights" *à la* Freud or Jung, Marx or Lerner, Sartre or Saroyan, Frost, Dewey, Auden, Mann, or whomever else the producer's been reading; or they are Dali paintings, surrealist fun-houses with endless doors leading the spectator to inward "awareness" and self-consciousness, and far away from a simple ninety-cent seat in a simple mansion of leisure-time art and entertainment; or they are expressionistic shotguns peppering the brain of that deplored "escapist" with millions of equally important yet completely unrelated pellets of message—messages about the human personality and its relations to politics, anthropology, furniture, success, Mom, etc., etc. The trick consists in taking things that don't belong together, charging them up with hidden meanings, and then uniting them in an uneasy juxtaposition that is bound to shock the spectator into a lubricated state of mind where he is forced to think seriously about the phony implications of what he is seeing.

Most readers will remember the calculated moment in *Sunset Boulevard*—the kept man in the fashionable men's shop, ashamed of buying the camel's-hair coat with the ex-star's money. Up to a certain point, this scene was unfolded in a straight narrative line, and then Director Wilder pulled his Gimp-string. The camera moved in for a very close close-up, the atmosphere became molecular and as though diseased—and there was a sleek clerk whispering to the slightly ill gigolo: "After all, if the lady is paying. . . ." Thus Wilder registered spiritual sickness and business-world corruption in an adlibbed shot that had all the freshness of an old tire patch, consisting as it did, under the circumstances, of naive moral gibberish that no adult in his right mind would mouth. This indirect shot, with its laden overpantomiming going back to and beyond Theda Bara, offers a classic example of what the Gimp can do for a director, helping him avoid monotony (by switching from storytelling to symbolic "pseudo-action"), explaining hidden content, and insuring his position in movies as a brave, intransigent artist.

One of the most confusing films of all time, *People Will Talk*, dealt with an unflaggingly urbane gynecologist, a liberal-minded doctor who cured patients with friendliness, played with electric trains, scoffed at radio programs and packaged food, and generally behaved like a Lubitsch portrait of an enlightened college professor. One scene showed him making vague epigrams and looking down his nose at overconscientious note-takers in an anatomy class. Obviously all this suavity needed some excitement, and so Director Mankiewicz jerked his string and provided the well-analyzed doctor with a weird trick that you'll never see again in a movie. The doctor undrapes the corpse on the slab before him, and—surprise!—you are looking at a naked brunette, not only the most ravishing person in the movie but the whitest and least dead-looking. While the doctor talked on about heartless people and gracefully did things with the corpse's Godiva-like tresses, the audience was so shocked by the beauty and lifelikeness of the corpse that it started thinking all sorts of things about how society nags the individual, even unto death. (Visually, in the best Gimp tradition, this scene was bewitching for its pure unusualness; Cary Grant's classy erotic playing with the dead girl evokes a compound of evil, new kinds of sex, and terrific grace.)

The Gimp is the technique, in effect, of enhancing the ordinary with a different dimension, sensational and yet seemingly credible. Camera set-ups, bits of business, lines ("They don't make faces like that any more") are contrived into saying too much. Every moment of a movie is provided with comment about American society. "Original" characters are sought, the amount of illogical and implausible material is increased, to such a point that movies which try to be semi-documentary actually seem stranger than the Tarzan-Dracula-King Kong fantasy.

We are getting such characters as the abortionist in *Detective Story*, a close-mouthed Dutchman dressed like a low-paid, respectable clerk from an early Sinclair Lewis story about department store life in the Midwest. To make him look as though he has emerged from the bowels of common life in America, he is given a pinched, deathly pallor and a sickly personality that hardly allows him to breathe, much less talk. The apparent intention was to set up a significantly ordinary, true-to-life, entirely evil, grass-roots American; the result was a surrealistic creature who seemed ready at any moment to throw up. Thanks to the canny acting of George Macready, possibly Hollywood's most impressive character actor, this sour figure provided the film with its only good moments.

Two recent pictures have made especially adroit and unrelenting use of the Gimp. In *A Place in the Sun*, Director George Stevens, not content with letting a climax of violence follow naturally upon an inevitable train of events, treats us constantly to macabre darkenings of the landscape, metronometimed hootings of a loon, and about six other sensational effects reeking with recondite significance. The story is about a not quite bright social climber, and Stevens so buries him in symbols of money, dominance, and sex that every last member of the audience must become involved with the vague meanings of the boy's daydreams. Wherever he walks, there is sex or wealth—usually both together —written out so big that no one can miss it: billboards that out-Petty Petty, languid and sophisticated aristocrats, a Gus Kahn love lyric coming from a midget radio. And of course his dingy furnished room in a depressed urban area must have a window facing on a huge neon factory sign standing for wealth and achievement.

In one protracted example of contrivance, a luscious babe in a Cadillac flashes by the boy as he hitchhikes on some spacious highway, and then comes a broken-down truck chugging straight out of *The Grapes of Wrath* to pick up the disappointed hiker. Immediately, the audience was saying to itself one or all of these things: "This is about the unfair distribution of wealth in the United States," or "His spirit is crying out for joy, ease, and love," or "He has a complex about being raised in a poor, harsh, confined neighborhood." Whenever any particularly delectable symbol crossed the boy's line of vision, he would freeze up with yearning, refusing to act, not answering questions for minutes on end, his wispy shoulders almost but not quite jerking, and occasionally one dead word straying out of his twisted mouth. There were eccentric scenes in which the boy met up with a deputy cop or a suspicious boatman, who—with the help of acting that was probably coached by Emily Brontë, and camera angles that gave the actors height and took away width—looked like ominous scoundrels from the Dark Ages, and showed you Society intimidating the Outcast, American Justice breaking the Common Man on the wheel.

Symbols are a dime a dozen in Hollywood's storehouse, and Stevens bought up the stock; police sirens, train whistles, double-shots of a boy's face and a remembered kiss, the lame leg of the sadistic district attorney (which makes him more formidable), a shadow going over a face to indicate an evil thought. Such things may seem to come from real life, but actually they are the products of medieval imaginations capable of grasping glaring features of contemporary life only in cliché terms. These creators have entrenched themselves within a vicious circle of decay: having helped to create and foster the world of lurid wealth, romantic love, and Big City glamor, they now express despair and chaos by exaggerating the same corny symbols they originally invented.

It has always been obvious that the movie camera not only reflects reality but interprets it. This fact used to imply the deepening and enrichment of an intelligible structure of plot and character. What is happening now is the complete disappearance of reality in the fog of interpretation: the underground "meaning" of every shot displaces the actual content, and the movie-goer is confronted with a whole crowd of undefined symbolic "meanings" floating entirely free. Shove the camera up against the pimple on an actor's face, and you automatically produce an image of immense importance: it will mean *something*—no matter if you don't know exactly what, and no matter if you have made it impossible to tell your story. Just as comedians now manufacture their humor out of immense card indexes of gags, so movie di-

rectors dip into their mental gag file of disconnected bits of social
significance, amateur psychiatry, and visual shock effects.

   In *A Streetcar Named Desire*, Elia Kazan pulls the Gimp-
string so mercilessly that you never have one plain character or
situation, but vast bundles of the most complicated sociological
phenomena. For example, the hero, a sharp-witted Polish me-
chanic, conveys heavy passion by stuttering the first syllables of
his sentences and mumbling the rest as though through a mouth-
ful of mashed potatoes, a device that naturally forces the spectator
to sociological speculation; disgusted with the fact that the hero
has apparently been raised in a pigpen, the spectator is impelled
to think about the relation of environment to individual development. This hero of Kazan's is getting ahead in his work, is a
loving husband, makes "those colored lights" with his sexual
genius, and is possessed of a delicate moral sensitivity. But all
these bourgeois attributes have to be matched with their opposites
for the sake of excitement, and so Kazan pulls his string and you
see the Polack slobbering, licking his paws, howling like a trog-
lodyte, hitting his wife so hard that he sends her to the maternity
hospital, playing poker like an ape-man, exuding an atmosphere of
wild screams, rape, crashing china, and drunkenness. And to make
sure every two-year-old will understand how bad life is in this
Grimm's fairy tale hovel, Kazan hammers his point home with
continual sinister lights, dancing shadows, gaseous oozings.

   With its freakish acting, nightmare sets, and dreamy pace,
Streetcar may seem like traditional Hollywood poeticism, but
looked at closer, it becomes very different from movies of the
past, and in the same odd, calculated way as *A Place in the Sun*,
People Will Talk, etc. For one thing, the drama is played completely in the foreground. There is nothing new about shallow
perspectives, figures gazing into mirrors with the camera smack up
against the surface, or low intimate views that expand facial features and pry into skin-pores, weaves of cloth, and sweaty under-
shirts. But there is something new in having the whole movie
thrown at you in shallow dimension. Under this arrangement,
with the actor and spectator practically nose to nose, any extreme
movement in space would lead to utter visual chaos, so the char-

acters, camera, and story are kept at a standstill, with the action affecting only minor details, e.g., Stanley's back-scratching or his wife's lusty projection with eyes and lips. On the screen these grimly controlled gestures appear huge, florid, eccentric, and somewhat sinister. Again, there is nothing new about shooting into incandescent lights and nebulous darks, but there *is* something new in having every shot snotted up with silvery foam, black smoke, and flaky patterns to convey decay and squalor. Never before has there been such a use of darkness in masses as we find in the new films (at least not since the Russians, who probably didn't have any lights). All this to jazz up a pseudo-drama in which nothing really happens on the screen except dialogue in which you see two faces talking, then a close-up of the right speaker asking, then a close-up of left speaker answering, then back to the two, etc. The spectator is aware that a story is being told, but mostly he feels caught in the middle of a psychological wrestling match.

Though there has never been so massive a concentration on technique, the fact is these films actually fail to exploit the resources of the medium in any real sense. Kazan, Stevens, and their colleagues have been shrinking films down to an almost babyish level in situation and grouping. With slumbrous camera movement, slow choreographies of action, sustained close-ups of enigmatic faces surrounded by areas of gloom, and drifting dialogue that seemed to come out of the walls, Stevens in *A Place in the Sun* had time only to unreel in grandiose terms a kiss, a seduction, and a drowning that would have taken him all of five minutes to examine with the straight story-telling technique he used in *Penny Serenade* and *Alice Adams*, both of which he made in the 30's. *Streetcar*, for dramatic action, shows one big character—a neurotic Southern girl on the last lap to the mental ward—in one main situation: talk, talk, talk with an uninhibited couple in a two-room apartment. *The African Queen* was shot entirely in the Belgian Congo, but the characters do almost nothing that couldn't have been done on one studio set with the aid of some library shots.

Movies have seldom, if ever, been so physically overbearing

in their effect. The scenarios are set up so that the story can be told with a small cast, little movement, and few settings. The camera fastens itself on the actors with such obsessive closeness that every moment becomes of overwhelming importance and threatens to disclose some terrifying psychic or emotional fact. The effect becomes even stronger and more curious when the actors occasionally move across the room and this all-revealing eye just barely moves to keep them in focus—as in *Something to Live For,* when a worried advertising ace paces his office, while the camera seems to move back and forth no more than a fraction of an inch. One has the feeling that nothing is any longer of importance except a magnification of face, gesture, and dress, and that these can tell you all you need to know about life in our time.

All this seems to have started in an exciting if hammy 1941 picture called *Citizen Kane.* This grim mixture of suspense thriller and tabloid obituary, in which most of the surface facts paralleled events in the career of William Randolph Hearst, combined the thunderous theatrical trickery of Orson Welles with a reckless use of darkish photography and funny angles by a top cameraman named Gregg Toland. Toland threw into the film every device ever written into the accomplished cameraman's handbook— everything from under-cranking (to make the people in "news-reel" clips jerk and scuttle) to crane-shots, two-shots, floor-shots, and his favorite perspective shot in which figures widely spaced and moving far off down long rooms were kept as clearly in focus as the figure closest to the audience. This stuff helped make an exciting film, though marred by obvious items of shopworn inspiration: camera angles that had been thoroughly exploited by experimental films, and the platitudinous characterization of Kane as a lonely man who wanted love from the world but didn't get it because he had no love of his own to give. This unpeeling of a tycoon was clearly the most iconoclastic stroke in major studio production since the days when D. W. Griffith and his camera-man, Billy Bitzer, were freeing movies from imitation of the stage. Orson Welles's bold jumbling of techniques from theater, radio, and film led inevitably to a shock-happy work that anticipated everything that has since become fashionable in American films.

Oddly enough, this film, which had the biggest cultural build-up before release since Eisenstein's Mexican film, made little impression at the time on Hollywood's veterans. Only a few years ago did the ghost of *Citizen Kane* start haunting every "A" picture out of Hollywood. Before the advent of Orson Welles, the most important thing in motion picture technique had been the story, the devising, spacing, and arranging of shots into a plot line that moved easily from one thing to another. Welles, more concerned with exhibiting his impudent showmanship and his deep thoughts about graft, trusts, yellow journalism, love, hate, and the like, fractured his story all along the line, until his film became an endless chain of stop effects. At every instant, the customer was encouraged to pause over some Kubla Khan setting, some portentously lit floor-shot of an actor, or some symbol (the falling-snow toy, the bird screaming in escape), and think in the terms of what it had to tell about a publisher's immoral pursuit of love-power-respect. The plot was simple enough: a famous man said something ("Rosebud") just before dying in his castle on a mountain, and "March of Time" sent out an inquiring reporter to make a story out of it. Eventually we did get the answer, not through the flash-backed memories of those interviewed—Kane's oldest friend, his newspaper manager, the girl, the butler in the castle—but in a final nerve-tingling shot, privy to the director and audience, of the "Rosebud" sled of Kane's lost, barren childhood. The story was presented in such complicated ways and made so portentous with the shadows of meaning cast off by a hundred symbols that you could read almost anything into it, including what Welles had put there. There were certain dramatic high points like the rough-cut in the "March of Time" projection room, the kid outside the window in the legacy scene, and the lurid presentation of an electioneering stage. But in between these was a great deal of talk, much less action, and almost no story.

Welles bequeathed to Hollywood, which had grown fat and famous on hurtling action films, a movie that broke up into a succession of fragments, each one popping with aggressive technique and loud, biased slanting of the materials of actual life. He told his story backward—which was nothing new—and slowed it even more by breaking it into four situations that didn't flow together but settled stiffly and ambiguously into a sort of parallel construction. He also complicated and immobilized each shot with mismated shock effects that had never been seen before in Hollywood. For example, the ominous figure of Kane was shown in the dark alongside a clearly lit pseudo-Grecian statue and a vast undone jigsaw puzzle that the cameraman had cleverly shot so that it seemed strewn over a marble floor. The spectator had trouble arranging these disparate items into a convincing visual whole, but his brain was mobilized into all sorts of ruminations about avarice, monomania, and other compulsions. Even the devices for moving the story along were complicating and interrupting: again and again, you went from the first part of a sentence spoken at one time and place to the last part of the same sentence spoken years later; this made one less conscious of time passing than of a director stopping time to play a trick on reality.

Welles also showed the Hollywood craftsmen how to inject trite philosophy, "liberalism," psychoanalysis, etc., into the very mechanics of movie-making, so that what the spectator saw on the screen was not only a fat, contrived actor screaming down a staircase, but also some exotically rendered editorializing contributed by everyone from the actor to the set designer. The movie opened and closed on the iron fence around Kane's castle. In between this repetition, which spelled out the loneliness and baronial character of a tycoon, were similarly meaningful images: Kane in his castle among the boxed accumulations of his collecting; hopeful and innocent Kane gesticulating in front of a huge electioneering poster that showed him as a sinister demagogue. And always, practically on top of the cameraman, his unreal figure suggesting a blown-up cue ball adorned with the facial features of Fu Manchu, with nothing inside him but a Freudian memory giggling around in the fumes cast off by Welles's ideas about how an American big shot goes wrong.

The hidden meanings and the segmented narration were the two most obvious innovations of this film. Toland's camera provided the third, and it was anything but what you'd expect from a film that was advertised as using an unbound camera. Toland's chief contribution was a shallow concept of movie space. His camera loved crane-shots and floor-shots, but contracted the three-dimensional aspect by making distant figures as clear to the spectator as those in the foreground. To accomplish this, Toland had to arrange his actors in widely spaced, parallel arrays across the screen. He also had to immobilize them and cut them off from the natural obscurations of scenery and atmosphere. His powerful lens did the rest. The spectator was faced with an image that exaggerated the importance of the figures it showed to a point where the deep space between them seemed to have been negated. The chief visual effect was the microscopically viewed countenance, one into which you could read almost anything. Almost as important was the static grouping of figures, amounting to a reversal of everything Hollywood had previously perfected in the creation of fluid groupings in unbounded space.

Citizen Kane and its Gimp-effects were generally laughed off by highbrows in Hollywood and elsewhere. Their opinion of the film was that it was too obviously theatrical and exhibitionistic to be linked to the main journalistic path of cinema. But one had the feeling, during the war years, that as Hollywood turned out dozens of progressively more realistic action films—Western, war, detective—it was more than a little concerned with what Welles had done in the symbolic enriching of a movie through florid mannerisms. For Hollywood directors and actors couldn't forget that Citizen Kane was crazily three-dimensional in the manner of a psychoanalytic hour and that it did start you thinking at every moment of ambiguous drives hidden inside each character. Citizen Kane seems to have festered in Hollywood unconscious until after the Wylers and Hustons returned from their government film chores; then it broke out in full force.

In the acclaimed films of the early postwar years (The Lost Weekend, The Best Years of Our Lives, The Treasure of the Sierra Madre, Champion), one began to see Welles's theatrical innovations effectively incorporated into certain films that otherwise tried to look like untouched records of reality. There still had to be a long training in what is known as "semi-documentary" technique (movies shot in real streets with non-studio make-up, natural lighting, spontaneous pantomime) before Hollywood could link Welles's florid symbolism with enough of the appearance of actuality to make it appear moderately reasonable. But by now the lesson has been learned, and the ghost of *Citizen Kane* stalks a monstrous-looking screen. The entire physical structure of movies has been slowed down and simplified and brought closer to the front plane of the screen so that eccentric effects can be deeply felt. Hollywood has in effect developed a new medium which plays odd tricks with space and human behavior in order to project a content of popular "insights" beneath a meager surface.

Thus has a revolution taken place in Hollywood, probably unbeknownst to the very men—directors, actors, and critics—who have led it. If the significance of the New Movie is understood, it may well be that Hollywood will never be able to go home again. Any attempt to resurrect the old flowing naturalistic film that unfolds logically and takes place in "reasonable" space seems doomed to look as old-fashioned as the hoop skirt. For better or worse, we seem stuck with an absurdly controlled, highly mannered, over-ambitious creation that feeds on everything in modern art and swallows it so that what you see is not actually on the screen but is partly in your own mind, partly on the screen, and partly behind it. You have to read these pictures in a completely different way from the one you've been accustomed to. They are no longer literally stories or motion pictures, but a succession of static hieroglyphs in which overtones of meaning have replaced, in interest as well as in intent, the old concern with narrative, character, and action for their own sakes. These films must be seen, not literally, but as X-rays of the pluralistic modern mind. But the popular ideas deliberately half-buried in them have the hard, crude ring of Stone Age tools, though most of them come out of psychoanalysis and the Popular Front morality plays of the depression. The most ambitious of the current film-makers got their higher, and highest, education in the New York of the latter 30's and have never lost the obsessive need to "improve" the world through art. They are by now too sophisticated and weary really to believe that this will work, but the hangover of conscience, regret, guilt, and frustration still produces in their movies the new Worried Look. They have lost the spirit and convictions of the radical 30's, but the characteristic feelings of those years re-

main, expressed vaguely in a bleak, humorless, free-floating, and
essentially pointless misanthropy—social significance gone sour.
There may be nothing wrong with misanthropy as a working view-
point, but when, as in *A Place in the Sun*, it takes its conception
of workers, tycoons, and debutantes from a world of ideas fantastically unrelated to current American experience, it is merely a
negative sentimentality. The emotional impact of a technique
committed to elegant, controlled, mismated power effects is as
modern as ammoniated toothpaste; but the popular ideas to which
this technique is wedded seem almost as dated and provincial as
those in *Damaged Goods* or *A Fool There Was*.

Greenwich Village:

Decline and Fall

by Milton Klonsky

Rabbi Joseph ben Shalom of Barcelona maintains that in every change of form, in every transformation of reality, or every time the status of a thing is altered the abyss of Nothingness is crossed. . . . Nothing can change without coming into contact with this region of pure absolute Being which the mystics call Nothing. . . . It is the abyss which becomes visible in the gaps of existence.

—Gershom Scholem

ONCE last summer I was crossing north on Sheridan Square, thinking of nothing; suddenly the green light turned red, and there, dodging in the middle of traffic with me, I caught sight of a man whose face was so blotched, pitted, and scabbed by disease that, modestly (having been ravished before by so many obscene stares), he cast his eyes down with the refined coquetry of a beautiful woman. Where did he come from? And what was he doing out there in the broil of midday?—this phantom escaped from the undermind! When I reached the curb, I looked for him up and down the seven streets that radiate from the hub of the Square. But he had already disappeared, leaving behind him only a sulphurous after-image which, even now, still burns and holds its shape. What a scream, I mean what a laugh if this image of mine were his only claim to being—yet I choose to regard him with a straight face.

Now in the rational light uptown, above 14th Street, which is cut off from the Village like the Ego from the Id, I would have seen him for what he was. "There is the world dimensional," as Hart Crane called it, "for those untwisted by the love of things irreconcilable." But downtown, everything obvious is immediately

16

suspect; and, obviously, the most hidden secrets are dressed in the loudest fashion, if you know what I mean. Even the streets of Greenwich Village have so many twists, dead stops, gaps, trailing ends, and sudden inspirations out of blank walls that it sometimes takes years of free association to find your way around.

There is no straight way. Nobody wants to be tagged—you're *it!* Intellectuals without glasses, poets in business suits, gynanders and androgynes, the shapes and figures blur and metamorphose like the images of a dream. *Come out from behind that beard! Ovid, old Roman spy, you haven't changed, who do you think I think you are—Sigmund Freud?*

Where was I? I was standing on Sheridan Square one night waiting for the electric horse on Jack Delaney's marquee to jump over the neon stile. But just as the lights turned, I saw, out of the corner of my eye, a drunk walk on his hind legs like a dog, stagger, fall on all fours, and heave up on the street. One of the Bleecker Street Goths who hang around this neighborhood pushed him from behind with his foot so that he slumped face down in his own stew. When he tried to jack himself up on his elbows, he was shoved down again, even harder than before. Standing there, I identified myself so closely with the poor croak that it was almost as though I had been kicked, and I who was sprawled out on the street with my head in vomit. But I knew it would be dangerous to interfere, so I swallowed my disgust and walked diagonally away across the Square.

Wherever you go you run into these young toughs, the "internal proletariat" of the Village, each one of them with a little fuse of violence smoldering under his shirt. They issue every night from the ranges of ulcerous tenements along Bleecker, Christopher, Macdougal, Sullivan, etc., in order to escape from the squalor of immigrant family life in crowded cold-water flats. Since the "nice" girls of the neighborhood are called in by their parents before the long Village night is even half over, they are forced to gather on the corners by themselves in male packs. Then to see Othello walking hand in hand with Desdemona, or the lay sodalities of fairies (a caricature of themselves), makes them ache with jealousy. They even grudge the sexual freedom of the Village artists and intellectuals who, like themselves, are barred from the commercial mills uptown. But here at least the artist and the conscientious objector to American culture have some sort of status. The Goths have none. Therefore, the drunk must eat his vomit.

Sometimes I'd come across them pitching coins against the wall of the Christopher Street poolroom and then, while the next pitch was held up until I passed, they'd look me over. *Was I a Jew? How did I do? Did I show any fear? What was I doing here?* Their philosophy is as hard as the cement under their feet. Everything is a racket; the game of life is to beat the racket; and anyone who says no is a liar or a sucker. Their true heroes are the bookies, the prize-fighters, and the racketeers who once rose out of their own ranks and now operate the Nite Clubs and park their Cadillacs in front of the poolroom. One question they can never figure out, and so what never fails to impress them, is this: why anyone with a chance to play for the blue chips uptown, or why any girl born with a privileged face, should choose to live in these slums? And every year they see new recruits coming down.

The Village attracts its own from every state of the mind: some for the faded romance of La Vie Bohème; some to be free of their parents; some out of acedia or wanhope; some to trade in free love; some for art's sake; some because they are zebras on the white plains; some to hide from their failure; some because they'd rather be in Paris; some to do something about *it*; some for a change of mind or heart—but almost all to escape from the stunning heat and light and noise of the cultural mill grinding out the mass values of a commercial civilization.

But not all who live in the Village are at home there. There are also writers, private secretaries, dancers, copy writers, actors, illustrators, and musicians on the make, who come down from the provinces to be close to the Big Time and leave as soon as they can. Graduates of the toney Eastern colleges for women such as Vassar, Bennington, Bryn Mawr, and the rest comprise one of the steadiest sources of recruits. But after a brief flurry of excitement and uplift, these also dry up fast like summer rain. And then there are the fellow-travelers of Bohemia, whose home base may be anywhere at all, but who keep up with the Village line through the auspices of friends. Not to mention an etceterogeneous muster of characters for whom any classification would be inherently contradictory.

The places where all these people live range from the plush and marble apartment hotels on the Gold Coast of lower Fifth Avenue to the cold-water tenements with communal toilets and no baths that once housed the masses of immigrant workers at the beginning of the century. Here and there a few of the old type of one-family brick houses still stand, relics of the Henry James and Lillian Russell era when Washington Square and its environs was the hub of New York society. Most of these have been split into two- or three-room flats, each one inhabited by its own colony of extraordinarily sensitive roaches with long, delicate, trembling wands and Hamlet-like refinements of indecision, a breed peculiar to the Village. The interiors are furnished in a style which, through the years, has become almost as standardized as Bronx Department Store Gothic or Terre Haute monde moderne: chairs and tables and couches wavering between junk and the antique like the houses themselves; framed reproductions of Rouault's "The Old King" or Picasso's "Woman in White" or that picture by Henri Rousseau of a lion in the moonlight sniffing the feet of a sleeping gypsy; floors painted red, yellow, green, brown; collapsible shelves loaded with books on psychiatry, books of modern poetry, books of prints by the Paris school, some second-hand or inherited, but most of them borrowed and never returned; and so on. With only minor changes, it is recognizable as the period style formed at the end of the First World War—the time Greenwich Village first became self-conscious—and reflects all the nostalgia for those good old days.

As seen from the fox-hole perspective of the Village during the 20's, America was a No Man's Land, the haunt of the Cyclops. Only in Europe could the good life be found:

> *Là tout n'est qu'ordre et beauté,*
> *Luxe, Calme, et Volupté.*

The boulevards of Paris were as crowded with Villagers as Washington Square in the Spring.

By the 30's, the spiritual homeland had shifted a thousand miles to the East amid the gilded domes and cupolas of the first Workers' State. (It was at this time, incidentally, that young Jewish intellectuals from the outlying boroughs of New York entered the Village as a group.) The depression fell like an incessant damp, cold and miserable and everywhere. What remained of the enthusiasms of the 20's was sublimated into political passion: Dionysius was reborn as Nicolai Lenin. And, conversely, the café and speakeasy society of those days was transformed into cafeteria society—Life Cafeteria, Stewart's, the Waldorf—where, until far in the night, the history and destiny of mankind was measured out with coffee spoons. To the Bleecker Street Klans on the other side, who sat in the steam of tobacco smoke and watched these tables seethe and boil with Marxist pronunciamentos, appeals, denunciations, charges, and countercharges, all this talk and all this fervor were just so much sucker bait.

Still, in those first years the marriage of bohemian freemasonry and the camaraderie of the WPA was almost perfect. The open collar and the grimy pants served both as well. But afterwards the foundations of this union split so wide (corresponding to the political divorce in the Workers' State itself) that, when the bastard Stalinist type appeared with his slogans, his cast-iron frame of mind, his dog faith, and his carefully cultivated mediocrity, it was a shock to recall his parentage. And the radical splinter groups that followed with their perpetual cries of "Rape!" and their tedious apocalypses—what could be expected from them?

By the end of the 30's Lenin's mummy had begun to stink.

Not the Revolution, but the Great War itself—that was the apocalypse so much dreaded and so long anticipated it was almost a relief when it came. Greetings! "Bababadalgharaghtakamminarronnkonnbronntonnerronntuonnthunntrovarrhounawnskawntoohoohoordenenthurnuk," as James Joyce said. But ah, those days of innocence! O lost Arcadia! I never saw so many drooping fawns and dying swans. The war put a stop to all that. And nothing could ever be the same any more.

While the war was going on, every night in the Village was

Saturday night. Soldiers and sailors of all the Allied armies jammed the bars and the main streets of Greenwich Village hunting for a wild time. But that time was gone. With the moral dikes broken everywhere, and the whole country engulfed by the flood, the Village, strangely enough, was left high and dry. All the tabooed "dirty" words had been rubbed clean by everyday use. Of course there was as much freedom in the Village as before; but since this was equalled and even surpassed by Main Street, where was the defiance and the revolt against convention which, previously, had been the spur? The celebrated Village campaign for sexual independence had ended in a strange victory: free love was driving the professionals off the streets. And the baby-faced V-girls walking arm in arm with sailors down Broadway were wearing their mothers' high heels. In this situation, only the operators of the honky-tonks on Sheridan Square and in the side alleys made sure, somehow, that the sinister reputation of Greenwich Village was preserved.

The good old days when nobody had a job and nobody cared were over. Even the panhandlers who wander down to the Village from the "smoke" joints on the Bowery would touch artists and intellectuals on the street who were never good for a nickel before. And now that there was so much money around, apocryphal stories of the Depression were revived with nostalgia: how this musician had split his personality and collected four pay checks from the WPA music project as a string quartet; how someone else had lived off the Waldorf Cafeteria for a year by demanding a free cup of hot water for a second cup of tea without buying the first, and then, by pouring in enough ketchup, had brewed a thick bowl of tomato soup on his table, etc., etc. But for the majority of Villagers, rejected by the Army on psychoneurotic grounds, the slush money to be had uptown was irresistible; and, without too much loss of face, some erstwhile bohemians were even able to join the great herd shoving at the trough. This was not altogether a betrayal of principle. It was, I think, a means for absolving the secret guilt of not being in uniform. For them the despair within had at last been equalled by the hysteria without, thus providing a precarious common ground for a *modus vivendi*. But a return later on to the past life was almost impossible, as most had, in the meantime, contracted a new apartment, an analyst, a wife, or other expensive habits.

Perfect circles of friends drifted apart and disappeared like smoke rings. And one by one the old hangouts were lost. George's Bar (the ancestor of the San Remo today) was taken over completely by sailors and their quail; and even the last remaining forum of cafeteria society, the Waldorf, fell to the Bleecker Street Goths, who now had it almost completely terrorized. Boredom followed everywhere you went: boredom, barroom hysteria, confessions regretted by morning, cracked marriages, affairs over in a week, violence for reasons forgotten during the violence. . . . Then the war suddenly ended.

After the block parties and the parades under the Arch, it was wry to see the new recruits to the Village come down expecting to find the Golden Age of the 20's or the Silver Age of the 30's, but hardly prepared for this, the Age of Lead. Morale was worse than in the army. It was impossible to rent an apartment without "pull" or a great deal of cash. Through their GI loans, some managed to open new book shops with a room in the back; and there you could see them sitting all day and part of the night surrounded by second-hand books and piles of old literary magazines—*Partisan Review, Kenyon, Sewanee, View,* etc.—chatting with friends and customers most of whom came to sell rather than to buy. A dull business, once the edge had worn off.

What they had dreamed while regimented in the army was a vision of the palmy days of Paris Bohemia with a slight admixture of the American Frontier—but by now, alas! the Left Bank had been eroded by sentiment, and the frontier had contracted to the five senses of the individual. The underground names and passwords of a generation ago were already shopworn, with the new ones kept under the counter. It was also harder to break into certain Village cliques by mere brilliant talk and the flash of personality alone. Somehow the crass slogan of American business— "How much does he make?"—had been taken over by the Village: "Where does he show?"—"What has he published?"—the bark of an official dog. Artists and poets did their "work" like everybody else.

During the war, Greenwich Village had been exposed as never before to the total glare of American mass culture, a light that had long blinded everyone with excess of light. Then, with the liberation of Paris, came the first influx in five years of the new paintings by Picasso (with their cartoon shapes) as well as work by Braque, Bonnard, and young French painters such as Dubuffet; the poetry of Eluard and the cryptograms of Queneau; and, most astonishing, the Existentialist philosophy of Sartre and Camus, which drew heavily for its examples on the tough-guy heroes of American fiction and gangster movies. The anticipation was nothing compared to the let-down. And when European artists and writers again came to America, guided by their customary arrogance toward the natives, they were given a close look. They were like us—only smaller, fussier, dingier, and even (O Ghost of Henry James!) more innocent of the facts of life. Despite all their bitter experience, they had not yet been through the mill of a total commercial civilization—and that was the Real Distinguished and Distinguishing Thing. Their day and night were not ours.

Europe had already probed the nerve ends of modern art to the points of their most exquisite attenuations, from Mallarmé to Proust, from Redon to Mondrian. By seeking to re-barbarize their own culture through American jazz, movies, comic strips, etc., European artists and intellectuals had in the end redirected America up its own alley. (A final irony is that, even in this, America is still following the lead of Europe.) But now there was no turning back.

In the past, these debased forms of popular culture had been something to be poked with a long stick. Now that they had acquired such foreign respectability, their very coarseness was subtly admired. O Polyhymnia, sacred slut, sing for us (if you don't mind) of the furious drives of Dick Tracy, L'il Abner, and Moon Mullins struggling in their boxed and aimless worlds; and of the shadowy Olympus of Hollywood where the old forms of Greece are overthrown by a mechanical Prometheus; and of the soap dramas on the radio where the drabness and stupidity of life is celebrated, and the movements of the bowels are announced with trumpets. . . . Maybe the old alienation of artists and intellectuals in America could be adjusted by a common bondage. Maybe

this was the way out at last. But even if this were true, the sad
fact remains that a way out is not necessarily a way in, nor is
"culture" a revolving door.

The way of alienation is the Jew's badge of Greenwich Village, a way apart that orients itself by negation. Life here is the
ghetto life, indrawn, with its own tastes and smells, rank and dark
and protected as an arm-pit. The native loneliness of Americans
is so intensified in the Village that, paradoxically, it becomes a
social cement that holds it together. For what is feared even more
than alienation from American life is self-alienation, the loss of
identity in the melting pot, reduction to the lowest common
denominator of dollar and cent values. It is from this fear that
Greenwich Village protects its own. Under cover of the most
ideal persuasions of self-denial, there is always a private need.

The radical movement of the 30's was engaged not only with
politics but with more personal considerations: political parties
were places where you met and made your friends. And the same
function was served by the arty societies of the 20's. But times
change—now's now and then was then.

Free and easy love in the Village is a thing of the past. The
night wanderer from bar to bar searching for the rare encounter
finds only wanderers like himself, always on the prowl, always
restless, never satisfied. The more intellectual can spend hours
sitting in the gas chambers of the New School, bored to extinction, but hoping to meet a true friend in such cultured atmosphere. The fairies are the most driven—their nervous cruises down
8th Street, 4th Street, the Park, and back again are like a man
pacing up and down a room. And even when all these find what
they want and still want it, the gossip spreads so fast and the
Who's Had Who in the Village is so faithfully compiled—although nobody cared enough to snoop before—that a lasting relationship is rare.

If the most important single event in the erotic life of Man
during the past century has been the gradual disappearance of
animals from the cities and farms, then the next—although probably there is no connection—has been the emergence of Woman
to the rank of full and equal partner. Women in the Village are

often as aggressive as the men, who are inclined to be somewhat backward as a result. The illusion of emancipation, however, satisfies most. On the corner of Greenwich and 6th Avenues stands the House of Detention, or jug, for women, which hides its grim interiors behind the facade of an apartment house—even numbered, 10 Greenwich Avenue: a demure symbol and monument of the suffrage movement. Like the men of Greenwich Village, women here suffer from the fact that love is not an immolation of the self, but the proof of it: *Copulo ergo sum.* And those causes and movements which once supplied additional proof are no longer viable.

Without any unifying political or artistic center, the Village has fragmented into small groups who go to the same parties, hold the same views, and know each other too well. The Society of Neurotics Undergoing Psychoanalysis is the only one at present with something of the old catholicity, yet with this important difference: it is a secret society, and the membership is hidden even from those who belong. Still, it's a connection. And it takes only a minute for those who are, or who have been, or will be analyzed to smell one another out. First, the shy query: Have you been analyzed? Then: How many years? And next: Who is he? How much does he charge? And then: What party?—Freudian, Reichian, Adlerian, Horneyan, Jungian? This last question is charged, and the wrong answer can explode any further conversation.

For when the political cliques of the 30's lost their passion and died, they never really died but rose to the bosom of the Father and were strangely transmogrified. Psychoanalysis is the new look, Sartor Resartus, but the body underneath is the same.

A competent analyst can read their minds like a book by Freud, which is what some of them become after two or three years on the couch. The desperation, however, is real. Looking into themselves, they've seen the Gorgon. It does no good to pat its ugly snout, or to feed it lump sugar. The monster sits deep inside covered by the muck of the undermind and with its eyes always open. In order to charm it to sleep, or to pierce its heart by a sharper insight, they lie on the psychoanalytic couch in a dark room with Perseus on his rocker behind them, his pen in hand, taking notes. *O why was I born with a different face? Why can't I find a lover? or a job? or a friend? Why don't people admire me? Why do I hate the sound of clocks? Why can't I dream? Why can't I get up in the morning? Why do I bite my toenails? Why don't you ever say anything? O tell me it's true and it's not true! Show me the open way! Make me feel that everything will be all right.* So it goes on. Job, covered with boils and sitting on a stone in the field, asked the same questions.

There is a circle apart, however, even from the Village which is itself apart, where all the answers kiss the questions and all those who are afflicted with wanhope or acedia can make peace with themselves. I mean the jazz-narcotics coteries, the "hipsters," so-called. These are drawn from the spiritually dispossessed who form the underground of Village life. Since they are unalterably against The Law, they have their own rites and passwords and worship their own forbidden God—The One Who Puts Out The Light. The Hipster societies—if they are such, since nobody in them thinks they belong—may be considered the draft-dodgers of commercial civilization, just as Villagers, in general, are the loyal opposition or "conscientious objectors." They take no stand, for any stand would have to be inside the group and therefore against themselves, against their negative principle. The mood which infects them all is, perhaps, a tender American version of that underground nihilism which erupted in the forms of Dada and fascism in Europe—anti-art and anti-morality. What they believe in is benzedrine, "tea," and jazz.

Jazz and "tea" (marijuana) form a bridge to Harlem, the other ghetto uptown, and many on both sides use it to cross over. The midpoint is 52nd Street where all the cats, black and white, can get together in the cellar clubs to dig the latest jive and to hear Dizzie or the Bird or the Hawk blow their valves. Black jazz is the only art whose moods and ecstasies reflect their own, whose pace is equal to the terrible inner speed of the drug. When marijuana loses its drive there are some who learn how to saddle and ride the "horse" of heroin. But once on that nightmare, as everybody knows, there is no dismounting until the other side of the Bar has been crossed. For such release, life itself is a handicap.

Around the track of all these gyres and circles in Greenwich

Village, no matter where we start from we arrive at the same place in the end—beside the point. Without a common focus, images are fractured on everybody's point of view; and meanings shift without pivotal reference. The boundary between inner and outer reality is blurred. What is real or good or beautiful is a matter of taste. Since for our time, and in the Village especially, truth itself has become a sentiment, the search for an Absolute is maudlin. All the beards of authority have been cut off, and anything goes: Ovid is Freud is Karl Marx is Joe Gould is I AM. Which brings us by a commodius vicus of recirculation back to Sheridan Square and environs, like a barber's pole forever disappearing into itself.

I cut diagonally away across the Square, leaving the drunk on the sidewalk, and headed for the cover of darkness in the movies. The theater was packed, people were standing five deep behind ropes, yet, somehow, probably because I was alone, the usher signaled for me to follow as soon as I arrived. While we were walking down the aisle, a sudden blow of laughter from the audience struck me so hard that, even without knowing why, I laughed along with the rest.

My seat was in the middle row, the best in the house, and, what was even more uncanny, two others right next to it were vacant! I smelled them, I looked under them, I felt them—nothing was wrong. But why wasn't anyone coming down the aisle? There was another blow of laughter, and then another even harder, the effect augmented by itself. I looked up at the screen. *A man was being hit over the head by a lead pipe.* Although he seemed in agony, every time he screwed his eyes and made mouths the laughter from the audience became louder. A woman was whispering behind my back! I turned around, but quickly she looked the other way. ME? Now the whole house was screaming. *A blindfolded man was about to walk into an open sewer.* I shut my eyes, but his after-image remained. The beam of the inner eye cast his figure on my mind with as much power as the projector upon the movie screen. As I wavered, two women in gray and black came down the aisle. There was no other way out. I ran up the stage, and, while my shadow wavered on the screen for a moment as though undecided whether to follow, plunged into the abyss of nothing. The man tore the bandage from his eyes and clutched at me as I passed. But the film of reality which separated us was as wide as the abyss itself.

Down Fifth Avenue and under the Arch I ran to the cement circle in Washington Square. It was a bitter night without stars or a moon and the park was deserted. But from nowhere someone called "Klonsky!"—my name. I saw him then as he came loping towards me, his face so flat and black I could hardly separate the features. "Give me some skin, man," he said, "I want you to dig some of this new charge."

Ah well, ah well, it was my friend Saggy, an old viper out of Harlem, always frantic, always high, the kind of tea-pusher who'd pull a hype on his own mother if he knew who she was. Under his sleeve his wrist was pocked with a thousand bites of the needle. He took out a long white fuse of tea from his pocket and bit open one end. Then he lit up with a deep sigh of smoke and, as the image of the burning match reflared upon his eyes, I saw in that sudden flash of insight that they were pitch-black! they had no whites!—like the sooty fire-place with the orange flame burning inside it before which I am writing.

Our Middle-aged
"Young Writers"
by Seymour Krim

OPEN the pages of any of our literary magazines, look at the Contributors' Notes column, and the chances are good that you will find at least three out of the twelve contributors identified as "young writers." It can be quite a shock to meet one of these Young Writers and find him baldish, drinking celery tonic for his heartburn, worried about his third child, and in general a victim of cranky middle age. And when one looks a little more closely at this wry jest of the Young Writer in our times—who seems to average nearer forty than twenty—one discovers some interesting aspects of the present period in American letters.

Let us think back to what Young Writer meant in the flowering 1920's—the era that celebrated youth and glamorized the profession of literature. It meant a young man or woman under thirty, and usually about twenty-five or so, who wrote works of a "creative" nature. It included E. E. Cummings, Ernest Hemingway, F. Scott Fitzgerald, John Dos Passos, and others when their early work appeared and each of these men was in his early or middle twenties. Apart from their actual age their work was also "young" —fresh, tangy, brash, and completely different in tone and point of view from the older generation of, say, Theodore Dreiser (although there was only one Dreiser, to our loss). Independent, vigorous, and ready to gamble, they lived up, or down, to their cocky youth.

Now consider some of our current writers who are identified as "young," either in the Sunday book review sections, in literary conversation, or in our own minds: J. F. Powers, Paul Bowles, Michael Seide, Delmore Schwartz, Eudora Welty, Saul Bellow, Jean Stafford, Ralph Ellison, Bernard Malamud, Mary McCarthy, Carson McCullers, Alfred Kazin, J. D. Salinger—these are some better-known names, chosen at random. All of these writers are at least in their mid-thirties, and the quality of their work is hardly young in any sense. They are a sophisticated, complex, embattled group with none of the high-dive leaping—eyes shut and a whistle on the lips—that characterizes truly young writing. It is plain, then, that in this time the definition of literary youth has been extended—distended, in fact—but it is not so plain what the reason is.

When we call someone young we are talking not only of his actual years but of his total bearing, his "maturity" or lack of it. Today, many of our most sensitive and serious talents are maturing as writers at a much later age than their opposite numbers in the 1920's or even the 1930's. This naturally extends their youth in our eyes. Their output is on the whole very small compared to the generation of the 20's, and this, too, enters into the idea of "youth," rightly or wrongly. A traditional sign of maturity is vigorous production with a clear-sighted goal in view. But that is precisely what has been so hard for our harried old-Young Writers to achieve.

Unlike the generation of American prose writers following the First World War, who broke fresh ground, our finest younger authors have not been anything like pioneers in the older sense. The dramatic union of American experience and European perspective after the first war brought into our prose literature a newness of sensibility (E. E. Cummings), a poet's concern with language as a means of rendering fresh aspects of experience (Djuna Barnes, Hemingway), a technical audacity designed to give immediacy to the violent realities of American life (Dos Passos, Faulkner), as well as other fresh contributions. Here was vitality, daring, and above all the intoxicating sense of "new vistas," as Hart Crane phrased it for a generation. Today's serious Young Writers, on the other hand, came of literary age directly after this outburst of creativity, and faced a new set of problems. As artists they were required to absorb all the radical changes that had just taken place in our literature; not only those radical changes named above, but the even more formidable contributions—evocative of the whole spirit of modern Western civilization—made by such men as Joyce, Proust, Eliot, and Thomas Mann. With so much to learn—whoever wanted to do justice to *Ulysses* or *The Wasteland* had to study five other subjects as well—and so much to speculate about, these writers needed more time to *think* than their immediate predecessors, who *acted*. The creative urge, as it was once innocently called, had to be swallowed down or at least sidetracked, and men and women who wanted to do nothing but "write" found themselves becoming students instead.

Thus our most sensitive literary minds remained "younger" than writers the same age who absorbed less, probed less, experimented less, but hardened earlier. The contrast between Jerome Weidman and, say, Eleanor Clark is instructive: both are approximately the same age, yet Weidman matured as a writer more than ten years ago (and has been going downhill since) while the more discriminating Miss Clark is still developing, and has just published only her second book to Weidman's thirteen. History, we might say, has forced our better writers to behave like perpetual graduate students—to extend their knowledge at the sacrifice of accomplishment—and this imbalance has kept their youth alive if only in the traditional sense that maturity is earned by resolution and commitment, which is difficult to achieve if you are not sure what to resolve and commit yourself to. Born under the constellations of experimental literature and difficult thought, this literary generation had to sweat out perplexing problems which the "beautiful and damned" Fitzgeralds and Hemingways, for all their gifts, were never faced with.

But apart from this there is, I think, a stronger reason why Miss Clark or any of her "group" can still be called Young Writers with some legitimacy. That reason is this: with psychoanalysis and the values it has filtered into the literary life, we have come to feel with a new sharpness that "youth" is symbolized by economic, emotional, or intellectual dependency, and "maturity" by the ability to make a living, to stand on one's own feet—in a word, to be "independent" in a tangible sense. Oversimplified as these catchwords may be, they provide us with a clue. Our most serious writers are not independent in this everyday sense—as their analysts enjoy pointing out to them. They are unable to make a living from their own work. They remain dependent on friends, family, wives, part-time teaching jobs, and many other uncertain sources of income. They are rarely able to assume the traditional burdens of adulthood in the sense of earning enough money to own a home (or even a decent apartment), to establish and govern a family, or to develop those parts of the personality that lead to authority and decisiveness in practical affairs. This means that our dedicated writer in his mid-thirties is often truly "young" in many of the ways that the world and perhaps you and I as *people*—not as artists or intellectuals—consider important. Many of these writers, for reasons we will look into, have been cut off from an area of life—often deliberately—that forces ordinary people to develop muscles, so to speak, on the plane of action.

This phenomenon, I believe, is for clear historical reasons peculiar to the generation of American "highbrow" writers we have been discussing. They were the first home-bred group of writers to bear the full brunt of European-inspired "modern" writing—its implications and standards—and, wanting nothing but the best, they tried to live up to what they *thought* were its injunctions. With Joyce, Proust, Kafka, and others as guides and heroes, the most earnest members of this generation deliberately sacrificed certain aspects of living to attain what they thought was a higher goal. The specialization of modern art seemed to imply a special way of life as well; one lived outside conventional society, and was therefore immune to criticisms of personal behavior or weakness which applied to the majority of people. What we now call "neurosis" or "frustration" was often not only accepted, but positively embraced, as the inevitable and almost holy martyrdom of the artist; the sufferings of a Flaubert or a Cézanne were as romantically sanctified as the corpse of Lenin, offering a possibility of personal identification which gave purpose to one's life and ennobled one's personal pain—not merely allowed one to bear it, or even forget it. In other words, certain attitudes were cultivated to the exclusion of others by the most self-aware members of this generation, with High Art, modeled on the achievement of the European greats of the first quarter of the century, serving as the highest criterion of one's life and thinking.

Now that we have entered an era with another prevailing point of view—that of psychoanalysis—it is easy to say, and many unthinking people do, that the philosophy outlined above provided a perfect rationalization for personal inadequacies. In several cases it probably did just that; but in most the point of view was not only sincere but courageous, and the dedication to the life of art meant, not self-deception, as certain too gullible exponents of psychoanalysis now maintain, but, more often, an ultimate commitment in terms which *then* were meaningful and hence faith-giving. In any case, however, the point to establish here is that whatever the motives of each individual in sublimating his life to a specific, European-inspired, early-20th-century conception of High Art, the prevailing attitude precluded the development of a different point of view, and of different parts of the personality not thought to be of the highest value and hence either scorned or ignored.

What seems to have happened now is that many members of this generation of Young Writers find themselves unprepared for the life around them in today's America, either as writers or people. And their earlier ideals, modeled on a particular time and attitude, are no longer relevant, by the testimony of their own lives. Instead of finding fulfillment—passion, significance, completeness, whatever word you wish—in their work and being reconciled to their isolation, as the pioneers (from Joyce to Hemingway) seemed to have been, they have too often ended up feeling themselves orphans of American life—unwanted, ignored, no longer sure of their direction. And they are too sensitive and too intelligent not to see how pretentious and irrelevant is the old notion of the artist as High Priest—how "square" and romantic against the ironic realities of American life as they know it.

It seems safe to say that the Young Writers we have been discussing have undergone a true change of heart. They are surrounded by a much more complex, challenging, and highly organized society than were their fellows of the 1920's—those who helped give them their aesthetic standards and who brought home from the European experience an attitude of superiority towards America which has lasted until this time. Many of our writers have now come to feel that American society holds values unlike

any they could have imagined before, and they have begun to
see their own separation from America no longer as a badge of
honor but as a serious deprivation. They have also begun to question the value of their own poverty—a poverty which could be
borne with good humor only so long as the fundamental premise
of *purpose* was unquestioned.

Thus it is that writers once piously "alienated" from American life have begun to seek "integration." No longer does their
safety, as artists or men, lie in that highbrow exclusiveness which
once divided the world neatly into the minority of intellectual
haves and the majority of have-nots; the criteria on which that
division rested have lost their bite since American mass mediums
(like *Life* and TV) have begun to popularize, and will do so increasingly, some of the very values which were once the property
of the chosen few. No longer can the individual rationalize his
personal deficiencies under the guise of Art; the ideas of psychoanalysis, whether we accept them or not, have taken the
bloom off any rhapsodic ideas of the suffering artist. And no
longer can American culture in the gross or popular sense be dismissed as beneath comparison with European advance-guard culture, for American life on even the low level has become more
significant and interesting to the serious writer than European art
on the high. All signs seem to point one way: writers now want to
participate more than ever before in American life, and are beginning to measure themselves against certain standards of American success which they once despised.

This has reached the point where many who used to look
down upon the big, so-called national magazines as a matter of
course now regard the challenge of *Collier's* or *Saturday Evening
Post* "professionalism" with new eyes. The emphasis now is less
on the falsity of "slick" stories, or the intellectual poverty of both
readers and writers who commune within the glossy pages, and
more on proving to oneself that one can master this form of
popular expression and break out of the solitary confinement
which serious writers have endured for the last decade. It is not
that our writers think more highly of popular writing than they
once did; it is that they think *differently* about it, and with their

revision of values one now sees complimentary essays about someone like J. P. Marquand, an eminently successful popular writer who was able to "beat the racket" in a way that appeals to writers who suffer from lack of money, fame, and an audience, and from an isolation which except in the strongest leads to self-doubt. Once these same writers would rather have been caught reading Somerset Maugham—embarrassing enough!—than praise Mr. Marquand publicly. Now they get a sense of accomplishment out of selling their work to the big magazines which they often can no longer feel in publishing a story in a little magazine.

Here is a decisive change of attitude, one that breaks sharply with the best literary traditions of this country for the last twenty-five years, and it seems to be proof that this is a crucial transitional period in our literature. Involved in this change of attitude is the growing reaction of our writers against the little magazines, which for the last quarter of a century had served as the foremost literary showcase of the avant-garde. These journals, begun by Ezra Pound and the British rebel Wyndham Lewis in London around 1915— and then carried to Paris by Pound, and subsequently to America —pioneered in printing the work of the great European experimentalists and the expatriate Americans of the First World War generation. The little magazines thus became invested with romantic significance for the generation we have been discussing, a significance that remained to them even during the Marxist era.

For more than twenty-five years the little magazines were looked upon as the only outlets for really significant short work in fiction. This is not true today. The little magazines have come to be regarded by many of our best Young Writers as repositories for amateurism in fiction; creatively they no longer hold the "glow" and sense of purpose they once did. Rejected stories from the sleek bourgeois magazines—bourgeois in lack of daring, lack of purpose, like the New Yorker, Harper's Bazaar, and Mademoiselle —frequently find their way into the little magazines nowadays, so that those once creative mediums now often display either inferior conventional fiction or amateurish "unconventional" stories unredeemed by freshness or by pertinence to the needs of their readers.

But the important point to be made is that the little magazine is no longer the home of the advance guard in creative writing because that very advance guard is no longer meaningful in the older sense, and the breach has not been filled with any creative or critical leadership that might be as pertinent to our current needs as was the leadership of Pound or Joyce to the needs of a quarter of a century ago. This being so, and with confusion of literary values rampant in the pages of the little magazines themselves—to the extent that there is no longer any acceptable criterion as to what constitutes a piece of "good" or "bad" fiction, and worse, no attempt is being made to establish new standards —it is no wonder that some of our Young Writers feel they have backed the wrong horse and regard the once philistine national magazines with a fresh eye. The cost of living, in both the literal and figurative sense, has gone up and no longer admits of lip service to a literary ideal which is not rooted in life as it is lived today.

It seems clear that the change of heart of the Young Writers would not have shown itself so decisively if there had not been a corresponding lack of vitality in the editorship of the little magazines—once the outlets for freedom of artistic expression, animated by purpose and dedicated to a responsibility for the best that the literary imagination could conceive. Today not only is there lack of aggressive purpose and life-giving passion—if one can judge by the often unnecessarily involved and pedantic tone that drones away within the pages of the major little magazines—but literature itself is often treated as a rather boring and irrelevant concern, inferior to philosophy or gossip and important mainly to show how much greater were dead European writers than living American ones—or if some live American is singled out, it is because, by some chilling logic, he resembles a dead Russian. (Apropos gossip, several of the so-called stories in recent issues of *Partisan Review* are little more than expansions of "Did you hear that So-and-So . . . ?" involving Greenwich Village personalities—to this Homeric height has the "best literary magazine in America," as Edmund Wilson once called it, ascended.)

No wonder, then, that into the lap of the generation of writers discussed here have fallen problems that will admit of no easy solution. Writers who once looked to the little magazines for the kind of leadership and sense of purpose which in the past they seemed to have were deceived; as always, they must supply their own. In an age of increasing possibilities and complexity, the major literary magazines have let us down badly. They have kept to no discernible course in either the encouragement or the publishing of creative work. They have ignored the problem, crucial to any magazine editor, of being vitally interested in and then going out and getting the liveliest new American prose writers, either because they are out of touch and have a point of view formed twenty years ago, like the editor of one review, or because they are literature-weary and clannish, like the editor of another, or because they are just plain not concerned, like the leading editor of a third, who said in this writer's presence that he was more interested in "ideas" than fiction, and implied that he wished he didn't have to publish the stuff at all.

Nor are these the only sad charges to be leveled against these so-called upholders of the best literary traditions of this country. In the deluge of articles published in our literary magazines on Existentialism, Psychoanalysis, Marxism, The Negro, and The Jew, very little attempt has been made to relate these provocative ideas *technically* and *concretely* to the ultimate *act* of literature, which is, after all, the point of a literary magazine. The result is that the editors of our magazines often lament the fact that their contributors don't send them "exciting" or "meaningful" creative fiction—which is their own fault to the extent that they haven't encouraged in their pages the kind of thinking that brings it about—and our gifted writers have been swamped trying to absorb many provocative ideas, ranging from the Leibnitzian nature of comic strips to the Kierkegaardian nature of God, and relate them to the seemingly boring struggle of making literature. What has happened in such an environment as the literary magazines have been (perhaps unwillingly) encouraging is that the creative writers have begun to doubt the value of art and have become ashamed that they are not experts on everything from Symbolic Logic to the Principles of Gestalt—it should be no secret that the artist's ego is his faith, and when abstract ideas are the means to achieve prestige he will try to outdo Husserl himself.

Who is to say that our literary magazines, which hitherto have been the self-proclaimed guardians of the highest literary tradition, are not in part responsible for this state of waste and self-doubt on the part of our writers? Have they tried to reassess the value of fiction in an age which threatens it? Have they made a basic distinction between the function—and, if you will, grandeur—of art and that of ideas, no matter how provocative the latter might be in an analytical period like ours? Have they tried to combat, in this age of specialization, an increasing eclecticism which devours thought from all sources—a dangerous tendency in a time when each department of knowledge is highly technical —and inspires confusion because it follows no guiding principles and attempts to construct no consistent point of view?

Surely it is true that the province of literature has necessarily broadened in this time, and that much of it will be concerned with "ideas"; but just as surely, this will necessitate a stronger faith in that container of ideas, literature itself, which must be recreated with the total life-needs of each generation. And yet, at the zenith of this country's vitality, with its character struggling to be molded in art and its imagination demanding expression in art, our major literary magazines do not rise to the occasion. Where our needs, as writers, "intellectuals," or men, demand order and purpose more than ever before because of the ear-splitting jangle of the times, we receive from our literary magazines no sure sense of purpose, no certainty of taste or direction, no critical leadership based on *literary* values, and none of that concern for the creative work of a new generation which distinguished little magazines in the past.

Where the literary artist, whose great gift is his imagination, should be encouraged he is discouraged, his imagination is disparaged, and he is intimidated by the very critics who should be his protectors and who eventually will even "learn" from him, though you would not guess it from their false omniscient tone. It should therefore be no surprise that many of the aging Young Writers, whose destinies were once allied with the little magazines by common purpose and common values, have left or are leaving the fold. Nor should it be a surprise that the few among them who have never lost faith in Art—for the simple reason that they

are artists, that is, men who will literally create their brothers'
values in the light of their imaginative grasp of the truth—have
done so by turning their backs on the distracting contemporary
holler and giving themselves up to the first law of creation, silence.

*(Editor's note: Mr. Krim's point is
further elaborated in the following letter
published in* Partisan Review)

In a recent review of fiction Delmore Schwartz felt called
upon to uphold the Old Lady. He gave what seemed like a reasonable defense of the vitality of the form, but what is interesting
is that he felt pressed to say a word in her defense, as if reassuring himself that everything was all right. The sad fact which
we have all uneasily felt, if not defined to ourselves, is that everything is not all right. We may read our quota of contemporary
novels each season, but the crucial symptoms are being shown
every three months in our quarterly magazines. Where once we
made for the short stories with interest and eagerness we are now
often bored by the very idea of a story; I ask the reader to honestly
check his own experience on this point. In addition, many of the
writers who once had an almost sacred attitude toward fiction are
now turning their typewriters to the article-of-ideas.

Here is a phenomenon which can't be explained away by saying that good writers are not appearing; that is probably true, but
the reason they are not appearing is a general one and the words
"good" and "bad" are inadequate to the problem that confronts
us. This problem goes beyond individual writers and covers something more crucial. Short stories in the "little" or literary magazines were once read with keen interest because they were pertinent to our lives: aesthetically, morally, personally—the whole
kaboodle all at once. I remember fifteen years ago, as does everyone of my generation, the way we read *Story* magazine from
cover to cover; these were "literary" stories, the very kind which
usually bore the pants off us today. Today, as each of us knows,
we pick up the latest quarterly and leaf through for a lively-look-
ing article; that is, one with intellectual pace, pace enough to
keep up with the *speed* of our minds.

The italicized word is my first clue to the deadness and irrelevance of almost all the short fiction we have been seeing. For many reasons—all the answers to which I don't know, nor do I think anyone does—our minds are racing far ahead of the imaginative expression we have been seeing on the page. For most people 30 or under this not only holds true for the fiction they have been getting, but is proven by the amount of skipping they do in reading great books of the past. Out of sheer curiosity I have asked a number of people, writers and just ordinary neurotics, about their reading habits and practically all confess a tremendous impatience with past works. As one painter told me: "Balzac takes thirty pages to describe the birth of a child; I want it in a sentence—so I can get on with the story, but more important, with my life. I have only so much time to read; I work eight hours a day, teach one night a week, and have to paint, play husband, entertain myself, etc. the rest of the time."

Thus along with speed we have a changed sense of the value of time—one obviously relates to the other—as a second clue to the datedness of our fiction. Painters seem to have felt this before other artists; one line now suffices for the delineation of a form where once there would be much detail. But as significant as our changed time-sense and its effect on our sensibilities, in accounting for the tediousness of fiction, is another factor: the unprecedented variety of our mental lives. "My mind is like a kaleidoscope," one writer said to me—and then he went home and tried to write a more or less traditional story. No wonder it bored him and everyone else who read it.

Let us publicly acknowledge what we have all privately experienced: our minds are fantastically active, and speculate as a matter of course about things that are without precedent. The extent, pace and "strangeness" of our daily thoughts—the mind examining and speculating about itself, for example—ranges far beyond what is recorded in past literature.

Now it stands to reason that a fiction which doesn't imaginatively project a variety, speed and awareness compatible with our mental life is going to be regarded as academic by us. Our imaginations, both as individuals and artists, build on the materials at hand: the fantasies that people nowadays take to psychoanalysts have to be incorporated in our fiction, literally or by tone, to give that fiction a relevance to our mental lives. Do not think that by this I mean the Kafka-type fantasy, "modern" as that is compared to the antique fiction we have been getting. The materials of contemporary American life are what our minds play with and it is out of that tension that an enormously pertinent and exciting fiction can be built.

We can take a hint of the kind of fiction we could have from the recent probers into so-called popular culture in America. Here is a "new" kind of criticism which appeals to our minds because it joins the kinaesthetically exciting physical environment of our daily lives to our complex and keenly felt variety of ideas. We have read this kind of criticism with an eagerness and participation that we used to get from reading new American fiction. This is because it has an immediate pertinence to our lives: it lifts the mass culture to our own level by seeing it with our entire arsenal of new ideas. Thus the culture which dins at us every day is made intelligible to us on *our own terms*: think what an enormous release this is to us as human beings! The release in criticism that the popculturists are giving us is, I repeat, just a hint of the kind of pertinence, excitement and real meaning that a new fiction can give us.

We are not getting these things now. The most accomplished "young" short-story writers that we have, those like J. F. Powers and Eudora Welty, do not speak to us as a vital fiction should and once did. We can admire their art, but it has no intimate meaning for us as individuals; this being so of the best, think of the foolishness of ordinary writers continuing to write the one-dimensional realistic story, except for purposes of entertainment. For purposes of art—that is, for purposes that relate to our actual lives today as we live them, hence conceive them—these stories are irrelevant. Much of our non-fiction, as I suggested before, has more actual life in it.

To sum up: the arts of the short story and novel in America have lagged far behind the life we are actually experiencing, especially when you think of the imagination—the sense of possibility—as the most important part of our experience. The "realistic" story as a container and expression of this life has become too flat and shallow, a form that is unable to speak to us any

longer in a pertinent way. We must have a fiction—nay, a fact!—
equal to the intellectual pace and new sense of possibility which
our minds have become tuned to. Otherwise I can't see our novels
and stories being important to us who are, alas, real not fictional
people. Our fiction now is addressing a fiction of ourselves—not
what is actually going on, nor the new visions of beauty and order
which contemporary necessity has inspired.

The Rhetoric of
Intergroup Liberalism
by Don J. Hager

A RECENT volume in intergroup relations (Cole and Cole, *Minorities and the American Promise*, Harpers, 1954) opens with this sentence: "Social change is in the saddle riding mankind." And later follows with: "Poor human relations are sand thrown into the gears of society. . . . For many Americans the current times are not conducive to producing one of their better moments." One ponders whether the grating impact of these sentences on the ears stems from something more than curious syntax and tortured metaphor. At least the title of the book avoids the vulgarity reflected in that of another contemporary volume, *When Peoples Speak to Peoples* (American Council on Education, 1953).

It is often difficult to assess the voluminous literature produced in the interest of improving intergroup relations. It is difficult because while the reader often shares the authors' liberal sentiments and beliefs, he suffers a complete disenchantment when those commendable sentiments emerge as wearisome clichés and importunate substitutes for analysis and social reality. But how does one explain this obsessive recourse to evangelistic rhetoric and moral exhortation? Is it something more than unwitting anti-intellectualism? Is it that the author has not yet discovered that social problems can be both moral and scientific? Or, is it simply that the specious omnipotence of the winged word has so captivated him that he is impelled toward the unsophisticated, the unintelligent, and the merely hortatory approach to intergroup affairs, e.g., "He who cheerfully throws in his lot with his fellow Americans and tunes his ears to the rhythm of their common life cannot fail to sense one vibrant note: it is freedom."

In many respects, the role of this brand of liberal matches

his bizarre rhetoric. He is fearsome to behold in his stance as a defender of "minority group" rights. His quiver bulges with intergroup "messages" hafted to such arrows as "dynamic democracy," "ever-enriched living" (homogenized?), "wholesome attitudes," and "greater intercultural equalitarianism." He is generally a devotee of "mass media" (*à la* Madison Avenue) and of the "educational" approach to group conflict. If it were possible to sell stock in improved intergroup relations, he'd be a wow. But he is continually unnerved by his inability to dent community power structures and the economic realities that give rise to prejudice and discrimination. For him, discrimination is real but the conditions that give rise to it are not. He knows that something is wrong with Mr. Wilson's celebrated remark confusing General Motors with the general welfare but he is not quite sure what it is. And more than likely he favors the "Great Crusade" because it reduces the economic and political complexities of the "cold war" to a rather simple and unambiguously defined struggle between "the forces of atheistic Communism and the forces for good."

But these are digressions. For we still face the question of why intergroup literature predicated upon commendable liberal sentiments is often transformed into something that dismays rather than attracts. This question invites inquiry into the assumptions and premises that provide the undergirding for a type of literature addressed to the problem of group conflict. In many respects, these assumptions and premises represent the point of widest cleavage between developments in intergroup literature and social scientific theory and research.

The thrust of much intergroup literature appears to be unrealistically directed toward the elimination of conflict rather than toward the development of ideas and techniques for harnessing conflict to *socially productive* communal ends. The emphasis on elimination of conflict tends to shut out the social value of conflict, of the dissenter and the critic. Conciliation is valued to the detriment of the intelligent resolution of problems (governmental agencies are not immune to the "conciliation" virus—the annual report of a state anti-discrimination agency pridefully states that the agency has tried to do its job "in an atmosphere of cooperation. The alternative . . . is . . . an atmosphere of conflict." These are not, of course, the only alternatives).

Uncontrolled social conflict can be destructive. But the development of the necessary agencies of control is not enhanced by ruling conflict "out of order" or by ignoring the role and function of conflict in a democratically constituted society. The fact is that in a modern industrial democracy, characterized by a large mobile population that is motivated by socially acceptable (but often conflicting) aims, loyalties and ambitions, and which is imbued with a philosophy of self-betterment and individual worth, conflict is a full and functioning *part* of the democratic order. The important task of creating and maintaining a social atmosphere (e.g., promoting civil rights and liberties) hospitable to socially productive conflict is not to be accomplished by denying the efficacy of conflict in the advancement of human progress. Nor do peoples mature by obsessive attachment to such verbal nostrums as "unity," "harmony" and "brotherhood." "If we desire to reduce prejudice and discrimination," writes Gerhardt Saenger, "we should perhaps not so much emphasize the evils of prejudice and discrimination, as the advantages of the democratic approach."

There are those who hold that since conflict is "bad" and has no place in a "healthy" society, the people who engage in it must be "misguided," *i.e.*, they have the "wrong" social perspective or are the victims of ignorance. Consequently, they argue, it is inevitable that "education" (including the use of mass media) should appear to be the proper corrective. If, after all, conflict is due to "misunderstanding" or a lack of communication, then obviously, they say, one must proceed to conquer ignorance and the irrational by employing the rational. This is not only demonstrably poor pedagogical practice but ignores the impressive body of evidence that has been accumulated concerning the extremely limited capacity of educational and mass media programs to (a) "change attitudes," and (b) to create "a climate favorable to improved intergroup relations" (this is the current last line of defense for the uncritical advocate of mass media programs—a proposition that rests on no evidence whatsoever).

And since the research and criticism that spells out the deficiencies of the educational approach to group conflict has been well publicized and distributed, one is left to speculate about the reasons for its continued use. In the absence of evidence to the contrary, at least two motivational alternatives come to mind: (1) that sponsoring an educational program (institutes, workshops, pamphlets, posters, etc.) in intergroup relations appeals to many persons precisely because it extracts no commitment, policy or performance from its supporters, or (2) that such programs serve as a device for advertising the sponsoring agency—in these times, a dubious and expensive form of fund-raising. And organizations thus committed can only be embarrassed by the rapid downfall of segregation and discrimination brought about by court decision, law and legislation.

The educational and ameliorative approach to group conflict is frequently attached to one of the most misleading and mischievous theories of intergroup conflict. According to this point of view, conflict and tension arises between groups or nations because they do not "understand" one another; therefore, peace and tranquility are best achieved by promoting "understanding" among peoples. If understanding is achieved, if misunderstandings are exposed and reconciled, then conflict, tension and war will disappear from the human scene.

The assumption that conflict springs primarily from "misunderstanding" (or a "lack of understanding") is buried deep in the literature and method of intergroup relations. It is still the bulwark of certain well-intentioned intercultural and interfaith programs. It often guides research and policy in the field of international conflict. The potency and ubiquity of this point of view has not, however, gone unchallenged. First, it is clear that many serious and persistent forms of conflict do not derive from any demonstrable failure to "understand" cultural differences in tradition, language, religious and historical experience. Nor does "understanding" necessarily bring about the desired state of peace and reconciliation. One can understand, for example, that the Roman Catholic dogma of papal infallibility (in matters of morality and faith) is a part of the theological structure of the Church, an article of faith. But understanding this fact does not make the dogma any more acceptable to non-Catholics nor is it likely to prevent disagreement on this point if the occasion should arise.

Second, the sheer fact of cultural, linguistic, racial or religious differences is rarely the chief source of group conflict or hostility (the Cole volume makes the curiously anachronistic statement that "Whenever conflicts arise among groups, the crux of the problem centers in racial and cultural differences" and, in so doing, lends credence to the erroneous proposition that such differences are inherently conflict-producing; not to mention the fact that investigations into prejudice and group hostility during the last decade emphasize the relationship between these anti-social manifestations and socio-economic status, social mobility, and the like). In addition, numerous observers have pointed out, for example, that wars are fought between nations sharing the same cultural tradition (and often, the same "racial" or genetic ancestry). Goodwin Watson suggests, moreover, that in recent wars the cultural differences among allies have been greater than those between enemies. It is highly unlikely that "misunderstanding" causes either war or group conflict; it is even more unlikely that "better understanding" will prevent them from occurring.

Third, the notion that increased understanding necessarily promotes greater friendship among groups or nations suffers from still other deficiencies. It reflects a certain social immaturity in that it assumes that the issues which precipitate conflict between groups are wholly imaginary and without significance. This reductionist tendency is often manifest in the gratuitous assumption contained in the statement that "After all, Judaism, Catholicism and Protestantism are *merely* different ways of worshipping the same God." This is not only a patronizing and unintelligent observation; it dismisses all regard for the right of collective individuality—the principal and irreducible tenet of cultural pluralism.

Fourth, to the extent that individuals and groups become convinced that conflict and hostility are primarily due to a "lack of understanding" then, to that extent, they have permitted themselves to become intellectually disarmed, *i.e.*, they are incapable of recognizing or dealing with the economic, political and ideological sources of conflict. Fifth, understanding is not always necessary in achieving many pragmatically desirable community goals, e.g., equality of opportunity in housing. Jews and Gentiles, for instance, need not "understand" one another (in the cultural sense) in order for both groups to subscribe to the principle of equal rights and liberties for all. It is entirely possible for members of different groups to meet on equal-status terms in the pursuit of common objectives without necessarily becoming involved in a program of "mutual understanding."

And finally, it is something of a paradox that many avowed advocates of cultural pluralism will often abandon this principle and succumb to the ecumenical urge to reduce or destroy the integrity of group differences. In this case, "understanding" takes the form of denying the reality of group differences in the interest of achieving the dubious benefits of "mutual understanding"— and the values of individual and collective self-expression are lost. This is not to denigrate the role of understanding which, in a critical sense, is the power to make experience more intelligible by analyzing it in the light of valid and appropriate general concepts. Such analysis is the sole guide for the intelligent selection of alternative courses of action.

Opposition to prejudice and discrimination derives necessarily from an ethic, and in the case of many persons from a particular religious ethic. However, the remedy for these social evils is not to be found in the realm of values and opinion but rather in the province of scientific investigation and objective analysis. Despite the overwhelming evidence that prejudice and discrimination are a consequence of *social conditions* and structures, intergroup literature continues to substitute various forms of personal salvation and responsibility for analysis. There is also a tendency to overwork the device of pointing to the discrepancy between the "Real and the Ideal," that is, between prejudicial and discriminatory behavior on one hand and democratic ideals, on the other. No one denies that this discrepancy exists and Myrdal made it the central theme of his monumental work on the American Negro.

But it is mandatory that one do more than point to the discrepancy between ideals and behavior. The problem is to explain why the discrepancy exists (on other than moral grounds). One must analyze belief systems (ends) and social institutions (means) and attempt to explain, sociologically, why institutional pressures, clashes between values and interests, etc., often actively interfere with the full attainment of social ideals. If not, then of course the onus for perpetuating the discrepancy is placed solely on the individual; a kind of nineteenth-century psychologism which derives all social problems from the vagaries of personal will and desire (or from a lack of personal morality). In short, people should change, not institutions or social systems. This may or may not be a commendable approach to the problems of human existence, but its capacity to eradicate injustice and inequality is ephemeral.

Probably the greatest weakness in the type of intergroup literature being discussed here is its studied avoidance of the relation between economic and political power structures and the fact of prejudice, discrimination and conflict. To some extent of course, this avoidance is a function of program and commitment. If emphasis is placed on "education," "good will" and the doctrine of personal culpability as forms of social therapy, then a head-on clash with community power structures is averted. And, too, there is the accompanying tendency to regard differences in "race, creed and color" as the only differences with which we need concern ourselves.

This blind spot concerning the role of economic power and political ideology in the perpetuation of conflict is often revealed when this approach is extended to the field of "international tensions" and the "cold war." The 1954 report of a national organization dedicated to improving group relations observes: "But today we are engaged in a deadly struggle between the forces of atheistic Communism and the forces for good . . ." In this case, concern for the important issue of religious liberty is scuttled by the implication that it is the primary issue in the struggle between the totalitarian and free worlds, a kind of modern Holy Crusade.

This point of view is not only misleading; it is strategically fatal to the democratic cause. For religious liberty is a desirable consequence of political liberty. The lack of religious liberty in

Soviet Russia reflects a lack of political as well as other liberties. The cause of the free world is not advanced by quasi-theological pronouncements dividing the universe into believers and non-believers.

It is anticipated that each individual brings certain promises and assumptions to bear on social problems and issues. To some extent, these intellectual predispositions help to define the problem as well as to determine how it shall be managed. But all assumptions are not equally valid or verifiable and this observation is particularly pertinent to those we make about human behavior. For our enthusiasm and liberal convictions do not necessarily guarantee the validity of thought or performance. And, fortunately, as modern man seeks satisfactory solutions to common problems, he is no longer forced to choose between the irresponsible exhortations of the romantic and the unimaginative descriptions of the fact-gatherer.

Ecstatic in Blackface

The Negro as a Song-and-Dance Man

by Bernard Wolfe

AMERICANS, *Life* observes, are not only free to *pursue* happiness; they also believe they *are* happy. "Happiness is somehow a part of their culture, a kind of virtue." But, for that very reason, the average American's estimate of his own well-being is likely to be padded: "There is always considerable pressure on the individual to persuade himself that he is happy . . ."

Wary of this subjective pitfall, the editors of *Life* in 1948 organized a forum to examine the American joy-level. It was the unanimous conclusion of the experts that we "are not doing so well" with our pursuit of happiness; that "there is a failure in America to achieve genuine happiness." This "failure" was traced through several areas of mass experience—our work incentives, our standard of living, our advertising, the state of our "serious" arts, our movies and other mass media.

These are vital departments of our lives, admittedly. But can they tell the whole story to the diagnostician of joy-quotients? Here the pursuit of happiness is uniquely oriented toward fun, the good time; and it has produced a uniquely systematized fun-culture. That fun-culture generates other, richly indicative mass interests and activities which the *Life* panel overlooked. Above all, it generates certain telltale ways of singing and of dancing.

Every community calls out a string of "unnecessary" sounds and movements from its members. In these mass rituals of voice and body the whole subjective state of a people can be read, its fulfillments and its frustrations. These "nonuseful" exercises must be doubly revealing in America—for here they have become overwhelmingly Negroid in both content and form.

"The plaintive and derisive songs of an oppressed people," an anthropologist notes, ". . . have become the background of the whole society's pleasures and distractions." And, according to our

51

foremost dance critic, the Negro "has certainly given us at least the basis for all our popular dances." Apparently, if happiness is "a kind of virtue" with us, song and dance are two of its most coveted forms—and these forms we consider almost a monopoly of the Negro, worth borrowing from wholesale.

Strange, this "esthetic" commerce across the rigid barriers of caste. In two key areas, at least, the pursuit of happiness narrows down pretty much to a pursuit of the Negro; becomes, in fact, a mass touching—even fondling—of the Untouchable . . .

I

"The Negro as He Really Is"

The Negro's "esthetic" vaulting of caste is obviously encouraged and even sponsored by the white man. That circumstance, one suspects, may hold the key to many mysteries of the jazz and jitterbugging arts. And the most tantalizing mystery of all, surely, is the identity of the elusive personality that hovers behind these arts.

Who, exactly, *is* the Negro who sings these "plaintive and derisive" songs for white consumption, dances these "unrestrained" dances? Are we being treated here to a display of "the Negro as he really is"—the essential, distillate Negro, propelled by trance, emotionally supercharged, spontaneous—his dynamic "un-European" self surging out to us through its "natural" media, itchy feet and throbbing vocal cords?

We like to think so. We pride ourselves on knowing the "real" Negro, the "authentic" Negro; and, over long decades, we have come to equate him with one of our primary Europe-evading folk heroes—the ecstatic song-and-dance man. But does the Negro "give" so freely, through his muscles and his mouth, simply because he is "being himself"? Or is it rather because white America, craving a song and dance it cannot generate itself, so ardently wants him to?

We sense the broader cultural backdrop that sprawls behind the Negro song-and-dance man: it is the whole formalized and institutionalized American joy-quest. The pursuit of happiness, of course, is far more than an abstract political guarantee; in living terms it is a mass striving which fans out to embrace, ultimately, all those things Americans pursue in the hope of being made happy. Under the fun-oriented sway of this mass endeavor come "the whole society's pleasures and distractions"—the sumtotal of our activities over and above our food-getting and rent-paying. And almost everywhere in these "nonuseful," "nonpecuniary" reaches of our culture the image of the Negro crops up with jumping-jack persistence, blithely hurdling caste fences.

It is no secret that our entertainment industries have always featured the Negro prominently, and nearly always in set "happifying" images. From postcolonial times on there has been a strong Negroid component, not only in our song and dance music, but in our vaudeville, drama, cartoons, popular humor, and related fields; and today it shows up, sometimes overwhelmingly, in movies, best sellers, jukeboxes, dance halls, and so on. But this cultural Negrophilia spreads far beyond the amusement industries. If the entrepreneurs of these industries play up Negro themes it must be because there is a steady current of mass interest in them, and that interest must make itself felt in other areas too.

It does; standard amusement fare quite aside, America is inundated with many more tangible kinds of commodities to which one stock Negroid image or another is attached. One afternoon's browsing through any fair-sized shopping center will turn up an imposing array of these mass-produced images: on food labels, wallpaper, napkins, nylon stockings, perfumes, bandanas, charm bracelets, earrings, sweaters, men's shorts, lamp shades, ash trays, figurines, the billboard and magazine ads for a wide variety of food and drink. A good deal of our standard decor, in fact, both modern and traditional, is dominated by the Negroid motif. All this, of course, in addition to the Negro's highly visible presence in many best sellers, children's books, dolls, toys and masks, on post cards and greeting cards.

Most of these articles are useful, true enough; but the Negro image is not built into them for its "use-value." It pleases us in some "nonfunctional" way—amuses, titillates, entices. It is somehow essential to certain of our pleasures and distractions, adds a rousing fillip to others.

In certain standard and stylized forms, then—most often radiating from an ecstatic grin—the Negro image is a central feature of our "pleasure"-culture. And when such a motif endures so doggedly in the culture of a nation, we can guess that it is heaved up from the more profound "fun-loving" depths of the mass mind; there must be some deep-set mechanism behind its constant display.

An urgent methodological problem is posed here. Can any one instance of this pariah-display—the lindyhop craze, say, or Uncle Remus, or the minstrel show, or jazz—add up to very much unless you see the general process unwinding behind the particular instance?

But most of us who are drawn to the Negroid components in our culture are swept away by our enthusiasm for the immediate. That goes equally for the jazz cultist, the devotee of Katherine Dunham or the Savoy Ballroom, the fan of Amos and Andy, the member of Kiwanis or Rotary who performs in his lodge's minstrel show year after year, the collector of pseudo-African masks and bric-a-brac, the follower of Lillian Smith or even Richard Wright, or the housewife who buys those cute doilies with beaming Negro mammies parading across them. We rarely see that our momentary pursuit of this or that Negro-in-effigy is part of a more inclusive and enduring pursuit. Intent on having our particular "needs" catered to, we seldom ask why we so often require the Negro—generally in quite unreasonable facsimile—as the caterer.

We have many fat volumes on jazz now. Most of them, it seems fair to say, suffer from this myopic inability to peer beyond the local and specific. Arguing heatedly for or against this or that form of jazz, their authors most often miss the real point—that the things they embrace or reject, as well as the embracers and rejectors themselves, are all part of a very complex and pervasive cultural process.

What is that process? Perhaps it might be defined as *the mass production and consumption of stock images of the Negro in the pleasure-culture of white America*—including, of course, the image of the Negro as an ecstatic song-and-dance man. From beginning to end this process is sparked by an intense, at times almost obsessive, cultural interest in the Negro—in the midst of a caste situation whose whole premise is that the Negro, as pariah, hardly deserves a second glance.

It may be objected that this syncretic view makes a hopeless jumble of quite unrelated things. Addicts of Negro music and dance, for example, will certainly argue that, whatever happens when Negroes produce jazz and jitterbugging and whites consume them, it is not at all the same thing that takes place when Aunt Jemima beams plumply and irresistibly at the American housewife from a box of pancake flour.

The jazzuits would grant, probably, that when the image of the Negro keeps showing up on greeting cards and food labels, or in the movies and on the radio, it is worth taking a sharp look at. That image is obviously manufactured by the white man, who controls these media, for the consumption of whites, and thus does not involve the Negro *creatively* at all. The white man would appear to be dramatizing his own composite picture of the Negro, the distillate Negro, or hiring live Negroes to dramatize it for him.

But, we shall be told, the case is different with jazz, jitterbugging, zoot and jive. In such "spontaneous" overflows the Negro is stepping out as an unshackled creator in his own right—he is voluntarily, and without cues, putting on display *his* music, *his* dance, *his* fashions, *his* lingo. For once the Negro is "being himself" instead of conforming to a model laid down for him by the white man. And whites either accept his "spontaneous" cultural creations or reject them, without influencing in the slightest the creative process or the "genuine" ad-libbing Negro personality behind it.

The jazz and jitterbugging enthusiast, then, insists on a distinction. There are in our pleasure-culture certain areas in which whites produce images of the Negro for their own consumption, or hire Negroes to act out those images. And there are other areas in which the Negro appears as *himself*, creating himself in his *own* image. The Negro song-and-dance man is hailed as such a self-creation; his sounds and movements are taken to reflect only his own "insides." When this "uncued" ecstatic appears, it is alleged, the whites hug the sidelines as mere passive spectators, memorizing his ad libs for future use.

But in these pariah-elite exchanges the emotional traffic is not always one-way; it sometimes happens that the "spectator" is really the star performer—by proxy. Most often, despite the claims of many whites to an uncanny sort of racial omniscience, their concept of "the Negro as he really is" turns out to be a coy fiction, designed to camouflage the Negro as the white world sees him and forces him to behave. By a devious interracial irony the "creative" Negro, far from being his own spontaneous self, may actually be dramatizing the white man's image of the "spontaneous" Negro "as he really is." Ad libs, too, can be cunningly cued; even ecstasy, or what passes for it, can be an extremely learned response.

No doubt the Negro sings and dances lavishly, unstintingly, to a degree that is unheard of elsewhere in America; and out of his "effortless" creations have come our most characteristic forms of song and movement, the only ones we did not import from Europe. But what we take, in the singing and dancing Negro, for his own self-portrait may very well be a composite portrait which the white world has slapped together haphazardly out of its own emotional leftovers and flung over the Negro. We may be creating, via the Negro's musculature and larynx, what we could not create in our own persons. So that the "happifying" Negro ecstatic we pursue so hotly may be a lot closer to us than we think; he may be our own phantom self—in blackface.

For what pariah can "be himself" when, everywhere he goes, he must pick his way between mountains of images of him, produced wholesale by his masters? Our culture is, and has always been, clogged with these mass-produced images of the "distillate" Negro; and they must act as effective brakes on the Negro's "authentic" self, even—especially—in his singing and dancing. In two related ways they prevent the Negro "ecstatic" as creator and performer from "being himself."

II

The Manufacture of Spontaneity: Image, Reflex, Falseface

More and more we are coming round to the view that the pariah in any caste society is in large part molded by the master's image of him. The anti-Semite, says Sartre, creates the Jew.

The Indian Untouchable, for example, believed that he was genuinely untouchable—he "knew" that any Brahmin master who came in contact with his person would be contaminated, perhaps even mortally. In the same way, the Australian primitive "knew" that it was fatal to let his eyes fall on that taboo object, his mother-in-law; he knew it so well that, when the enjoined looking took place by accident, he sometimes dropped dead in his tracks. This is a very potent and steadying form of "self-knowledge," derived from unblinking contemplation of the "self" in the mirror of one's culture and resting on absolute faith in that mirror.

The Hindu Untouchable doubted the evidence in the mirror no more than did the Australian bushman; but their "reflections" were utterly unlike each other in emotional impact. Any accepted member of a community senses that those who define him consider him a projection of themselves, and approve of him as long as he continues to resemble them. The mirroring thus works both ways: mirror and thing mirrored are indissolubly one. The pariah, on the other hand, finds that those who define him consider him the negation of what they value in themselves: he is an object of contempt. The Other looks upon a candidate-peer as a fragment of itself; upon the pariah as totally and irrevocably unlike itself. Where one is beckoned with the promise of endorsement, the other is waved aside as an abomination.

The pariah is not unique, certainly, in not deriving his full sense of identity from "within." But he differs from everybody else in his relation to the authoritarian "without." For he is defined in very considerable measure, not by his open-armed fellows, but by the stand-offish elite—in terms of everything it despises. A caste man, a community member, identifies himself with those who define him; but the outcast, by definition a "thing apart," learns to feel a kinship with everything that is rejected by his definers—and at their insistence.

Still, there was probably little sullen resignation in the average Untouchable's attitude. He looked upon himself, quite simply, as a man made of a certain unalterable type of clay; if a Brahmin touched him by accident he was as horrified as the Brahmin by this "violation" of his personality. And, it goes without saying, he never dared offer his song and dance to the Brahmin, for he knew that his cultural excrescences were as tainted as his own person and that cultural touches were as abhorrent as physical or social ones. Mirrors, if they are not too badly cracked, can be very convincing.

Here, obviously, we are groping toward the unconscious levels, extending down to the deepest reaches of being, on which the underdog personality is conditioned, kneaded—twisted, if you will—by the emotional climate of the culture looming overhead. For the pariah has few norms of his own to sustain him; the norms under which he is born and lives out his life are those laid down by his masters; he can hardly help but see himself, to some degree, through his master's eyes. His master's eyes are mirrors; his sense of selfness is largely a reflex of what he sees there.

In part, then, "the" Negro must be a "reflex being"—what Gunnar Myrdal calls a "reactive personality"—led by the encompassing glare of his culture to think that he is, after all, something like the lowly thing his masters think he is. But the caste system has never taken such totalitarian hold of the American unconscious as it presumably did for long decades of the Hindu; if it had, jazz, jitterbugging and jive could never have evaded their cultural quarantine in the gallion and the ghetto. It follows that there must also be a more conscious level of personality shaping —one quite unique with the American Negro—on which an entirely different order of "distortion" takes place.

For possibly two thousand years and more the Hindu Untouchable acted not simply *as if* he were a carrier of contamination—he acted as he did because he *"was"* such a carrier and "knew" himself as such. America has never been able to convince the Negro—or itself—of his pariah identity in that all but absolute sense. Even if no other inconsistencies had showed up, our unflagging *cultural* interest in the Negro would by itself have plunged all our caste premises in doubt. For if the pariah is really so unworthy, why do we ogle and ape him so? Why do we rain social blows and heap cultural caresses on him so indiscriminately? The pariah who feels himself wooed even as he is warded off, beckoned and banned all at once, understandably is thrown into a certain confusion about himself.

In part, too, the Negro must sense that he deviates from his

master's official picture of him, the one on which the whole structure of caste rests. He gleans that, far from being *merely* an
abomination, he is in some way an object of considerable admiration and envy too. But in a world controlled by whites, he
must conceal his inner departures from the official norms they
have worked out for him; everything depends on it. If he is not
wholly a "reactive personality," he must pretend to be. When the
reflex falters, a false face must be clapped on.

Unless, of course, the white man will not take offense at such
personality "lapses." That happens in very special cases, as when
Brer Rabbit turns into Bigger Thomas—or when New Orleans
jazz, largely an accommodation to the mask, suddenly erupts into
bebop, a partial jibe at the mask.

There is, then, a nimble interplay of image, reflex and false
face across the caste lines which is death to all real spontaneity.
It is nowhere more striking than in the entertainment fields featuring the "spontaneous" Negro.

Understandably: the Negro is everywhere required to play a
part, whether reflexively or maskedly, and in the entertainment
areas he is paid for his prowess at play-acting. Traditionally the
Negro performer has been, at his master's behest, merely the
distilled essence of the Negro pariah as officially defined. Even his
song and dance have been belittled, by him as well as his white
audience, as dallyings of the essentially worthless. That did not, of
course, prevent the whites from borrowing them.

We do read Richard Wright, of course; we do listen to bebop.
But, by and large, except in certain flitting masochistic moods,
whites will not seek out Negro performers in order to have their
cherished racial images torn to shreds. Entertainment is no longer
entertainment when the consumer's psyche is ruffled rather than
soothed. Generally speaking, we prefer the masked aggressions of
Brer Rabbit to the naked ones of Bigger Thomas.

On the stage and the bandstand, therefore, the type-Negro,
professional distillate of his "race," retains his mask. He per-
sonifies the amiable unworthy—with a most interesting set of
motor and oral tics. And usually he dispenses a carefully re-
hearsed and lavishly packaged kind of "spontaneity," of the sort

which whites look for in "the Negro as he really is." And he brings it off with such deceptively "natural" ease that the white spectator can go away convinced that he has been observing "the Negro as he really is." So, for that matter, can the Negro himself, in many cases. But the real manufacturer of this spontaneity is the white man in the audience.

All this is as true of the whites who admire and lionize the Negro as it is of those more numerous whites who are scornful of him. Negrophiles, no less than Negrophobes, have their own pet notions as to what the Negro "really" is, and become incensed when the flesh-and-blood Negro shatters these notions. Witness the indignation of the white cultists of "primitive" New Orleans jazz when young ghetto Negroes step abruptly out of the Southern folksy-Negro mold to create the supersophisticated music of bebop—or when the barefoot levee stomper slips into ballet shoes and enrolls in Martha Graham's classes.

The Negro, the "distillate" Negro, soon learns his lesson. Whether or not he feels at one with the white man's image of him, he had better act as though he did—at least, he had better "conform to type" when he ventures forth before a white audience. Even the slave who built underground railways and fomented revolts often looked on the surface like a very docile Uncle Remus or Uncle Tom—the genial, good-natured "Negro" whom whites loved to portray on the minstrel stage. And anybody who has seen Negro entertainers relaxing among themselves, with their professional masks off, knows how shrewdly and devastatingly they will in private mock the "type" personalities they are obliged to assume when they're "on."

But in all this routine hypocrisy the Negro performer is only echoing the experience of his people. Most Negroes in our culture spend most of their lives "on"; the eyes of the white community seldom wander far from them. Every Negro is to some extent a performer.

Reflex, or the simulation of reflex—jazz, like most of the Negro's cultural creations, has traditionally teetered between these two extremes. Yet there are those who make a cult of this or that Negroidism without noting this dizzy shuttling between genuine robotism and mock robotism in the Negro performer; who consider the object of their interest, whether he acts reflexively or calculatedly, "the Negro as he really is."

Aren't they missing the whole point of the performance? Instead of grasping the phenomenon that unfolds before their eyes they themselves become part of the phenomenon—for their eyes cue the performance. The more they relish the Negro on the stage as "authentic," blinding themselves to the degree of calculation in the performance, the more must the Negro performer cling to the masks which they take for real faces. It makes no difference whether he feels at home in them or not. His audience does not recognize that order of subjective problem. The relationship across the footlights is not between subject and subject, but between subject and object.

Myrdal sums up this proliferating irony in a suggestive phrase: *the tyranny of expectancy*. The white man's expectant imaging is the tyrant that bludgeons the pariah's personality into being what it "really" is in a caste situation, whether as automaton or as masquerader. But anybody who does not see the subtle dividing line between reflex and false face, who overlooks the point at which *because* becomes *as if* and conscious intent creeps into the performance, has closed his eyes to the real meaning of most Negro art forms. At the same time, he guarantees that the Negro will continue to create himself in everybody's image *but* his own.

The truth about the Negro performer is that he is required to be a *Negro impersonator*. This truth has been hauled out into the open and even made into a public joke in our popular culture: for more than a century, whenever an occasional Negro *was* allowed to perform in a minstrel show, he too had to blacken his face with burnt cork and whiten his lips with cornstarch. But here, once more, what is a joke in mass culture only reflects a quite unfunny fact in mass experience. The very same idea has long been codified in Southern caste etiquette, which requires each individual Negro to personify the white man's image of the composite Negro. This type-casting of a whole race, however, does not take place only in the South: many Northerners, too, feel no reticence in addressing *all* Negro porters and bootblacks by the generic name of "George."

Myrdal records more than one case of a white Southerner

who actually could not recognize Negroes as Negroes when they dropped the role of impersonator. And Negroes, aware of this irony, sometimes toy with it mockingly in their social maneuvering —late in 1948, for example, the newspapers carried front-page stories about a Northern Negro scholar who, wearing an outlandish piece of Oriental headgear, travelled widely through the South, eating in Jim Crow restaurants and chatting boldly with the white help. It may help us to understand the new music of bebop if we remember that quite a few Negro bop artists have become converts to Mohammedanism: they assume Arabian names, study the Koran, salaam to Mecca at sunset—and sometimes even appear in public wearing turbans, so that unsuspecting whites will take them for something other than "distillate" American Negroes. Needless to say, the deception often works.

The Negro must be keenly aware of the white ears cocked all about him, and of the white eyes that "see" him before he appears. In his music and dance, above all, he must be doing a Negro impersonation for the benefit of these preset ears and eyes —much as, to borrow Parker Tyler's neat idea, Mae West has made a career out of female impersonation. To some extent, of course, the impersonation is for the Negro's benefit too: it often quiets his fear of being rudely stripped of identity altogether, left faceless and amorphous.

It might be said of jazz and jitterbugging that they are rituals of dissembling carried out by mouth and muscle, often so convincing that the Negro himself is taken in by his own play-acting. Often—but not by any means always. What we see in the Negro performer is not *simply* the ready-made personality we have draped over him. More accurately, what jigs into sight is the Negro's *caricature* of the white man's composite portrait.

The moment his performance takes on the quality of *as if*, the Negro performer slips from the reactive to the active: object metamorphoses stealthily into subject. Now creation of a sort *does* become possible, and the Negro begins to contribute something of his own to the final effect—most often, at first, as a retoucher. Increasingly he adds dabs of satire to the white man's ready-made image, corresponding to the taunts he invents behind the mask.

These touches, now growing bolder and bolder, announce that a radically new Negro culture is somewhere in the offing.

For the purely passive, pliable, reactive side of the Negro is steadily losing ground to the consciously manipulated mask which he dons as part of a deliberate act. That is, the extent to which he really feels himself to be what the white man thinks he is is dwindling, and the extent to which he *pretends* to be this or that, to achieve certain effects among certain groups of whites, is on the rise. And in that murky inner space where the mechanical fades into the willful lies the source of most Negro art forms. If the shift is ever completed the mask will be thrown off entirely and a startling new crop of art forms will mushroom forth: bop and its new dance form, the applejack, already point the way. The puppet is striving desperately to become its own prime mover.

The Lena Horne who flashes her sultry smile on the screen bears little resemblance, certainly, to the dead-serious Lena Horne who tells an interviewer: "Once I had as much hatred for the whites as they had for me. I'd like to be treated like everybody, not like a freak. I resent having to be normal abnormally." And, in fact, Negro entertainers like Miss Horne are beginning to balk at the standard "distillate" roles they are given to play, even at the risk of their careers. The insurrection against the tyrannical image is gathering momentum: the lazybones Negro comedian, significantly, has just about disappeared from the stage and screen.

It amounts to this: the American caste system, which never set too well on the national mind, is now losing its hold entirely on the Negro's inner life. If he still goes through the motions of caste ritual, on or off the stage, it is now a maneuver rather than a reflex, carried off with all sorts of subtle interpolations not called for by the script.

These interpolations more and more come to be the real content of the Negro's cultural "gifts" to his masters in this transitional phase. Above all, his much-mimicked song and dance are increasingly colored by them—when, indeed, they don't reject the falseface entirely. For now and then, even today, the newer Negro art forms afford us something quite unheard of in our entertainment fare: a fleeting glimpse of what goes on behind the Negro mask.

The ingredients in the Negro personality—passive enslavement by the white man's tyrant image; active and quite deliberate outward conformity to that image, increasingly tinged with satire —have been shifting rapidly in our own century. Even before our unheeding eyes they have gone through drastic reshufflings: Li'l Black Sambo yields to Joe Louis, Louis Armstrong to Dizzy Gillespie, Bill Robinson to Pearl Primus, Bessie Smith to Marian Anderson. And, here and there, something new is in process of being timorously added: a rebellion against both reflex and falseface, a disowning of the white man's image entirely.

It is very much as though the Hindu Untouchable, breaking painfully out of the crust of his culture, had suddenly realized that for two thousand years he had been a sleepwalker enacting a vast lie as though it were gospel truth. If he decided to keep up the masquerade for quite practical reasons—or simply because, as yet, he had no fully composed face of his own in reserve for such emergencies—it would now be on the basis of *as if* rather than *because*. And no doubt he would inject a little "face-saving" satire into his rendition of the role.

The unique thing about the American Negro is that he has *never* been fully able to take what he saw in his culture's mirror for gospel truth. All along, from the day the first slaver discharged its human cargo on American shores, his life has had overtones of *as if*. No doubt that not-quite-real quality of his daily experience has had a lot to do with crystallizing the Negro's engulfing sense of the absurd and his penchant for sheer nonsense. A burgeoning giggle can be traced in the Negro dance from the beginning— from the plantation shuffle and cakewalk to the triple lindy and the applejack. There was already a leavening of irreverent laughter in New Orleans jazz, even in the earlier blues; and bop is, above all, a satirical music.

Indeed, the stylized grin that motored the Negro's song and dance, and which we took for a simple beam of ecstasy, may have been, from the start, less transparent and more enigmatic than we had imagined.

III

Bohemia and the Ghetto

The sociology of jazz, as of all cultural transactions between the castes, is clear enough. There is, first of all, the general phenomenon: the white world, violating all of its caste conceits about the pariah's worth, constantly places images of the Negro before itself or encourages the Negro to impersonate those images. Almost always, of course, these stilted pictures embody stubborn preconceived notions, rooted in a subsoil of *white* need and yearning which deserves the most careful study.

Most of these notions are derogatory, inspired by the Brahminlike conviction that the pariah is worthy only of being shunned. But we do not single-mindedly shun him; on the contrary, we fill our fun-culture with images of him which, although they portray him mainly as an inferior, by their very numbers betray our excessive and very un-Brahminlike interest in him. Why this glaring discrepancy?

Perhaps because we are not entirely convinced of the Negro's inferiority. Among our motley notions about the Negro there is one in particular which is far more laudatory than derogatory. Echoing a set of profound white folk passions such as the Brahmin never for a moment entertained about his Untouchable, it defines the Negro as an ecstatic both muscularly and orally—a natural-born, endlessly spontaneous song-and-dance man. In *that* role the Negro fascinates us.

It follows that in his song and dance, however much this ready-made personality may chafe him, the Negro must impersonate the song-and-dance man said to be lurking in him. Whatever touches of his own he adds to the animated picture—sly interpolations, satirical asides, nihilistic nonsense, mock emotionalism, dabs of caricature—must be applied around the edges, blended imperceptibly into the background. And outright flinging aside of the image, any wiping off of the standard grin, will be tolerated only in special circumstances. So it happens that even the aggressive, image-rejecting music of bebop, as it leaves the ghetto to penetrate into the white world, takes on more and more protective coloration, its unsmiling taunts being increasingly camouflaged by an "innocent" and "high-spirited" clownishness and by a studied frenzy that can be taken for "primitivism."

"The social effects of art seem such an accidental thing," Ortega y Gasset notes, "so remote from the esthetic essence that it does not quite appear how, starting from them, we can ever hope to penetrate into the inner frame of styles." Yet when he set out to study the European music which begins with Debussy, Ortega found that he could make no sense of its "esthetic essence" without first looking into its "social effects." "The problem was strictly esthetic, and yet it turned out that the shortest way of tackling it started from a sociological fact: the unpopularity of the new music."

But how to get at the essence of the Negro's music—and of the dance which accompanies it—from the spirituals and stomps to New Orleans, swing and bebop? One may have to start with another sociological fact: the *popularity* of this new music and dance. For these sounds and movements are popular, in a variety of watered-down forms, on a truly massive scale—among precisely those who shun their creators in daily life. And this paradoxical fact, woven so deeply into the American ethos, can hardly be lost on their alert creator. It must have very much to do with the kinds of sounds and movements he creates; it may, indeed, provide the framework for their "inner frame of styles."

What if an elite poaches culturally on its own pariah over many decades? It can happen that the social effects of the pariah's creations seep back into them to infuse their esthetic essences; that the sociological all but floods the esthetic.

In Negro music and dance, assuredly, the profounder truths are more often sociological than esthetic. That is precisely the cramping limitation of all pariah culture, especially of that intended for export across caste lines. For its content is ultimately the creation of its intended audience, and the apparent creator is most typically only a middleman between the white as tyrannical psychic impresario and the same white as passive side-lines consumer.

The Negro's role in all this is hardly one of "self-expression."

He simply dispenses to his masters the wish-filled image that emanated from them in the first place—while adding more and more pointed comments under his breath.

The core of the jazz cult, to be sure, has always been made up of intensely "esthetic" whites who prefer to wave away the drabber and more sober facts of life coming under the heading of sociology. In many cases their flight to the Negroid is dictated by this urge to evade the grubby social realities which, according to the victimization myths they have about themselves, invade and choke their own daily lives. The magic circles of Negroidism in our culture—Harlem, 52nd Street, jazz, jitterbugging, the marijuana-cocaine-heroin-benzedrine-seconal cults—are for such whites an area of refuge from reality; ostensibly from social reality, actually from their own masochistic misreading of that reality. There only incorrigible "ecstatics," whose vast internal funds of spontaneous joy enable them to sneer at the sociological, are looked for and cherished.

In these very special joy areas the Negro is regarded as a capsule of undiluted "estheticism," immune to the arrows of outer circumstance. Why it should be thought that the Negro, smothered by the harshest set of social circumstances in America, should be the only American fully insulated against circumstance, is a little difficult to understand; but perhaps what is wanted here is the most dramatic demonstration that can be had of the-subjective-conquering-the-social. Feeling crushed by circumstance themselves, Negrophiliac whites prefer to see the Negro as a presocial creature in whom the romping subjective is king; the Negro must be defined from "within" because we feel ourselves so thoroughly puppetized from "without." The theory would seem to be that the Negro is lucky to be a pariah: banished to the outskirts of the community, he thus evades all the pressures and batterings to which one is subjected at the center and which are lethal to the "inner spark."

In this view estheticism—which here means little more than emotionality, instinct-release, the good time: in short, the stock forms of happiness we pursue—is a luxury of the periphery. It denotes a carefree pleasure-bound state which must be given up when one becomes "serious" and enters into the life of the work-a-day community. In our wistful social geography, the esthete is the dweller on the outskirts. The white esthete, or would-be esthete, is shocked, therefore, and even feels betrayed, when his fringe-Negro's joyous brow becomes furrowed by the sober concerns of the orthodox: by "serious" dance and "serious" music, among other things. This, to the white, smacks of selling a priceless birthright. It amounts to trading ecstasy for respectability, sex for prestige, spontaneity for technique, folk vigor for sophisticated gentility, the solar plexus for the prefrontal lobe.

But there is a vast irony here which escapes the white esthete entirely. He does not see that his attempt to evade the sociological through jazz cultism is in itself a sociological fact of no mean importance—which makes such "evasion" all the more impossible for his Negro folk hero. His antisociological attitude only helps to mire jazz more deeply than ever in the trap of social circumstance.

By turning to Negro art forms to side-step harrying social "irrelevancies" the white joy-seeker helps to perpetuate an image of the Negro artist as a "natural" singing and dancing creature who is impervious to the pummelings of social forces. He seeks the mythological Negro—an inveterately thick-skinned idol who is nourished exclusively from "within," who lusts and exults come what may, whom "nothing gets down." And for the Negro jazz musician the presence of such an esthete in the vanguard of his audience is a *sociological* fact he can't blink. This esthete must be catered to, under penalty of splintering his pure-joy trance and driving him away.

Something of the sort, in fact, has happened to the white devotees of New Orleans. They are today mortally offended by bebop, whose essential grimness and blatancy have unmistakable sociological overtones, echoing the strife of the restless ghetto; they miss the apparently unembattled, presocial "complacency" of levee music, imbued with the I-don't-give-a-damn of the "serene" drifter on the fringe. And bop, as it expands its white audience, is progressively distorted by the squeamishness of many whites about "circumstantial" concerns. Originally an outcry against social circumstance, expressing the ghetto's hunger for the "serious" culture of the orthodox white community, bop is

increasingly obliged to disguise itself as a spasm of "self-deter-
mined" ecstasy. From its increasingly "unserious" antics one
would never guess that the whole driving force of bop is an overpowering lust for respectability.

The "irrelevant" fact remains that jazz, the quite remarkable
creation of the American pariah, has a massive cult built around
it by the white elite. And the esthetics of any jazz form, as of any
dance generated by it, must remain an enormous question mark
until within its "frame of styles" is seen the interplay of image,
reflex and masquerade which goes on constantly within the caste
structure of America.

But is this to say that the Negro is not capable of true
estheticism? Quite so. The esthetic, in any really subjective sense,
flowers only among those who, having passed freely through the
community and tasted of all its sober concerns, can afford to turn
their backs on it and commune with themselves. Sartre argues,
perhaps too categorically, that the Jew, so long as he is surrounded
and defined by anti-Semites, is perforce a social creature, and that
his anxieties are social rather than metaphysical in nature: he cannot contemplate his relation to the universe so long as he is
haunted by his daily relations with other men. But if this is an
oversimplification about the Jew, who after all has some alternative norms of his own to fall back on, it must apply with full
force to the Negro, who after three hundred years of slavery and
pariahdom has few norms except those handed down to him from
above.

In the situation of daily terror created for him by American
caste life the Negro must be a uniquely harried being. A socially
produced anxiety spread-eagles over his entire existence, negating
in advance every attempt at a genuine plunge into the subjective.
And the Negro produces unique sounds and movements of anxiety,
rituals of tension and malaise; but social reality is their spring-
board, and social reality their target. Negro song and dance are,
in their innermost frames, laments for the *smothered* subjective.

Very possibly the Negro has a breath-taking bent for the
truly esthetic, all the more remarkable for enduring in an environment which has never favored "nonuseful" pursuits. But like the
proletarian—we recall the many dismal Stalinist efforts to pre-

cipitate a "proletarian culture"—he will never be allowed the luxury of esthetic preoccupation until he has groped his way to the very center of the community, feasted liberally on all its prestigious orthodoxies—and then, of his own volition, departed. The social fringe can become a bohemia only for those who gravitate there out of choice, surfeited with the sober life behind, never for those who are exiled there from birth because of alleged incapacities. There is some stubborn blind spot in the American mind which makes it easy for us to confuse bohemia with the ghetto; our cultural Negrophilia would be impossible without that fallacy. But the fallacy is much more easily maintained by the weekend tourist to the ghetto, who never relinquishes his social mobility, than by the permanent resident there, who is rooted to the despised spot.

The ghetto is always being eyed and eavesdropped on here. No pariah drenched in such cultural limelight is simply "spontaneous," just "being himself." His dance is designed for the ring of eyes peering over the caste fences, and his music is very subtly molded *at the source* by the white ears into which it will be funneled. And whatever the Negro adds of his own to these "creations" is by way of spiteful comment on those eyes and ears, not a spurt of the self-centered subjective.

From Little Nemo to Li'l Abner

by Heinz Politzer

ON the heels of the Truman election came the publication of Al Capp's *Life and Times of the Shmoo*. If, as has been said, Mr. Truman's victory was Franklin D. Roosevelt's greatest hour, then we can easily discern in the almost unprecedented success of Mr. Capp's comic-strip creation a revival of some of the basic ideas underlying the New Deal: the anti-trust spirit, love of the simple man and the underdog, optimism toned down by a thorough knowledge of reality.—"And so, side by side, the two li'l shmoos waddle off into the sunset, confident that they —and billions of their children—will live happily ever after." (But the bulk of the Shmoo nation had been wiped off the surface of the earth only a little while before.)

The Shmoo seems to have laid bare one of the emotional drives inherent in our democracy, and the pollsters might have done better to investigate the right funnies instead of the wrong statistics. However, there is a strain in the Shmoo that goes deeper than any single historical conjunction. "When yo' looks at a Shmoo as though yo'd like t'*eat* him—he *dies of sheer happiness*!!" (Italics and exclamation marks are Capp's.) The Shmoo is ready to immolate himself without any sense of sacrifice, simply out of overflowing love and helpfulness; and if the American people have adopted him for the moment as a sort of national symbol, they have voted for precisely this loving-kindness, which he represents with the exaggeration of a fairy tale.

The master, discoverer, and champion of the Shmoo is Li'l Abner. Li'l Abner is a Simple Simon, a Lucky Hans, a hillbilly. But he is also a giant-killer, the declared enemy of the strong and evil, with a stone for Goliath always ready in his sling. Behind his face stands another, more significant, face, and Coulton Waugh (in his book, *The Comics*) simplifies the matter when he attempts to reduce the resemblance to Henry Wallace. Li'l Abner is, in the unconscious depths of his being, a protestant; the world's in-

71

justice, which he senses more than perceives, leaves him no rest. At the same time, however, he preserves a confidence in the victory of the good, a remnant of the pioneer spirit. "The Lord— and Mammy Yokum—is with you, and He'll help you." America today is well mirrored—and gladly so—in Li'l Abner. In him is reflected our ardent avowal of youth, but also a rather stubborn attachment to crude juvenility; a sympathetic identification with the victorious simpleton, but also a certain indifference to the development of personality—the simpleton remains a simpleton.

For Li'l Abner is not only a hillbilly, a strong man and a roof-raiser, he is also an illiterate. And his creator wants him so. When, for some petty political reasons, Li'l Abner was excluded from the pages of the Pittsburgh *Press*, Al Capp was heard to comment: "You know, one of my friends at the *Press* told me that when they left me out of the paper, they got fourteen thousand letters of protest. Who ever would have thought that so many people who like my strip are actually able to write?"

Beneath this cynical utterance lies the businessman Al Capp's sober evaluation of the public whose daily spiritual bread he provides.

The comic strip of this century, like the *Biblia Pauperum* of the Middle Ages, works as an agent of civilization on an amorphous mass of readers not much more educated than the populace of those earlier times. The *New International Encyclopedia* gives the following information about the *Biblia Pauperum:* "A sort of picture book of the Middle Ages, giving on from forty to fifty leaves the leading events of human salvation . . . each picture being accompanied by an illustrative text or sentence in Latin. . . . Before the Reformation these books were very popular among both the clergy and the laity. Owing to their genuine popularity the printed copies were soon sold out. . . . The pictures. . . . were copied in sculptures, in wall and glass painting, . . . and thus became of importance in the art of the Middle Ages. . . ."

The pictures in the *Biblia Pauperum* were devised for the sake of their texts, but the pictures infringed more and more on the message and in the end made it superfluous. Historically, the dissemination of these books was one of the steps that led to schism in the Catholic church and the rise of Protestantism; it is easy to imagine a Roman cardinal, taken with foreboding, lifting his arms to hurl the anathema at these comic strips of his time (whether he later thumbed through them, we cannot tell). With these picture books, art began to abandon its place within the rigid structure of medieval society, changing not only its audience but also its themes and ultimately its function. The *Biblia* were the first harbingers, not of popular, but of bourgeois art.

Like the *Biblia Pauperum*, the comic strips are based on the picture, not on the word—on the *how*, not on the *what*. The dialogue, the "balloon," is but the intellectual excuse for a medium essentially visual; it is the pretext literate people console themselves with for reverting to the atavism of picture writing. But there can be no doubt that in this very atavism lie the effectiveness and the revolutionary possibilities of the comic strip.

To be sure, the comic strips, unlike their medieval predecessors, have no message to proclaim. They owe their immediate origin to capitalist competition—the newspaper feud between Hearst and Pulitzer in New York in the 1890's. From the outset they were used to attract circulation, and their syndication in 1913 by Moses Koenigsberg spread them over the whole continent. At first, the upper-class originators of the strips poured anything they pleased into them and translated it into a crass and primitive picture language. The comics were originally addressed to children, and since educators at the beginning of the century looked on children as small, stupid, and rough adults, the producers of the comics chose the sensational, the luridly fantastic, and the exotic—cruelty with a happy ending. And this, in the main, still remains the case. "Amoosin' but confoosin'," as Li'l Abner would say.

Addressed to the immature and to those of immature culture, to the dwellers in the side streets of contemporary civilization, the comics inevitably embody a threat. For they contain the revolutionary possibilities latent in all means of mass enlightenment. Underneath all the pedagogic, aesthetic, and moral arguments raised against the comics lies the unexpressed and usually un-

conscious fear that most responsible people feel in the face of
any highly developed instrument for influencing the masses—and
mixed in with this, perhaps, is a bad conscience for having thus
far found no end appropriate to so potent a means.

Little Nemo and *Yellow Kid* revealed the condescension of
the upper classes. But almost at once the audience of the comics
began to project its own image into the thoroughly petty-bour-
geois, suburban world of the comics. In so doing, they conformed,
as in the *Katzenjammers,* to the stereotypes that the upper classes
have of the lower: the Katzenjammer characters are complêtely
naive, eager for adventures and happy endings; they are in fact a
vulgarization of the Tom Sawyer motif, which was folksy enough
in itself. It is only lately that the common man has reacted to the
challenge of the comics by making them revelatory of his *true*
nature. In the long run, the influence of the audience on the
creators of the comic strip, and on their creatures, could not but
leave its mark on this most democratic of art enterprises. Extending over the six plus one days of the week, exposed on every
one of these seven days to the participation and criticism of its
audience, the comic not only takes shape under the eyes of its
public, the public takes shape along with it.

The originator provides the skeleton; the artist—who as often
as not is also the originator—provides the flesh and clothing. Yet
the comic strip owes its earthly existence, its fantasy, its adventurous idiom, its melodrama and shameless sentimentality, its
awkward and well-concealed humanity, directly to its public. Instead of a message, the comic strip contains the mirrored image
of its readers. Thus it is that the comics come to be the folk play
of the American masses, produced on an infinitesimal stage built
by the technical apparatus of the time for the needs of a mass
public that breathes its own life into the end-product.

Accordingly, the comic-strip artist fulfills a function different
from his less fortunate brothers in the free, non-applied "fine"
arts. Indeed he may well be the only contemporary artist who
does fulfill a function; the others, if not caught in the snares of an
ideology, seem today only able to comment upon the problems
arising from their disrupted communication with the public. Like
his medieval colleague, the comic-strip artist has at least a path

laid down for him in advance, and thus he is free to concentrate entirely on the formal aspect of his task. And since his work, once he is hired, is secure (almost as secure as that of the master-builder of a Gothic cathedral), he also has the leisure and the breathing space to keep on refining and perfecting it.

Like the artist of the *Biblia Pauperum* again, the comic-strip artist is essentially anonymous. The modern artist and his work feed on his biography, on the conflict in which he is embroiled with society. His name, the embodiment of his biography, is indispensable, and his work is to serve in establishing and maintaining his name in history. But in the comic strips the fictitious character is more important than the hand that draws it. It can survive its creator, change fathers. The new "authorship" may bring about certain small changes in line, composition, and characterization which the attentive reader may notice, but they make little difference in the general effect of the strip. Here if anywhere in modern art, the old concept of school and master has been revived. The art product has thrust aside the artist; the artist's style is no longer his unique signature but rather an embodiment of the taste of the times.

The comic strips have developed two lines of evolution over the decades. One leads from *Little Nemo* to *Superman*, and represents what the industry as separate from the public considers suitable for mass consumption; it is *imposed*, reflecting the mood, the insight, and the cultural level of the entrepreneurs rather than of the audience. The other type, perhaps best exemplified by Walt Disney's *Mickey Mouse*, expresses the common-man comic-strip reader's sense of himself.

The art work in McCay's *Little Nemo* of 1906 has the bizarre baroque quality of American *fin de siècle*, the abstruse, imported beauty of the Hudson ferries and certain downtown subway stations. The representation of space is theatrical, the arrangement is that of an operetta or opera set. The color, highly differentiated out of regard for the printing techniques of that period, is full of the weary, satiated half-tones then popular in Europe.

Ignatz, on the other hand, the David who forever defeated Herriman's Krazy Kat and was the forerunner of Mickey Mouse, has the gaiety of the circus and of the small-town carnival, a vitality that drives the strip on from box to box. Here at last was the dynamic needed to make a strip a strip. The *Krazy Kat* strip is to *Little Nemo* as the movies to still photography. In order to remain intelligible, Herriman's dynamic figures require an optical concentration, an extreme simplicity as opposed to the vague overcrowding of McCay's static sketches.

Nemo is a dreamer, Ignatz and Mickey are creatures of action. Nemo is genteel, a cisatlantic cousin of Little Lord Fauntleroy; Mickey is a hopelessly immature small-towner, the little man of the people. The logical continuation of Little Nemo's dream world is the pseudo-scientific, pseudo-exotic world of *Buck Rogers* or *Flash Gordon*, strips that are obviously conceived as an assault on the nerves of their readers. The technical or scientific lore of these strips is there not to spread knowledge but to heighten tension by a merely *apparent* adjustment to reality; it is a technology not even limited by science. Utopia crowds out the reality of the day.

Ignatz needs no development. He stands there, round, bristling, impudent, and lewd. He heralds Mickey Mouse, but also the Sad Sack. He bears the imprint of a tradition that is older than the comic strip and extends far beyond the shores of America: the self-glorification of the little man through persiflage. He gives the strip folksiness, but also a true popular character. Originally he was conceived just as formally, or schematically, as other comic strip figures, but it turned out that the ordinary citizen was able to fill in Ignatz's outline with his own self-portrait. The principle of Ignatz's efficacy is not sensation but identification; he arouses less excitement than friendly recognition.

But the dividing line between suspense comics and funny comics is fluid. There are innumerable mixtures and conglomerates. Popeye with his seaman's Latin is a perfect take-off on the *Buck Rogers* type. But the parody is filled with its own kind of seriously intended melodrama. The *Little King* is a petty bourgeois in royal robes, his comedy derives from this antithesis. *Barnaby* is a hard-boiled realist, unimpressed in his encounters with the miraculous. (The fact that he is an American child accounts for his realism as well as his flair for the miracle, and sharpens both conflict and comedy.)

Another synthesis is represented by figures like Terry of *Terry and the Pirates* and Joe Palooka. They are conceived as stereotypes of what the masses now hold to be expressions of individuality; but, through the dialectic of the comic strip, they serve not only the interests of their manufacturer, but also the real life they claim to represent. In the course of the strips they define themselves personally as well as socially; they might indeed contain the possibility of furnishing characters for an American comedy, but the schematism of the strip that creates them deprives them of the breath of personality; Terry and Palooka are individualists in a huge crowd of individualists, as much alike as the houses in a suburban settlement. (America insists that all its citizens must be individualists, but all in the same way. What standardizes them is the very obstinacy with which they insist on their peculiarities, their hobbies, whimsies, and tics.)

But perhaps this contradiction is a motif of democracy as such. The comic strip grew out of the common man's urge to self-portraiture. It represents a compendium of the average American's modes of behavior in every stratum of American mass civilization for the last half-century. It is the comprehensive presentation of the general behavior of the American man, a history of manners.

The comics are less revealing when it comes to women. Here they have committed themselves to the French Doll, an expressionless mask in every conceivable costume. Woman has become a taboo, hidden behind a symbol. This would seem to indicate that American society, among the middle classes at least, is still predominantly masculine. The female character has life and individuality only when a woman does the drawings, as in Virginia Clark's *Oh, Diana*. Or the empty dream-figure that represents Woman becomes converted into its opposite and takes the shape of aggressive brutality, as in Popeye's Olive Oyl or in Maggie of *Bringing Up Father*. But here, too, the woman remains little more than a function of the male imagination.

I nearly forgot Mammy Yokum, the extraordinary mother of the extraordinary Li'l Abner. "Vaguely female," she is carved from the wood of the mandrake root; she is one of the great mothers who live on in the subconscious of the people, of every people. She is realistic and poetic in one. In this dwarfish, pipe-smoking, "vision conjurin' " matron, the people as such for the first time enter the American comic strip. Mammy Yokum stands in the background—or, rather, Li'l Abner is given a larger dimension proper to himself, like the saints in early medieval painting where everything incidental recedes—and yet it is she who fills the page after all; if she gives precedence to her son, she can well afford to do it, for she is the mightier of the two. Here we discern far more matriarchy and true feminocracy than in the pipe dreams of Blondie or Dixie Dugan.

Like all folk plays since the days of the ancient mime, the comic strip revolves around the stock figure. Intrinsically, the stock figure is the target of every possible identification, the schematic type into which every onlooker can project his own peculiarity, provided it does not shatter the general image. Through this projection, the stock figure is solidified and filled out, and achieves a kind of immortality; if, for technical reasons, it is removed from the stage of the comics, its departure becomes a public loss. That is why the comic strip, in its typical form, can afford to be as tedious, for example, as a novel by Dickens— where the reader also feels at home because the art is as slow and devious as life and shows him his own experience as he himself conceives of it.

Nameless as the creator of the strip may be, the name of his main character is vital; sometimes indeed the name is the whole content of the character. The register of names and destinies extends from Alley Oop to Yanitor Yens Yensen. Sometimes a name proves completely successful, as with the Katzenjammers, who carry the whole origin, atmosphere, and dynamic of their existence in their name. The German descent of the Katzenjammers not only contributes an invaluable linguistic touch; it is as though the strip wished to recall its own descent from the European picture book—in the case of the Katzenjammers from

Max and Moritz, the bad boys of the inspired sadist Wilhelm
Busch. Or a character's occupation may be added to reinforce his
name in establishing his personality and often foreshadowing his
destiny.

It is here that Abie the Agent comes in. Abie Kabibble is as
Jewish as the Katzenjammers are German: in him the ethnic
minority enriches the American scene by the peculiarity of its
speech, mentality, and group character. Abie is a *shlemiel* and a
realist, outrageously sentimental and stubbornly matter-of-fact,
the wandering Jew taking a short rest in the suburbs of the world.
But the suburbs are those of pre-World War I America. Abie
shows neither complacency nor self-hatred; his flat feet have
plodded into reality and there he has settled down. He is the
general underdog, proclaiming the philosophy of the socially un-
derprivileged. He, too, is the last, the best of all the game. In his
mouth, to be sure, this assurance has a faintly ironic ring.

Abie the Agent is the explicit contribution of American Jewry
to the comic strip. Elsewhere, Jews function more as a leaven and
a seasoning. Such artists as Rube Goldberg season the general
trends with their wit rather than reflect themselves. And with
Alfred Gerald Caplin who is Al Capp, American Jewry demonstrates its advanced position in American society. Al Capp has
only to express in his strip his own desires, drives, and anxieties—
like, say, Saul Steinberg in his cartoons—in order to answer the
desires, drives, and anxieties of all his contemporaries, regardless
of variety of origin or creed. By their very names, Abie and Li'l
Abner show the stages in the path American Jews have followed
in integrating themselves in the context of American civilization.

In its names, the strip often parodies the mystic possibilities
of nomenclature, sometimes in a way that is positively thematic,
as after the birth of Toots and Casper's Buttercup. But it also
exploits the magic of names: in alliterations like *Donald Duck*,
in rhymes like *Silly Milly* (who is by no means silly; with her, as
with the Marx Brothers, the nonsensical sometimes borders on
revelation); or in the pun, as in *Claire Voyant* or *Ella Cinders*
(=Cinderella). Or the name is eliminated and gives way to the
situation, as in *Mr. and Mrs.* or *Bringing Up Father*—both rela-

tively early products. But there the artist intervenes, substituting for the name the graphic formula of a physiognomy.

The faces and figures of the comic strip, like the names, are abbreviations of characters and lives. *Yellow Kid* and *Little Nemo* are still, from the point of view of graphic characterization, nameless and indistinct; the scene is smothered in detail. The umbilical cord attaching them to English book illustration and to stage design has not yet been cut. But *Mutt and Jeff* already has that clarity of outline, that economy of stroke, and that forceful grouping of light and dark surfaces which characterize the good comic strip and are essential to its speed.

Living parasitically on the body of contemporary civilization, the comic strip has sucked in as much of the art of the century as it could digest. It contains traces of impressionism and even of abstract art. (The concentrated form of abstract art is perhaps best suited to its essential character, if only the comic strip artist is intelligent and bold enough to discern this essential character.)

Picture language is symbolical by nature, accepted as the reality for which it has been substituted. In thus replacing reality, it creates a circle of the initiated who are united by the symbol they have accepted in common. This principle applies no less to the admirers of Picasso's "Guernica" than to the fans of Crocket Johnson's *Barnaby*. Strips like this last, or Otto Soglow's *Little King* or Disney's more advanced works, or even Hoff's *Tuffy*, show how readily the symbol as a pictorial element, no matter what liberties it takes with nature, can be accepted and understood by the public at large.

These strips also demonstrate the possibilities of modern non-objective art for popular consumption. All commissars to the contrary notwithstanding, realism and mass appeal are not identical; indeed, the intelligent selection and use of artistic symbols can make realistic detail appear not only superfluous but actually disturbing. From the artistic point of view, Paul Klee's "Twittering Machine" and Barnaby's Atom Machine for the manufacture of shoes have at least their remoteness from reality in common— except that Barnaby's fantastic contraption is placed within an accepted context, while Klee's exists in the glacial solitude of a violet vision. In the comic strip, the masses have begun to approach art and the dream and to put them to work for their own civilization.

Many comics are drawn with the left hand, the dreamer. To be sure, this dream is still unarticulated and heavily encumbered with the trappings of daily life; diffuse and awkward, stammering and drunk with sleep, it staggers along, then again it grows shrill and phantasmagoric, and always it remains in the fetters of business, of the syndicates.

Yet the comics, having risen from unconscious depths, must needs address themselves to the unconscious depths in their public. Graphically, they are derived from "doodles," those glosses that the unconscious, once it knows itself to be free from control, writes in the margin of the wideawake day. Doodles are the safety valve through which the soul liberates itself from the tension of concentration, the back door by which the creative urge, which has no recognized place in the economy of the American working day, sneaks out of doors. Moreover, since the successful comic figure openly proclaims its descent from the doodle, the reader can identify himself not only with the figure but with its creator as well: he might have drawn it himself.

Rarely have so many identified themselves so profoundly with anything so vague. Consider Superman. He has hardly more than his name in common with Nietzsche's blasphemous and iconoclastic phantasm; in fact one suspects that he originally owed his "super" to the "super-duper," the "ne plus ultra and then some" of advertising usage. This Superman is a Li'l Abner without Mammy Yokum and without popular background, a hillbilly without the fertile background of folklore or remnants of creed. He is a Goliath rather than a David, but a Goliath who has joined the side of the conventionally right. The most serious objection to him I have heard from the mouth of a child: that he is immortal, and therefore the amazing things he does are not miracles.

The emblem of his supermanhood is inscribed on his chest, not on his forehead. He is as guileless as Li'l Abner, but he lacks the primitiveness of the country boy; the old magic that flows from the contrast between city and country is missing. Li'l Abner is at home in Dogpatch, Superman in the universe—that is, nowhere. Superman is on the side of the right as well as of hygiene. He uses violence against violence. His eyes penetrate granite walls and steel plates, but he does not see what Mickey Mouse always sees: reality. Planets serve him and the elements lie at his feet, but in the main his accomplishments are limited to smoking out a small gang of criminals or outsmarting some master mind. The mountain labors and—with the help of modern technology— brings forth a stunt.

An example of the irony unintentionally provided by Superman is the sequence in which he magnanimously carries away a glacier in order to help a village with its drainage problem. His work done, he has to bring a new glacier from the North Pole, because nature, which *non facit saltus*, plays a trick on the winged lord of creation and floods the village. Superman has about him something of Goethe's Sorcerer's Apprentice, of Dr. Faust, of Hercules, and of Atlas. To be sure, Jules Verne and H. G. Wells also make their contribution to his costume and trappings, but essentially he owes his effect to the vanishing remnants of ancient mythology, that collective memory of mankind which has here been combined with utopian anticipation. He does not *embody* all this, for Superman has never achieved such density of personality as Li'l Abner, for example, but he does draw constantly from a plentiful, if shallow, reservoir of watered-down myths and pipedreams of the future.

Superman is a product of the last war, the shadowy but legitimate son of the Hitlerian age and the atom bomb. Although, as we have stressed, he comes in the wake of a long tradition, it is upon the miracle of technology that he finally calls in situations that can no longer be met with the implements of reality. The *deus ex machina* has become the *machine god*. Superman is the boy's dream in pictures, but through the dehumanization of the miracle and the substitution of technical for poetic fantasy, his face has acquired a terrifyingly unhuman, aggressive, and hard profile, foreshadowing a world in process of formation, a world that is certainly new but far less brave than it thinks and claims to be. Seen politically, Superman is the promise that each and every world problem will be solved by the technical trick. He is the Man of Tomorrow; so he says himself.

Fritz Lang, to whom the American film owes a number of real achievements, made two films in pre-Hitler Germany that show symptomatic resemblances to Superman: *Die Nibelungen,* whose Siegfried resembled our hero in build and physiognomy—bull neck and a blank face moulded of some soft substance; and *Metropolis,* whose setting is related to the background of the Superman strips—a city on the borderline between modern civilization and pseudo-scientific Utopia. Like Superman, Lang had caught the *Zeitgeist.*

Myths crumble, heroic figures can be watered down, but symbols and names cannot be used with impunity. And even though this bashful, amiable Superman is to the petty *Übermensch* who unleashed the Second World War as Robin Hood to a storm trooper, they have one thing in common: they both blur the transition from the technically possible to the miraculous-irrational, their efficacy rests on the vague hybridism of heroism and Utopia, of technology and the miracle.

Superman announces himself the ally of right, the people, and democracy. Prankster is his enemy, Lynch is a thorn in his side; he issues forth to vanquish the *tyrannosauros rex,* as Siegfried did to slay his dragon. But his credo, like the "balloon" in which he expresses it, is loosely attached and interchangeable. It is not the natural expression of himself, like Li'l Abner's far more modest self-avowals. He has merely put on his credo like his winged cloak. He lacks human reality; is it not precisely his mission to abolish reality?

Superman, in fact, is a figure of dual identity. He slips from the civilian clothes of his everyday life into the ceremonial garb of his miraculous deeds and back again; he is a quick-change artist, and even more amazing than the ease of his metamorphoses are his trifling reasons for undertaking them. But the dual identity motif is the schema of Dr. Jekyll and Mr. Hyde—a pattern bordering on that of the pathological swindler and criminal. For a popular figure, it is not without its dangers. The double face and the split personality are symptoms of a disease that has attacked our civilization. And, more often than not, it is also an attribute of modern dictators, perhaps of the tyrants of all epochs.

Superman has become anchored in those sections of the population that are most naive, most capable of enthusiasms, and most susceptible to revolutionary impulses. By the technique—general in the comics—of breaking off the text just before the climax, by creating new climaxes almost from day to day, it creates an excitement close to enchantment and frenzy. A toy, a puppet, Superman is a monstrous carnival figure combined of wishful dreams and present anxieties, of sensationalism and abused enthusiasm. Accustomed to change his identity, Superman has it in him to become a political figure. To play with him is to play with the dynamite of our times.

I do not know whether the comics are popular or folk art, primitive or "primitivistic" art; I do not even know whether the word "art" is in any sense applicable to them as they are today. But they are surely a democratic enterprise. An immanent need of the masses presided at their birth and helped to develop and round out their figures.

Accordingly, it is reassuring to see that after our entry into the war, the Superman of 1938 was followed by George Baker's *Sad Sack*. Sad Sack is not an unmixed joy to his public like the hero and swindler of the air. He is a little man in the lineage of Charlie Chaplin, and he is the little man's answer to the pathos and uniform of war. He is molded of clay, not blown up with air: an American Good Soldier Schweik, less subtle and malicious than Schweik (he ultimately accepts the cause for which he is fighting as *his* cause), but just as stubborn in asserting the rights of his private existence, which as a rule is identical with personal misfortune. The *shlemiel* and Hard Luck Joe is a healthy corrective to the unfettered pipedream of the masses; it is perhaps the only corrective that is possible throughout the whole breadth of our civilization.

We must see the comic strips for what they are: excellent means of communication. America has produced in them a technical miracle: precise, smooth-functioning, versatile, and, like everything that is technically perfect, always demanding new technical refinement. Absorbed in the production of this miraculous vehicle of modern communication, America has seldom asked herself who was going to ride in it and where it was bound for.

Every once in a while, when Americans take a good look at this product of theirs, they are seized by a fit of the shivers and feel almost that the best solution would be to throw the baby out with the bath. Aside from the fact that it would be impossible to prohibit the comics—everybody knows that, and the idea itself is merely a means of making conversation—such a step would deprive this country of one of the genuine contributions it has made to its own culture. America without comics would not be America.

It is, therefore, as shortsighted as it is ungrateful to see in the comic strip nothing but an incitement to crime and violence, and to forget, because of the magnetic emptiness of Superman and his like, the ironical urbanity of the Shmoo. Art has always had a certain similarity to the cactus. Many thorns are needed to produce, in a blessed moment, the blossom that crowns them all. The undeniably thorny horrors of the Gothic tales were needed to create a European poem like Byron's *Manfred*.

The violent controversies between psychoanalysts and other educators over the comic strips are likely to obscure the basic problem they pose. How can we channel the revolutionary possibilities inherent in this—hitherto almost aimless—means of mass entertainment and mass enlightenment so that a maximum of art is combined with a maximum of edification; how can we realize and develop the artistic possibilities latent in the comics even today? How can we rescue them in general from that complete lack of significant content which has vitiated so much real talent? In the end all these problems become one. In view of the latent powers of the comics as a means of social criticism and of their enormous circulation and technical perfection, what they still lack is the artistic genius to control these forces and drive them towards a goal.

Li'l Abner and his Mammy Yokum are about as far removed from the creative origins of real popular art as they are from realizing the artistic potential of the comic strip as such. Yet they are on their way, perhaps, to that realization, and have already found some good companions among the menacing crowd of slick and sloppy nightmares let loose by the syndicates on the imagination of the nation.

"I was sick of writing for kids, and adults with the minds of kids," condescending and calculating Al Capp meditated one day. "I got to know all the dirty tricks, and I knew that if I experimented and lost a great section of the featherbrained, Bam!-and-Zowie!-loving public, I could always go back to them. But I also knew that by experimenting I might get some of the usually non-comic-reading public—the people who had been appalled by the childishness and utter stupidity of most strips."

The future of the American comic strip as an artistic as well as a moral enterprise lies in meditations like these.

Plaint of a Gentile Intellectual

by Chandler Brossard

THERE is a new Alienated Man around. He is the Gentile intellectual in New York City. Hopelessly outnumbered by his Jewish colleagues on the New York intellectual scene, of late he has begun to feel that his back is against the wall.

It is tough enough for the Gentile born in New York, who is at least geographically, if not spiritually, acclimated, but it is at least five times that tough for the Gentile intellectual who immigrated here from some distant city. When he begins to acquire friends he finds, after a while, that somehow most of them are Jewish. (Somewhere in the process the few Gentiles were passed over.) Most, not some, of the smartest people he knows are Jews, and he soon begins to believe that the Jewish intellectual is the only intellectual who is really "hip," that is, in the know, and that the Gentile is "square," or naive.

So what does he do? The Gentile simultaneously accepts and rejects. Partly consciously, partly unconsciously, he starts assuming some of the wise style of the Jewish intellectual, to overcome what he thinks is his own naivety, in order to become part of the group surrounding him. The implications of this are almost infinite.

Strange things happen. His vocabulary becomes spiced with Jewish inflections and expressions (his friends teach him the correct pronunciations: he has an increasingly strong tendency to say *"nu?"* instead of "so?"). His gestures become sensual, curvilinear, and an elaborate and necessary part of his communication. His humor becomes less mirthful—so long, Mark Twain!—and more ironic, twisted, oblique, and gaggy. (If he is a writer this gag quality finally gags him insofar as his originality is concerned.) He cannot remember the last time he told a joke that did not involve a Jew or the Jewish point of view. He becomes much talkier than he ever was, and finds—sometimes with a helpless confusion, even distaste—that part of his enjoyment of any experience, often one of extreme privacy, is talking about it, exploiting it verbally. His own tradition was to withhold, to keep things to himself, not to make everything communal.

He feels, in effect, a kind of clown. His confusion is not helped by the fact that for the first time in his life he is now a member of a minority. It almost seems that he is a kind of extravagance of his Jewish circle; like an extra movie over the weekly ration, uptown and complete with vaudeville. He wonders whether he is ever really being accepted; he feels that his Jewish friends do certain things for each other that they do not do for him. Is he at the center or the periphery?

There was a lot of conversation and suddenly he looks up and sees that his friends have gone off to have a pastrami sandwich.

All this makes him re-examine what he thought were his friendships. He discovers that he has been misled by his Jewish friends' social ease. It was so painless for him to establish what he thought was real rapport: the Jews were so immediately warm and gracious and understanding, so *intime*, that he felt after a short while as if he had known them for years. He felt this way partly because it actually did take almost years sometimes to reach this same degree of relaxedness and confidence with another Gentile. And when it was reached with a Gentile, after a long and bruising feeling-out period, they had developed in the process a real friendship, and were committed to each other. So he experiences considerable shock when his Jewish friends, whom he mistakenly thinks have been with him through almost everything, suddenly treat him with the casualness of an acquaintance. But it is his own fault, he soon realizes: his friends had never signed a blood pact with him, he just thought they had.

It is only after a long groping period that he begins to understand his Jewish intellectual friends in New York. Particularly those in Greenwich Village.

Never before, for instance, has he seen so much concern with an individual style, so much intensive self-conscious development of a "personality."

He sees the young Jewish poet who wants to seem like an underworld character, talking and thinking out of the corner of his mouth, his every public move calculated to encourage this personality myth. While the other person in this cultivated schizophrenia is the soft, boy-faced poet protectedly experiencing his baroque emotional reactions to life unseen by the gullible public. And he looks on with suspended judgment as this poet shows him the way to turn an image into a gimmick.

He watches the under-thirty Jewish writer of Kafkaesque fiction who seems to have trouble choosing between the role of an American cowboy with blue denim pants and checked shirt, slouch-walking as best he can, prairie-swept, or on the other hand the avuncular academician from Minsk, with accents and gestures and style so rich and convincing you will almost swear he offered you a sip from that steaming glass of tea you are sure he was holding. And our friend the *goy*, remembering one story that sounded like a translation from the German, reads something else by this man that extends the confusion even further because it sounds like Ring Lardner.

Another of his friends wants to be known as an athlete, and is constantly proposing a boxing match at the gym, or a swimming race under water, or a run around the mile track, or a tennis match on an equatorial day. Actually he is quite frail, and is shy about being a painter.

The Gentile at first takes all this seriously. It is—or was—his habit to play it straight, to maintain a personality and behavior consonant with what he believes to be his real or true self. He then gets the feeling that his Jewish friends are smiling at him because he is so straight. What happens? He often winds up playing straight man to his friends at a nearly all-Jewish party. All those true words said in jest. . . .

After a while he stumbles into certain back corners of the lives of his Jewish friends.

He visits Coney Island. Here he sees the blurred shifting faces of his Jewish friends as they grew up. The whole place is one vast objective correlative—the Castles in the sand, the continually moving juxtaposition of youth and age and group sexual pursuit and sightseeing and shrieking on the broadwalk, the shooting galleries where the dead ducks flip alive at the next turn, the

three-for-a-quarter reproductions of posed absurdity, the hot dogs
with sauerkraut and onions and India relish, the sudden strength
that rings a bell on a tall pole, the giant laughing woman being
endlessly tickled by a machine.

He comes away wiser than he was, linking a gesture on the
boardwalk to a line in a lyric, a certain quick scene to a gibe he
had heard two weeks ago at a party, a barker's spiel to a book
reviewer's technique. He taps his pocket to see if his passport is
still there.

Then he visits a home in Brooklyn. The front living room
with the brand-new-looking furniture (the caul still protecting
the lampshade) stiffly arranged as if waiting for the principal
speaker of the evening. The strong, loving, almost masculine
mother who still hovers around her son even though he is now in
his late twenties. (Where was that caul? Over the lampshade?) He
senses with increasing uneasiness that the Jewish mother would
like to stroke him too as he sits there. He listens to his friend's
continual reminiscences about his childhood and his schooldays.
His finest years. And the combination of *Bubbe* and cookies turns
up with the regularity of a creditor. He, the *goy*, feels the compulsion to keep these objects and areas in his already finished past.
Perhaps because they were so depressing, so full of unexpressed
rage and unlove.

Now, perhaps, he understands the situation somewhat better.
He sees the Jewish intellectual in New York as a person actually
very different from himself, in cultural tradition almost opposed,
and then, perhaps for the first time, he discovers *himself* for what
he is traditionally. (His circle of intellectual friends has indirectly
told him he is actually the bourgeois, playing around intellectualism "for kicks"—though they say this with envy.) He has the
choice now of recognizing his background and origins, his differences, and living accordingly, or of denying them and reshaping
himself with the help, or proximity, of his Jewish friends. The
temptation to submit to reshaping is strong; it is hard to be different in these surroundings.

But if the Gentile submits, then his ambivalence becomes
acute, and he thinks his helpmates are patronizingly corrupting

him, and where once he may have considered himself, jokingly, as the All-American Goy, he now thinks of himself as the In-authentic Goy. But even this new alienation of his seems a Jewish literary brand of alienation, not his own raw brand.

If, on the other hand, he rejects the influences around him, his reaction is often stronger than is necessary, his behavior more separate, and he hears his friends remark that something is wrong with him lately, he is acting so strange. Those Gentile neurotics, they're so wild. He wonders if he even knows how to be properly neurotic. (Once he dreamed he had been turned into a goat and was about to be dispatched into the wilderness by his Jewish friends.)

What can he do? He does not intend to leave New York. (Everybody knows you can't go back home.) Paris? Who wants to go to Paris? He cannot afford, yet, to be psychoanalyzed. His friends kid him about the possibility of changing his name. One of them even suggested that maybe the American Jewish Committee would eventually set up a fund for the investigation of his dilemma. Meanwhile, here he is at *Commentary*.

Our Changing Ideals,

as Seen on TV

The Father on the Hearth

by Norman Podhoretz

AT least fifty plays are produced on television every week. About a third of these are detective and mystery stories; another large slice is devoted to whimsical tales with surprise endings. But the remainder constitutes a genre peculiar to television. It has developed its own style, its own conventions, and to some extent its own subject matter.

These TV plays are theatrical rather than cinematic, taking their cue from Broadway, not Hollywood. Movie stars rarely appear in them, though prominent Broadway figures often do; the casts consist of extremely competent actors most of whom, I imagine, consider themselves theater people. The direction almost always betrays the influence of men like Kazan—which is to say that it tries to combine realism of surface with self-conscious, sometimes arty, arrangements, movement, and overtones. Both dialogue and acting are more sophisticated than is usual in the movies. In general the productions are on a surprisingly high level, considering the number of plays turned out every week.

The tendency is toward low-key drama, a kind of domestic realism whose effect derives from its accuracy in reflecting the ordinary man's conceptions of the world. The very style of the acting—always plausible, always controlled, never permitting itself the least intimation of hamminess, rarely even admitting that it is artifice rather than actual conversation—restricts the drama to that level of reality which is easily accessible to common sense. A whole play may be based on a very trivial incident, chosen because everyone in the audience will have experienced something similar. For example, a teen-age boy takes the family car without his father's permission, gets involved in a minor accident, and doesn't come home until three in the morning. His parents wait up for him, anxiety-ridden, and when he finally returns, all is forgiven and the whole family goes to bed with the sense of having got through another crisis. This play is "true to life" in a way that popular culture seldom is: the audience has never had the stuff of its daily existence taken so seriously, and it responds with a new feeling of self-importance and dignity. Unlike the soap operas, which betray a masochistic relish in minor troubles, the point here is the relief people feel in being able to resume their usual routine: trouble teaches gratitude for the humdrum.

Depending for its effectiveness on its ability to remain content with the world perceived and comprehended by common sense, this kind of drama must resist appealing either to escapist fantasy or to the critical intelligence, never wandering above or below the staples of experience. Nowadays, to be sure, that can include a great deal of surprising matter. In a play about the relation between a mother and her son, suggestions of an Oedipus complex are offered in much the same way as characters appear wearing clothes: the writer, the director, the actors, take it completely for granted as an ordinary element in the family. It isn't a mysterious, sinister force (as it tends to be in the movies) but a tangible factor existing almost wholly on the surface and demanding to be observed. This means, of course, that it needn't have consequences; in this particular instance, it counted for nothing in the plot. That a son should be in love with his mother is an index of his normality, not of his monstrousness. This must imply, I suppose, that the audience has been trained to regard it thus, or is well on its way to doing so.

Life in these plays, then, is non-heroic: a world governed by common sense is a world where "everyone has his faults and his good points." No insuperable moral problems are recognized, for, in a universe ruled exclusively by forces visible to the commonsense eye, there can be no dilemma which resists the touch of good will and a spirit of compromise. Often a play will open with a situation in which right seems to conflict with right, but in the end someone is proved wrong or neurotic or misguided, and the difficulty immediately resolves *itself*. A common-sense ethos must always hack its way through to the simple truths which are supposed to lie buried beneath the ugly and delusory overgrowths of experience.

Though everyone in these plays has weaknesses as well as virtues, we find the weaknesses far less in evidence. If a man sins, he does so almost accidently, for sin is something that happens to people, not something they do. They make errors of judgment all the time, but they generally know nothing of pure or gratuitous malice. Only their virtues are essential to them; their sins are somehow external, reefs against which they have blundered in the fog. (The TV crime plays, on the other hand, become a repository of much that is omitted from domestic drama: crime is a violation of common-sense living, and therefore results in the criminal's exclusion from the sphere in which all slips can be made good.)

One would expect that a world made by common sense, ruled by common sense, and upheld by common sense, would be a pleasant world to live in. In many ways it is. It produces people whose passions are under control, who are well-bred, well-mannered, open, friendly, helpful, and above all, reasonable. More than anything else, they want to get along, they will do nearly anything to keep the peace.

And yet the optimism we find here is gray rather than flaming; it is overcast with a sadness that seems a new element in American popular culture. There is a distinct feeling that life is tough even for those who aren't harassed by the landlord and the grocer; and there is a shade of disillusion over the discovery that human possibility is not infinite—reverberations of Korea are in the air. The mood is more sober than what used to be called American optimism, and, as we shall see, far more honest.

Before the dislocations caused by 3D, Hollywood had been gravitating in several full-dress productions toward a similar form of drama (see Robert Warshow's "The Movie Camera and the American" in *Commentary*, March 1952). But the features characterizing the new genre—an insistent interest in domestic life, a *dramatis personae* entirely composed of ordinary people, a strict fidelity to the appearance of things, a quiet tone (everything is underplayed), a paucity of plot, and much discussion and debate —made it apparent that its real home was in television. Going to the movies is still more or less an occasion for most people, and an occasion demands something extraordinary. Even the size of the cinema screen insures that the movie world shall be larger than life (indeed, in answer to the small television screen, movie screens have become larger); perhaps for this reason, movies reproduced on television lose their bite. Watching television, on the other hand, has become an integral part of domestic routine, and the new genre serves an impulse to make the program a relevant and appropriate presence in the living room.

The living room, in fact, is the favorite setting of these plays, just as the favorite cast is a family. It is a middle-class family, neither unusually happy nor (as in the soap operas) continually besieged with trouble. Its most remarkable quality as a group is a negative one—fear is absent from the relations of its members and power thus becomes a corollary of love: it can only be had by free consent. The father guides and administers his household; he does not rule it. The plot always turns on some crisis that has suddenly developed, often in the family relations themselves: as in any family, its members are continually in the process of losing their illusions about one another, and the effort at readjustment is constant. Ultimately they emerge from their difficulties as more of a family, having restored a workable balance of power.

Almost always the father comes through as a sharper figure than the mother, who is supposed to have her being in and through her husband and children. A good woman is not so much *by* as *on* the side of her husband. If she asserts her personality too forcefully, we may be sure that calamity will result. Evil, when it makes one of its rare visits to these plays, is likely to come in the shape of a domineering wife or an overly possessive mother. As for the father, he is an earnest man, but his earnestness is mellow compared with the fierce unyielding grimness of his children or his wife's firm, uncritical loyalty to her feelings. Soft-spoken, controlled, never glamorous-looking, but always carrying himself with great dignity and self-assurance, he exhibits the palpable scars of a long combat with life. His humility, patience, and sadness are the products of many frustrations, and he is thus extremely skeptical of any comprehensive schemes or over-ambitious plans. Sometimes he is portrayed as a great disappointment to his children —for we live in an era where parents rather than children are perennially on trial—and in such cases the guilt and bitterness he feels are tempered by his pity for the son who will soon learn that all human beings are disappointing to those who make excessive demands on them.

We practically never see this new American father (as we used to in the movies and as we still do in television soap operas) involved in the big business deal, or embroiled in the problems of earning money: a comfortable income is taken for granted, while his career is merely a shadowy presence in the background. The great reality of his life, the sphere in which things happen to him, is his family. He carries his responsibilities willingly, without a sense of oppression, and the fact that they occupy him so fully, challenging all his resources of character and mind, never allowing him to get bored, is his most powerful proof to his son that the ordinary life is worth living. For this is the great lesson he is intent upon teaching. We find him telling his daughter that marriage, children, and love are far more important than fame and wealth; we find him insisting to his son that there is no disgrace in compromise. He represents reasonableness, tolerance, and good will: the image of American maturity.

Preserving the family from disruption is the role he is most often called upon to play. One species of disruption is conflict with his children. The conflict never takes the form of youth's rebellion against parental authority because the father's authority over his children is not given in the nature of things. Since he is a constitutional leader rather than an absolute monarch, his authority must constantly be reaffirmed at the polls. Nor can he assert it forcefully or arbitrarily: he must win the right to participate in his son's problems by making himself sufficiently attractive in the boy's eyes—good "public relations" is essential to his position. Interference with his son's private affairs being a matter of the greatest delicacy, he only presumes to speak in crucial matters. Otherwise he is there, looking on, setting an example, communicating through the silent power of his personality.

In an encounter with his children, he confronts them with a flexibility that often seems to be weakness but in reality turns out to be a wisdom based on the knowledge that human beings cannot afford to be too hard either on themselves or others. One play (already mentioned above) was about a young man of twenty who discovers his mother committing adultery while his father is away on a business trip. After wandering around the streets all night, the son staggers into his house, dishevelled, distraught, and looking a little drunk; to his amazement, he finds his father waiting for him. "Now listen, son, I know everything; your mother wired me and I took the next plane back. She told me the whole story." [1] The boy covers his face with his hands, unable to speak. "What are you going to do?" asks his father. "What do you mean, what am I going to do? What are you going to do?" "Well, what do you expect me to do—leave your mother and break up our home because she made a mistake?" At this suggestion that his father wants to forget the whole thing, the boy stares at him incredulously; it's impossible to go on living with an immoral mother and a weak-kneed father. Patiently and sympathetically, the father persists in trying to convince his son that their family is too important to be destroyed by a mistake. His wife, he explains, is going through a difficult phase; her son is grown up, she has nothing left to do, she thinks she isn't needed. Now she's upstairs suffering more than her son would believe, terrified that he may turn away from her. "Our job is to help her, not to kill her. I've got to be more loving, you've got to show that you understand her side of things. Will you do it?" And, of course, the play ends with the boy going upstairs to comfort his mother. This is an atmosphere in which adultery and betrayal breed not hatred, but new responsibility. Yet all this understanding disturbs one: is there no breaking point?

Occasionally there is, as when the father's worldliness becomes irrelevant (or worse) to his son's problems. A young man, caught violating the Honor System in his pre-graduation exams

[1] I quote from memory throughout this article.

at college, is about to be expelled by a committee of his peers, when he offers to turn in the names of the others who had cheated with him. The list of names is confided to the chairman of the committee, a brilliant student who is planning to marry a sweet young classmate and go into his father's business. On the list he finds his fiancée's name. Should he, before handing it in to the Dean, strike off her name? His father, guessing the boy's trouble, persuades him to do so: "You're going out into a tough world where nobody will care about you and your interests. You have to look out for yourself and the people you love. This is a small town, son; they never forget a scandal, they'll never let you forget that your wife was once expelled from college for cheating. Everybody cheats; the only difference between a respectable man and a cheater is that the cheater has been caught. Son, don't let your 'principles' destroy your happiness. Use your head, boy!" At first the boy takes this advice, but later, to the consternation of his father, confesses while delivering his valedictory address, and proclaims his own expulsion. The two young people leave the small university town together to begin a new life.

Though repudiated, the father in this play is not unsympathetically portrayed. He realizes that the Honor System places too great a burden on young people, and that there is something absurd—something that violates common sense—in allowing a trivial matter to ruin a life. He does not, as his own father might have done, advise his son to give up this girl who will disgrace him: the highest value is still preservation of the family, even if it hasn't quite been formed yet. And in this play the idea of family takes on a special significance. The world outside is assumed to be hostile (like the outraged student body demanding the expulsion of the cheaters), or, like the kindly Dean, helpless in the face of circumstances and the Rules. The world outside is mechanical, rigid, governed by cold standards of no one's making: even the Dean can't protect the students he would like to forgive. Within the family, however, a man has resources, for the family rests on love and reasonableness, and it is in the nature of love to persist despite circumstance, while reasonableness provides flexibility to liberate the spirit from the tyranny of Rules.

A person is most a person to those who love him; otherwise he is judged and disposed of.

That understanding and flexibility should be the father's greatest qualities is not surprising. What does surprise us, however, is that he rarely feels ambition for his children, merely wishing them to lead normal, contented lives. The only ambitious father I remember seeing is the one in the play just discussed, and he is also the only father who comes off badly in the end—as if ambitiousness were an act of *hubris* to be avenged. The drive for extraordinary achievement has always been considered notoriously American. An identity is something that must be earned, not inherited, and once earned it remains precarious and must be vigilantly maintained: if you lose your money, you also lose your name. This compulsion to prove that we are "saved" is probably a consequence of being born into a Puritan culture—many marks of status in America are simply secularized versions of what once were the symptoms of grace.

We seem, however, under the influence of psychoanalysis, to have reached a point where the most important mark of status has become not money, power, or fame, but a reasonably happy family life. Play after play insists that everyone is saved, that all are granted grace if they are but willing to accept it: adjustment is supposed to be available to all.

The way to justify the space you take up in the world is—as one father puts it—not to be *somebody*, but just to *be*. An adaptation of Dos Passos' *The Big Money* is used as a vehicle for showing the disastrous consequences of the pursuit of wealth; a young boxer who had been a foundling realizes that he needn't be compulsive about becoming a champion in order to give his infant son a "name"; a great soprano feigns the loss of her voice because she has learned that happiness lies in raising children and being supported by a responsible husband; a distinguished (divorced) actress gives up her career because she falls in love with a man who teaches her that what she really wants is a husband and family; a potentially great pianist is forced to admit that he is incapable of performing on the concert stage, and finds that being released from an immature ambition allows him for the first time to feel content in his marriage.

A particularly interesting example is a play about a widower, father of a fifteen-year-old daughter, who falls in love with a formerly great concert pianist. We are given to understand that some sort of illness interrupted her career, but now she is working steadily to stage a comeback. The woman is in her thirties, completely dedicated to music, living in a room which is stuffed with busts of great composers and that suggests the atmosphere of a mausoleum. Pressured into a date with the widower by a friendly neighbor, she reveals herself as socially inept. Her behavior is awkward, she can't dance, and she commits the great crime of being a killjoy by leaving the country club at midnight. ("I'm so sorry to have ruined your evening," she apologizes pathetically. "I knew I shouldn't have come. I'm just no good at this sort of thing. And now I have to get some sleep, because I have a long day of practice ahead of me.") The widower was an extremely good representative of his type: equable, quiet, observant (the camera kept finding excuses for giving us close-ups of his intently serious eyes), sensible, understanding, and completely at his ease in the many different situations the play showed him in. We soon discover that the widower's young daughter fancies herself a pianist too. Against the tactful urging of her father, she breaks a date for the junior prom in order to prepare for a high-school concert. Eventually, of course, the daughter and the ex-concert pianist become great friends. Father is disturbed, but for the moment does nothing, allowing her to study with the older woman. As soon as the high-school concert is over, he intends to be firm. The night before the concert, however, he is horrified to learn that great plans are being made for his daughter. "She reminds me so much of what I was like at her age. And she has talent. You can't stand in her way. I've sent for the Great Maestro to hear her tomorrow night. He'll convince you." After the concert, the Great Maestro tells his ex-pupil that her protégé is extremely talented, but that she'll never be anything more than a competent performer: the divine spark is missing. Father is pleased, but the woman refuses to accept this judgment as final. "There are other teachers. We'll get them to hear her. I *know* she has talent. She'll work hard, oh it will be very hard, but she'll make it, I know she will." The father shakes his head sadly. "Why did you stop giving concerts?" "Because I was ill." "No, you weren't ill. I know because I looked up the reviews. They said you had lost your genius, that you were a great child prodigy who never developed." "No, no, it's not true!" "But it *is* true, my darling. Why can't you face reality? Why won't you move out of this tomb and live?" Through her tears she whimpers, "But don't you understand? I have to be somebody." Then comes the clinching line of the play: "Why do you have to be *somebody*? Why can't you just *be*?" And she collapses into his arms. In the last act, the young girl tells her idol that she has to be somebody, but the redeemed artist repeats father's epigram, adding that "there are so many things in life for you. There's your first dance, and the first time you fall in love, and marriage and children." The child weeps hysterically and rushes out of the room, but father and stepmother-to-be embrace. "Don't worry. She'll be all right now."

The play hardly entertains the suggestion that there are circumstances in which a normal life is worth sacrificing, nor does the writer admit that there may be more than one way of finding happiness, or that there may be other forms of the good life which take place outside the family circle. All this is typical of serious television drama. It would be a mistake, however, to think that "conformity" is being urged, if we mean by that imposing a specific model of behavior. On the assumption that everyone really wants the same kind of things out of life, these plays argue, quite plausibly, that only childishness or neurosis (both of which are characterized by the excessive demands they foster) will prevent people from taking advantage of their inalienable right to pursue happiness. Nor is there any uncertainty about the content of happiness; the only problem is finding the surest, swiftest, and safest means to a predetermined end.

Yet, curiously enough, the most salient feature of this ethos remains its sadness. It presents itself as making a modest demand upon life, a demand so modest that life would be guilty of the cruelest perversity to deny it. Bearing in its countenance the lines and wrinkles of maturity, it is always opposed to the presumptuous, enthusiastic "idealism" of youth. Yet what could be more optimistic than the belief that contentment and security are within everyone's reach? When success is measured by money or fame, failure can be chalked up to bad luck; the whole man is rarely in the balance, for a certain distinction will be maintained between the private and public selves: the private self is there to fall back upon if the other turns out treacherous. But when success is conceived as an attribute of the personality rather than of the wallet, failure becomes the tenth circle of Hell. A new fortune can be made, but a man's personality is his essence—personality, in fact, is the modern word for soul—and if that proves befouled, then no good can come of it. In these plays personality itself figures as the goal of all striving; the object of ambition becomes not success but "successful living." The type of all failures is the neurotic, pictured writhing under his burdens like one of the damned; and appropriately so, for in this view of things, a failure of the personality is the last and most refined torture of the Devil. Perhaps some perception of this accounts for the resignation that overcomes the intrinsic cheeriness of the new ethos.

It would be foolish at this point to make any simple judgments of television drama as a whole. Its most notable achievements, I think, are the sharpness with which it has distinguished itself from the movies, the effort it has made to be honest, the success with which it has managed to be serious without being objectionably pretentious. Most important, perhaps, it gives pleasure as so many "serious" movies have failed to do—Hollywood's great fault is its inability to see any connection between "entertainment" and "significance." Apart from a few comic strips, television drama seems the only area of American popular culture that refuses to distinguish finally between the two. Because it isn't imitative, it gives a picture of American life whose accuracy may be difficult to measure but whose honesty is sometimes astonishing: there was a time when the play about the mother's adultery would have ended with the discovery that she hadn't really committed adultery at all.

It may be that this drama reflects the values and aspirations of the newly emerged middle class, now large enough to constitute a mass audience and powerful enough to set the stamp of its attitudes on an important segment of popular culture. Formed by psychoanalysis and nourished by the concepts of social work, this class shows a conspicuous distaste for violence and a remarkable lack of interest in the ungovernable passions of young love. It puts a very high value on the family, though not in order to retreat from the community. The family here is an expanding rather than a restrictive entity, the nucleus of community; it comes to mean all decent, sensible, and understanding people, "people like us," people, that is, who act *as* people and not as "forces." The retreat to the home, then, means a retreat from "environment" —from the competitive world of business and politics, which menaces amiable human relations and does not yield easily to compromise and good will.

Finally, this drama has contributed a new figure to the popular imagination. Attractive and disturbing as he is, the father may turn out to be a summation of the postwar ethos. In his benign firmness, in his mature sobriety, in his sad but determined sense of responsibility, in his unceasing efforts to keep the peace, we can detect the traces of the contemporary political climate. He reflects the feeling that the only safe oasis in a dangerous, cold-war world is our own home, a home which, though it may once have been taken lightly, must now be preserved at all costs if the battle is not to be lost everywhere. And in the long series of plays which turn on a rediscovery of the father by his son, we find, perhaps, the mark of a generation which has moved out of rebellion and skepticism into a patient and humble acquiescence; and we may here discover the role the new middle class seems to have marked out for its own.

The American Woman
as Snow-Queen
Our Self-Contemptuous Acceptance
of Europe's Myth

by Elizabeth Hardwick

THE muddy waves of American self reproach beat upon the European shores again. Nothing seems to have happened in thirty years. The postwar generation of young Americans is back in Europe, but it has skipped the last war and everything goes on reassuringly as before, the needle is stuck in a conversation from *The Sun Also Rises*. Comfortable with government funds or savings, there is nevertheless often a shy and wistful glance beneath the crew-cut—these new expatriates seek after all a place in time, the consolations of history. Conservative, like a reluctant old Victorian gentleman they cling to their past, the *bad* old times, an original stew of the 1920's and 30's. Sighing, they find themselves and their ideas among the dear, remembered deprivations of their parents' lives: starving, disenfranchised workers, the outlawed artist, apple-sellers on the street, fascism just around the corner, the shamefully rich owners of production insisting upon a new war. It is touching—so history is preserved in character.

But there is too much of it and in the historical attitude there are always footnote disagreements. It is easier to take simply one unchallenged notion—our own and the consequent European horror of the American girl, who is also away from home by the thousands, dog-paddling in the European waters, gasping and calling out helplessly, "Me, I'm different. Don't think I'm like the others, please!"

In a French café an alarmed and somewhat shabby French girl accompanies an American "painter" in blue-jean battledress. "She looks after him. She's not spoiled like American women."

The other Americans yearningly approve his luck. A Frenchman with a stunning companion arouses envy. No one knows quite what they may be talking about—the depths of this dialogue are not to be plumbed with hotel and restaurant French—but no matter. Who could fail to note that shot of stimulating benzedrine that *must* be in the French woman's conversation, her "active" listening, her artistic prodding here and there, her smile of comprehension and fascination? "What animation!" the American boys say, their eyes popping. And then there is the more earth-bound type of young American—oh, the Italian girl's exquisite, rumpled, and plump submission to fate!

"But your women are so cold!" the French say and we nod bleakly. The Italians shudder. "I'm afraid of them, they want so many things all the time. Our girls are not like that." Only the Turks, with their scarecrows in colored rags doing all the work in the fields, seem to feel a disgust with the native product equal to ours; and there it is not so much a comparison with foreign brands that arouses their scorn as the comparison with their male selves snoozing in the cafés.

No one could cast doubt on the obvious and tremendous charms of European women, but the licentious familiarity with the subject of American women that is commonly undertaken, the repetitive exchanges, fill one with gloom, this eternal dining on stale cake. Perhaps verbal liberties are the only conceivable ones, since the woman in reality is held to be so fleshless, bleak, and buried that other intimacies are unthinkable—the violation of a corpse. She appears as a creature of legend, the snow queen —tall, beautiful, appallingly splendid, all cleanliness and whiteness, living in her empty, silent, frigid palace. Her kisses freeze the heart, her wintry smiles hide a depreciation, her glittering, spotless, squeamish magnificence lulls one to the soft slumber that kills. Criticism and horror of her are the cries of the root and bud, the crackling of the frozen earth longing for a Latin sun; nature screams, but she does not listen. Unapproachable, self-isolated, she is nevertheless as restless and rapacious as a terrible cold wind, and, as in the fairy tale, the little boy can only be released from this glacial death by the hot tears of love—a foreign love.

This threatening apparition has the persistence of a folk belief, a native wonder of the world, exported along with the cow-
boys and gangsters to other countries. The foreign traveler to
America is no doubt fascinated. Skyscrapers, energy, wealth, automobiles—these at least can be seen; their weight, undeniability,
even their moral content (the obvious is also sometimes true) may
reasonably chagrin the stranger who prefers in well-known places
to refute common observation, even his own at times, in favor of
a fresh judgment. At first glance the American woman he has
heard about—and she is our own creation—is not on view. Something fantastically contrary meets the eye: the informal, independent, lively American girl whose manner recalls the old evan-
gelists swinging over the Sunday circuit. Far from realizing the
wicked somnambulist, she must seem self-confidently forward and
as incurably folksy as a peasant. But her very contrariness to expectation only serves to make the legend more profoundly appealing;
it becomes not a mere fact of experience but a serious, subtle
observation hidden to superficial knowledge. This naive, friendly
surface is a disguise, we are told, a marvelous baroque invention
masking a soul shriveled by Puritanism and vanity swollen by
leisure and power. Bold and generous in appearance, it was a
difficult act of the imagination for the American intellectuals, both
men and women, to discover that this ordinary woman was in
truth as greedy and anarchic as an infant. It is nearly impossible
to think of her as a mother, but even that has been made so
painless in her belief that a new conscience-stricken generation
takes lessons from the doctor in how to have a baby without modern aids, like a pioneer woman in a lonely cabin.

Mrs. Trollope describes the life of a rich Philadelphia lady
in the 1820's. The lady has a handsome house with elegant fur-
nishings, servants, and abundant leisure, but her existence is as
cheerless and repetitive as a squaw's. She does her needlework, goes
to the missionary society in the afternoon, where she has bare
bland conversations with other privileged Philadelphia ladies, and
no conversation at all with her husband, who returns from his
work in the evenings, "shakes hands with her, spits, and dines."
Mrs. Trollope regrets the lack of social drama in this destiny, yet
even this unbroken, dreary life, calm and endless as the prairie,

must seem one of excellent serenity to the young American man of the present—at least it spares him the frustrated expectation and consequent peevishness he professes to find in every American woman now.

The contemporary woman supposedly lives in a solar emptiness warmed occasionally by the dim sounds of the soap opera, and of this fearful nothingness she, and not her husband, is the complete master. Bored and idle, she may play bridge in the afternoon, but even the card game is only a pantomime, a wordless ballet simulating sociability, for she has no true friendship or communication with other women. Her evenings are more interesting because they suggest the rudiments of social intercourse, although always an exchange of remarkable hardness and intimidation. Silence often prevails because she cannot discuss business, politics, or art, but the silence is poisonous; it demands, defies, and dominates with the power of some querulous, bitter, festering law of her own spirit. The evenings end with a triumph, which means she has easily found a way to attack her husband's self-esteem before she retires to the twin beds. It would not be believed if it were suggested that this creature, in between barks and bites, does three times as much housework as the European woman of the same class and purse, who gloriously does none at all, enjoying placidly the comforts of a $12-a-week full-time French slave or the $12-a-month nunlike, dawn to midnight, devotions of the Italian domestic.

But this is only the *Vogue* model, captured like an Ivory Soap carving as the American Wife. There are other images of the American woman that haunt and belittle the American man and chill the Europeans—one is that absurd busybody knocking at the door of culture, or only killing time in the drowsy afternoon lecture hall, a sour figure with a roll of concert tickets in her over-the-shoulder bag. Even to see her toiling up the steps of foreign museums makes us wince—we have seen her before, so many times, in travel books and English novels, mispronouncing the names, grabbing it all with that overwhelming denseness and energy. Americans laugh shrilly at this yearning mind because of the closeness of the young men, particularly the articulate ones, to the sensibilities of the mother. Dancing lessons, piano exercises, the drawing box, illustrated classics, and children's encyclopedias —these things embarrass us sorely. The effort, the effort! we remember shamefully, seeing it all as rather priggish and unreal; in Europe, however, Americans begin to think learning and art are breathed in, unconsciously, from the atmosphere and even though the grossly unmoving modern pink and blue Virgin on the most beautiful, ancient altar is a slap in the face, we soon, by a miracle of hospitality, forget it and only our own contemporary bad taste remains.

But what is so much to be scorned after all in this culture-eager woman? Women are always, according to Schopenhauer, the guardians of the spirit; this hunger for art and excitement is a "natural" role, the very opposite of a humiliating compensation for sexual denials. We sympathize with the peasant woman in fiction who saves her egg money so that her son may become a gentleman in the city, or treasures some little book or picture or gift that will stimulate her children to a less laborious and more intellectual life. Yet the moonstruck wife of a prosperous business-man who clings to her pure and "inspiring" friendship with a weak but gifted young man, reads novels, and likes to discuss the theater is condemned as unbalanced. Her eager and, of course, too freely given appreciation of "fine things" in no way preempts the male prerogative, which is still the grand one of the highest creator of art, philosophy, and science. (That this should still be true for women, after the vote, freedom, wider experience, is one of the jokes of history.)

A recent European testimony, Simone de Beauvoir's *L'Amérique au jour le jour*, comes upon the subject of American women with a bald and instructive directness. A busy observer in her own right, this author's impressions are not confined to sight, but modified by her knowledge of prevailing intellectual opinion in America and particularly by American self-criticism. This criticism is a spectacular cultural achievement and to try to disavow it in the formation of one's own mind and opinion is altogether fruitless and stunting. Disagreement with a specific point of the acid verdict is not likely with us to be a wholesale endorsement of the national character so much as a criticism of a criticism, a yearly revision that seldom disturbs the basic text.

Mlle. de Beauvoir's first-hand impressions of American women are so cordial that they have, in this way, a kind of originality. She notes the women's clean hair, amazing health, the good humor of the college girls, their spontaneity, courtesy, good will, and their conversational freedom without impudence. With more than a hint of irony, de Tocqueville, a century back, declared himself "frequently surprised and almost frightened at the singular address and happy boldness with which young women in America contrive to manage their thoughts and their language amid all the difficulties of free conversation. . . ."

The amiable details in Simone de Beauvoir's picture have considerable weight, but in terms of the whole they are merely flashes of bright color that make an abandoned landscape seem more desolate. It would, perhaps, be impertinent for a stranger to ignore the attitude of the Americans to whom she talked and whom she had read, and so, against the uncertain evidence of the senses, the venerated, hostile opinion asserts itself. She notes the rancorous accent in which American men talk about women and remembers that it is a commonplace for them to say the women are frigid; she talks of the battle of the sexes, the frustration of the women, the absence of purpose in their lives, the fact that American men don't like them. And the most overwhelming statement is this: "The tragedy of those who have discovered passionate love in Europe and can no longer live with their cold husbands or wives is a stereotype."

The buzz of this theme song is certainly very loud among American intellectuals, but, at its best, it is a miserly way of expressing the American character even in its Puritan aspect and omits the fact that the Puritan heritage is complex, varied, culturally expressive. True, to the American, the voluptuary suggests the pathological—with us love is not an "art," nakedness not without its embarrassments, the body often an uneasy and improbable partner of the soul. We do not have the instinct or the habit of the rich and elaborate European flirtation, the gift for relaxed psycho-sexual drama. The American finds many things outrageously comical that are at the very heart of the European romance. Seeing this, not in *fact*, but in a parody comparable to the parody we present of ourselves for Europe, we cannot quite take comfortably the heavy-lidded coquetry of the middle-aged French couple (one of Europe's advantages being the recognition that ardent feelings do not disappear at twenty-five), the dark wisdom of the experienced matron with her opportune flatteries one moment and her tolerant smiles another, the luxurious, smothering drapery of the rendezvous, the hard-working charm and artifice that perfume the air. The scene seems to us all ludicrous movement, quickness, dramatic posturing, like one of those speedy silent films of the boudoir—heaves and sighs, black-eyed winks, muscular avowals. Our only equivalent is an imaginary and tired comedienne: the Southern belle with her ruffles, sky-blue costumes, flirtatious physiognomy—the decorations of a romantic pose which the "plain man" loathes because it is calculated and therefore, in his view, spotted and unappetizing like an overripe peach. Love can never be an art with us or even exceptionally artful, because we think it real only when it appears without human aid; it is rain from heaven, not the work of a clever imagination.

It is only a slight exaggeration to say that elaborate concern for "holding a man" or making a woman "feel desirable" are attitudes that would seriously wound the pride of Americans and can be, without humiliation, invoked only during a crisis, when a loss is threatened. In spite of the advertisers' effort to stimulate these activities, we are still not able to practice them with enough seriousness or fundamental belief to please the Europeans. Inclination is the only motive acknowledged as honestly relevant to relations between the sexes, and inclination is mysterious. It is not a drama or something earned or deserved; it is a gift, a sort of election. To marry for the most honorable human needs—loneliness, insecurity, desire for a family, *faute de mieux*—these are not quite enough and it may even be said that we feel, superstitiously, that the presence of these needs is hostile to true love. They inject a worldly and universal factor into a personal mystery—and to marry for money or physical comfort is almost a sin and certain to bring misery and repentance! Inclination is of course exclusive in its object, which is why Americans are so sentimental about love and so clumsy in the casual love affair. When a married person finds himself attracted to an outsider he is in agony and must make a choice immediately; without the choice, representing the exclusiveness of love, he cannot be certain he loves either one.

This intensely romantic conception, exclusive, mysterious, self-questioning, unworldly, and impractical, is not a rude and coarse hatred of pleasure, a narrowing of experience out of fear and shame, but a *kind of idealism* which seems to exhilarate and heighten the existence of most Americans. It closes its eyes to man's animal nature, is too pious and extreme, and carries its own doubt and despair with it, but it is just this that makes it the normal expression of a progressive, democratic culture. Love is not pure sensation or need or understanding; like the Bill of Rights, it is a noble possibility that both inspires and constantly accuses. That people are often able to believe they can live by this romantic idealism, contrary to "nature" as it is, reinvigorates it apparently. The picture of the old couple married fifty years gets a prominent spot in the small-town newspapers, and even our high divorce rate, offering the fallen another chance for the ideal, is an expression of it.

Tenderness and the permission of equality between men and women are the surest signs of love in America, but it is just this aim, which is not of course always our practice, that has come to be considered an insidious degradation of both men and women. It is felt that tenderness has degenerated into providing luxuries for the women and that the man who cannot do so suffers intense guilt. There is no doubt that success is highly valued in America, but American women also have a particular fondness for ne'er-do-wells and failures, of which there are always enough to satisfy the demand. I should imagine most European women would think this impossibly crude and unreal. The pride taken by well brought up, pampered American girls in the impoverished intellectual—anyone who can put a sentence together, read books, or listen to decent music—frequently amounts to slavishness. To love such a man, without hope of what is ordinarily meant by success, is evidence of having kept faith with the ideal, of having accepted a passion which is simply itself, unalloyed by worldly motive.

There is a dismal sadism and regression in the contempt for American women one finds nowadays in novels and hears in conversation. Their health, outspokenness, and much-exaggerated leisure are scorned; the ravaging labor of a peasant woman is raised to a high moral principal and with fantastic disingenuousness the poor, defeated European prostitute is sometimes believed to be humanly and aesthetically superior. What most startles one in these notions is the absence of a certain kind of painful emotion supposed to be typical of Americans—our feelings that the daughter who becomes a prostitute, the village without doctors, the hours spent beating the laundry on the riverbank, are the very heart of tragedy. We are often accused of triviality in this respect and perhaps we are the only country that wants to send the leukemia victim a present so that he may have his Christmas in November—a gruesome notion of the last pleasures of life, even a child's life. And yet our squeamishness about physical suffering and deprivation are a large part of what is most free and just in our character.

It's hard to know how seriously to take the chronic, soggy indignation about the "freedom" of American women. Strangely enough, only Henry James, an expatriate, considered a snob and an aristocrat, seems to have truly enjoyed the independence, luck, and "un-European" charms of this New World creature. To him her virtues and inadequacies were an invigorating and romantically honorable expression of the American spirit. He would have thought it cruel to expect her to deviate from the moral and psychological inhibitions of the whole culture, unimaginative to despise her aspirations and candor, and inconceivable that American men, born in the same culture, do not really like or understand her—all of which it clearly is.

A Portrait of the Hipster

by Anatole Broyard

As he was the illegitimate son of the Lost Generation, the hipster was really *nowhere*. And, just as amputees often seem to localize their strongest sensations in the *missing* limb, so the hipster longed, from the very beginning, to be *somewhere*. He was like a beetle on its back; his life was a struggle to get *straight*. But the law of human gravity kept him overthrown, because he was always of the minority—opposed in race or feeling to those who owned the machinery of recognition.

The hipster began his inevitable quest for self-definition by sulking in a kind of inchoate delinquency. But this delinquency was merely a negative expression of his needs, and, since it led only into the waiting arms of the ubiquitous law, he was finally forced to *formalize* his resentment and express it *symbolically*. This was the birth of a philosophy—a philosophy of *somewhereness* called *jive*, from *jibe*: to agree, or harmonize. By discharging his would-be aggressions *symbolically*, the hipster harmonized or reconciled himself with his society.

At the natural stage in its growth, jive began to talk. It had been content at first with merely making sounds—physiognomic talk—but then it developed language. And, appropriately enough, this language described the world as seen through the hipster's eyes. In fact, that was its function: to re-edit the world with new definitions . . . jive definitions.

Since articulateness is a condition for, if not actually a cause of, anxiety, the hipster relieved his anxiety by disarticulating himself. He cut the world down to size—reduced it to a small stage with a few props and a curtain of jive. In a vocabulary of a dozen verbs, adjectives, and nouns he could describe everything that happened in it. It was poker with no joker, nothing wild.

There were no neutral words in this vocabulary; it was put up or shut up, a purely polemical language in which every word had a job of *evaluation* as well as designation. These evaluations were absolute; the hipster banished all comparatives, qualifiers, and other syntactical uncertainties. Everything was dichotomously *solid, gone, out of this world,* or *nowhere, sad, beat,* a *drag.*

In there was, of course, somewhereness. *Nowhere,* the hipster's favorite pejorative, was an *abracadabra* to make things disappear. *Solid* connoted the stuff, the reality, of existence; it meant concreteness in a bewilderingly abstract world. A *drag* was something which "dragged" implications along with it, something which was embedded in an inseparable, complex, ambiguous—and thus, possibly threatening—context.

Because of its polemical character, the language of jive was rich in aggressiveness, much of it couched in sexual metaphors. Since the hipster never did anything as an end in itself, and since he only gave of himself in aggression of one kind or another, sex was subsumed under aggression, and it supplied a vocabulary for the mechanics of aggression. The use of the sexual metaphor was also a form of irony, like certain primitive peoples' habit of parodying civilized modes of intercourse. The person on the tail end of a sexual metaphor was conceived of as lugubriously victimized; i.e., expecting but not receiving.

One of the basic ingredients of jive language was a priorism. The a priori assumption was a short cut to somewhereness. It arose out of a desperate, unquenchable need to know the score; it was a great projection, a primary, self-preserving postulate. It meant "it is given to us to understand." The indefinable authority it provided was like a powerful primordial or instinctual orientation in a threatening chaos of complex interrelations. The hipster's frequent use of metonymy and metonymous gestures (e.g., brushing palms for handshaking, extending an index finger, without raising the arm, as a form of greeting, etc.) also connoted prior understanding, there is no need to elaborate, I dig you, man, etc.

Carrying his language and his new philosophy like concealed weapons, the hipster set out to conquer the world. He took his stand on the corner and began to direct human traffic. His significance was unmistakable. His face—"the cross-section of a motion" —was frozen in the "physiognomy of astuteness." Eyes shrewdly narrowed, mouth slackened in the extremity of perspicuous senti-

ence, he kept tabs, like a suspicious proprietor, on his environment. He stood always a little apart from the group. His feet
solidly planted, his shoulders drawn up, his elbows in, hands
pressed to sides, he was a pylon around whose implacability the
world obsequiously careered.

Occasionally he brandished his padded shoulders, warning
humanity to clear him a space. He flourished his thirty-one inch
pegs like banners. His two and seven-eighths inch brim was
snapped with absolute symmetry. Its exactness was a symbol of
his control, his domination of contingency. From time to time
he turned to the candy store window, and with an esoteric gesture, reshaped his roll collar, which came up very high on his
neck. He was, indeed, up to the neck in somewhereness.

He affected a white streak, made with powder, in his hair.
This was the outer sign of a significant, prophetic mutation. And
he always wore dark glasses, because normal light offended his
eyes. He was an underground man, requiring especial adjustment
to ordinary conditions; he was a lucifugous creature of the darkness, where sex, gambling, crime, and other bold acts of consequence occurred.

At intervals he made an inspection tour of the neighborhood
to see that everything was in order. The importance of this round
was implicit in the portentous trochees of his stride, which, being
unnaturally accentual, or discontinuous, expressed his particularity,
lifted him, so to speak, out of the ordinary rhythm of normal
cosmic pulsation. He was a discrete entity—separate, critical, and
defining.

Jive music and tea were the two most important components
of the hipster's life. Music was not, as has often been supposed, a
stimulus to dancing. For the hipster rarely danced; he was beyond
the reach of stimuli. If he did dance, it was half parody—"second
removism"—and he danced only to the off-beat, in a morganatic
one to two ratio with the music.

Actually, jive music was the hipster's autobiography, a score to
which his life was the text. The first intimations of jive could be
heard in the Blues. Jive's Blue Period was very much like Picasso's:
it dealt with lives that were sad, stark, and isolated. It repre-

sented a relatively realistic or naturalistic stage of development.

Blues turned to jazz. In jazz, as in early, analytical cubism, things were sharpened and accentuated, thrown into bolder relief. Words were used somewhat less frequently than in Blues; the instruments talked instead. The solo instrument became the narrator. Sometimes (e.g., Cootie Williams) it came very close to literally talking. Usually it spoke passionately, violently, complainingly, against a background of excitedly pulsating drums and guitar, ruminating bass, and assenting orchestration. But, in spite of its passion, jazz was almost always coherent and its intent clear and unequivocal.

Bebop, the third stage in jive music, was analogous in some respects to synthetic cubism. Specific situations, or referents, had largely disappeared; only their "essences" remained. By this time the hipster was no longer willing to be regarded as a primitive; bebop, therefore, was "cerebral" music, expressing the hipster's pretensions, his desire for an imposing, fulldress body of doctrine.

Surprise, "second-removism" and extended virtuosity were the chief characteristics of the bebopper's style. He often achieved surprise by using a tried and true tactic of his favorite comic strip heroes:

> The "enemy" is waiting in a room with drawn gun. The hero kicks open the door and bursts in—*not upright, in the line of fire*—but cleverly lying on the floor, from which position he triumphantly blasts away, while the enemy still aims, ineffectually, at his own expectations.

Borrowing this stratagem, the bebop soloist often entered at an unexpected altitude, came in on an unexpected note, thereby catching the listener off guard and conquering him before he recovered from his surprise.

"Second-removism"—*capping* the *squares*—was the dogma of initiation. It established the hipster as keeper of enigmas, ironical pedagogue, a self-appointed exegete. Using his *shrewd* Socratic method, he discovered the world to the naive, who still tilted with the windmills of one-level meaning. That which you heard in bebop was always *something else, not* the thing you expected; it was always negatively derived, abstraction *from,* not *to.*

The virtuosity of the bebopper resembled that of the street-corner evangelist who revels in his unbroken delivery. The remarkable run-on quality of bebop solos suggested the infinite resources of the hipster, who could improvise indefinitely, whose invention knew no end, who was, in fact, omniscient.

All the best qualities of jazz—tension, élan, sincerity, violence, immediacy—were toned down in bebop. Bebop's style seemed to consist, to a great extent, in *evading* tension, in connecting, by extreme dexterity, each phrase with another, so that nothing remained, everything was lost in a shuffle of decapitated cadences. This corresponded to the hipster's social behavior as jester, jongleur, or prestidigitator. But it was his own fate he had caused to disappear for the audience, and now the only trick he had left was the monotonous gag of pulling himself—by his own ears, grinning and gratuitous—up out of the hat.

The élan of jazz was weeding out of bebop because all enthusiasm was naive, nowhere, too simple. Bebop was the hipster's seven types of ambiguity, his Laocoön, illustrating his struggle with his own defensive deviousness. It was the disintegrated symbol, the shards, of his attitude toward himself and the world. It presented the hipster as performer, retreated to an abstract stage of *tea* and pretension, losing himself in the multiple mirrors of his fugitive chords. This conception was borne out by the surprising mediocrity of bebop orchestrations, which often had the perfunctory quality of vaudeville music, played only to announce the coming spectacle, the soloist, the great Houdini.

Bebop rarely used words, and, when it did, they were only nonsense syllables, significantly paralleling a contemporaneous loss of vitality in jive language itself. Blues and jazz were documentary in a social sense; bebop was the hipster's Emancipation Proclamation in double talk. It showed the hipster as the victim of his own system, volubly tongue-tied, spitting out his own teeth, running between the raindrops of his spattering chords, never getting wet, washed clean, baptized, or quenching his thirst. He no longer had anything relevant to himself to say—in both his musical and linguistic expression he had finally abstracted himself from his real position in society.

His next step was to abstract himself in action. *Tea* made

this possible. Tea (marihuana) and other drugs supplied the hipster with an indispensable outlet. His situation was too extreme, too tense, to be satisfied with mere fantasy or animistic domination of the environment. Tea provided him with a free world to expatiate in. It had the same function as trance in Bali, where the unbearable flatness and de-emotionalization of "waking" life is compensated for by trance ecstasy. The hipster's life, like the Balinese's, became schizoid; whenever possible, he escaped into the richer world of tea, where, for the helpless and humiliating image of a beetle on its back, he could substitute one of himself floating or flying, "high" in spirits, dreamily dissociated, in contrast to the ceaseless pressure exerted on him in real life. Getting high was a form of artificially induced dream catharsis. It differed from *lush* (whisky) in that it didn't encourage aggression. It fostered, rather, the sentimental values so deeply lacking in the hipster's life. It became a *raison d'être*, a calling, an experience shared with fellow believers, a respite, a heaven or haven.

Under jive the external world was greatly simplified for the hipster, but his own role in it grew considerably more complicated. The function of his simplification had been to reduce the world to schematic proportions which could easily be manipulated in actual, symbolical, or ritual relationships; to provide him with a manageable mythology. Now, moving in this mythology, this tense fantasy of somewhereness, the hipster supported a completely solipsistic system. His every word and gesture now had a history and a burden of implication.

Sometimes he took his own solipsism too seriously and slipped into criminal assertions of his will. Unconsciously, he still wanted terribly to take part in the cause and effect that determined the real world. Because he had not been allowed to conceive of himself functionally or socially, he had conceived of himself *dramatically*, and, taken in by his own art, he often enacted it in actual defiance, self-assertion, impulse, or crime.

That he was a direct expression of his culture was immediately apparent in its reaction to him. The less sensitive elements dismissed him as they dismissed everything. The intellectuals *manqués*, however, the desperate barometers of society, took him into

their bosom. Ransacking everything for meaning, admiring in-
surgence, they attributed every heroism to the hipster. He became
their "there but for the grip of my superego go I." He was received in the Village as an oracle; his language was *the revolution
of the word, the personal idiom.* He was the great instinctual man,
an ambassador from the Id. He was asked to read things, look at
things, feel things, taste things, and report. What was it? Was it
in there? Was it *gone?* Was it *fine?* He was an interpreter for
the blind, the deaf, the dumb, the insensible, the impotent.

With such an audience, nothing was too much. The hipster
promptly became, in his own eyes, a poet, a seer, a hero. He laid
claims to apocalyptic visions and heuristic discoveries when he
picked up; he was Lazarus, come back from the dead, come back
to tell them all, he would tell them all. He conspicuously con-
sumed himself in a high flame. He cared nothing for catabolic
consequences; he was so prodigal as to be invulnerable.

And here he was ruined. The frantic praise of the impotent
meant recognition—*actual somewhereness*—to the hipster. He got
what he wanted; he stopped protesting, reacting. He began to
bureaucratize jive as a machinery for securing the actual—really
the *false*—somewhereness. Jive, which had originally been a
critical system, a kind of Surrealism, a personal revision of existing disparities, now grew moribundly selfconscious, smug, en-
capsulated, isolated from its source, from the sickness which
spawned it. It grew more rigid than the institutions it had set out
to defy. It became a boring routine. The hipster—once an un-
regenerate individualist, an underground poet, a guerrilla—had
become a pretentious poet laureate. His old subversiveness, his
ferocity, was now so manifestly rhetorical as to be obviously harm-
less. He was bought and placed in the zoo. He was *somewhere* at
last—comfortably ensconced in the 52nd Street clip joints, in
Carnegie Hall, and *Life.* He was *in-there* . . . he was back in the
American womb. And it was just as unhygienic as ever.

Sex and Science:
The Kinsey Report
by Lionel Trilling

BY virtue both of its intrinsic nature and its dramatic reception, the Kinsey Report, as it has come to be called, is an event of great importance in our culture.[1] As such an event it is significant in two separate ways, as symptom and as therapy. The therapy lies in the large permissive effect the Report is likely to have, the long way it goes toward establishing the *community* of sexuality. The symptomatic significance lies in the fact that the Report was felt to be needed at all, that the community of sexuality requires now to be established in explicit quantitative terms. Nothing shows more clearly the extent to which modern society has atomized itself than the sexual isolation in ignorance which exists among us. We have censored the folk knowledge of the most primal things and have systematically dried up the social affections which might naturally seek to enlighten and release. Many cultures, the most primitive and the most complex, have entertained sexual fears of an irrational sort, but probably our culture is unique in strictly isolating the individual in the fears that society has devised. Now, having become somewhat aware of what we have perpetrated at great cost and with little gain, we must assure ourselves by statistical science that the solitude is imaginary. The Report will surprise one part of the population with some facts and another part with other facts, but really all that it says to society as a whole is that there is an almost universal involvement in the sexual life and therefore much variety of conduct. This was taken for granted in any comedy that Aristophanes put on the stage.

There is a further diagnostic significance to be found in the

[1] *Sexual Behavior in the Human Male*. By Alfred C. Kinsey, Wardell B. Pomeroy, and Clyde E. Martin. Saunders. $6.50.

fact that our society makes this effort of self-enlightenment through the agency of science. Sex is inextricably involved with morality, and hitherto it has been dealt with by those representatives of our cultural imagination that have been committed to morality—it has been dealt with by religion, ethical philosophy, and literature. But now science seems to be the only one of our institutions which has the authority to speak decisively on the matter. Nothing in the Report is more suggestive in a large cultural way than the insistent claims it makes for its strictly scientific nature, its announcement of divorce from all questions of morality at the same time that it patently intends a moral effect. Nor will any science do for the job—it must be a science as simple and materialistic as the subject can possibly permit. It must be a science of statistics and not of ideas. The way for the Report was prepared by Freud, but Freud, in all the years of his activity, never had the currency of authority with the public that the Report has achieved in a matter of weeks.

The scientific nature of the Report must be taken in conjunction with the manner of its publication. The Report says of itself that it is only a "preliminary survey," a work intended to be the first step in a larger research; that it is nothing more than an "accumulation of scientific fact," a collection of "objective data," a "report on what people do, which raises no question of what they should do," and it is fitted out with a full complement of charts, tables, and discussions of scientific method. A work conceived and executed in this way is usually presented only to an audience of professional scientists; and the publishers of the Report, a medical house, pay their ritual respects to the old tradition which held that not all medical or quasi-medical knowledge was to be made easily available to the general lay reader, or at least not until it had been subjected to professional debate; they tell us in a foreword for what limited professional audience the book was primarily intended—physicians, biologists and social scientists and "teachers, social workers, personnel officers, law enforcement groups and others concerned with the direction of human behavior." And yet the book has been so successfully publicized that at the present writing it stands fourth on the national non-fiction best-seller list.

This way of bringing out a technical work of science is a cultural phenomenon that ought not to pass without some question. The public which receives this technical report, this merely preliminary survey, this accumulation of data, has never, even on its upper educational levels, been properly instructed in the most elementary principles of scientific thought. With this public, science is authority. It has been trained to accept heedlessly "what science says," which it conceives to be a unitary utterance. To this public nothing is more valuable, more precisely "scientific" and more finally convincing, than raw data without conclusion; no disclaimer of conclusiveness can mean anything to it—it has learned that the disclaimer is simply the hallmark of the scientific attitude, science's way of saying "thy unworthy servant."

So that if the Report were really, as it claims to be, only an accumulation of objective data, there would be some question of the cultural wisdom of dropping it in a lump on the general public. But in point of fact, it is full of assumption and conclusion; it makes very positive statements on highly debatable matters and it editorializes very freely. This preliminary survey gives some very conclusive suggestions to a public that is quick to obey what science says, no matter how contradictory science may be, which is most contradictory indeed. This is the public that, on scientific advice, ate spinach in one generation and avoided it in the next, that in one decade trained its babies to rigid Watsonian schedules and believed that affection corrupted the infant character, only to learn in the next decade that rigid discipline was harmful and that cuddling was as scientific as induction.

Then there is the question of whether the Report does not do harm by encouraging people in their commitment to mechanical attitudes toward life. The tendency to divorce sex from the other manifestations of life is already a strong one. This truly absorbing study of sex in charts and tables, in data and quantities, may have the effect of strengthening the tendency still more with people who are by no means trained to invert the process of abstraction and to put the fact back into the general life from which it has been taken. And the likely mechanical implications of a statistical study are in this case supported by certain fully formulated attitudes which the authors strongly hold.

These, I believe, are valid objections to the book's indiscriminate circulation. And yet I also believe that there is something good about the manner of publication, something honest and right. Every complex society has its agencies which are "concerned with the direction of human behavior," but we today are developing a new element in that old activity, the element of scientific knowledge. Whatever the Report claims for itself, the social sciences in general no longer insist that they merely describe what people do; they now have the clear consciousness of their power to manipulate and adjust. First for industry and then for government, sociology has shown its instrumental nature. A government which makes use of social knowledge still suggests benignity; and in an age that daily brings the proliferation of government by police methods it may suggest the very spirit of rational liberalism. Yet at least one sociologist has expressed the fear that sociology may become the instrument of a bland tyranny —it is the same fear that Dostoevsky gave immortal expression to in "The Grand Inquisitor." And indeed there is something repulsive in the idea of men being studied for their own good. The paradigm of what repels us is to be found in the common situation of the child who is *understood* by its parents, hemmed in, anticipated and lovingly circumscribed, thoroughly taped, finding it easier and easier to conform internally and in the future to the parents' own interpretation of the external acts of the past, and so, yielding to understanding as never to coercion, does not develop the mystery and wildness of spirit which it is still our grace to believe is the mark of full humanness. The act of understanding becomes an act of control.

If, then, we are to live under the aspect of sociology, let us at least all be sociologists together—let us broadcast what every sociologist knows, and let us all have a share in observing each other. The general indiscriminate publication of the Report makes sociology a little less the study of many men by a few men and a little more man's study of himself. There is something right in turning loose the Report on the American public—it turns the American public loose on the Report. It is right that the Report should be sold in stores that never before sold books and bought by people who never before bought books, and passed from hand to hand and talked about and also snickered at and giggled over and generally submitted to humor: American popular culture has surely been made the richer by the Report's gift of a new folk hero—he already is clearly the hero of the Report—the "scholarly and skilled lawyer" who for thirty years has had an orgasmic frequency of thirty times a week.

As for the objection to the involvement of sex with science, it may be said that if science, through the Report, serves in any way to free the physical and even the "mechanical" aspects of sex, it may by that much have acted to free the emotions it might seem to deny. And perhaps only science could effectively undertake the task of freeing sexuality from science itself. Nothing has so reinforced moralistic or religious prohibitions as the concepts of science. At some point in the history of Europe, some time in the Reformation, masturbation ceased to be thought of as merely a sexual sin which could be dealt with like any other sexual sin and, perhaps by analogy with the venereal diseases with which the sexual mind of Europe was obsessed, came to be thought of as the specific cause of mental and physical disease, of madness and decay.[2] The prudery of Victorian England went forward with scientific hygiene; and both in Europe and in America the sexual mind was haunted by the idea of *degeneration*, apparently by analogy with the second law of thermodynamics—here is enlightened liberal opinion in 1896: "The effects of venereal disease have been treated at length, but the amount of vitality burned out through lust has never been and, perhaps, never can be adequately measured" (Article "Degeneration" in *The Encyclopedia of Social Reform*). The very word *sex*, which we now utter so casually, came into use for scientific reasons, to replace *love*, which had once been indiscriminately used but was now to be saved for ideal purposes, and *lust*, which came to seem both too pejorative and too human: *sex* implied scientific neutrality, then vague devaluation, for the word which neutralizes the mind of the observer also neuterizes the men and women who are being observed. Perhaps the Report is the superfetation of neutrality and objectivity which, in the dialectic of culture, was needed before sex could be free of their cold dominion.

[2] See Abram Kardiner, *The Psychological Frontiers of Society*, p. 32 and p. 441 n.

Certainly it is a great merit of the Report that it brings to mind the earliest and best commerce between sex and science—the best thing about the Report is the quality that makes us remember Lucretius. The dialectic of culture has its jokes, and *alma Venus* having once been called to preside protectively over science, the situation is now reversed. The Venus of the Report does not, like the Venus of *De Rerum Natura*, shine in the light of the heavenly signs, nor does the earth put forth flowers for her. She is rather fusty and hole-in-the-corner and no doubt it does not help her charm to speak of her in terms of mean frequencies of 3.2. No *putti* attend her: although Dr. Gregg in his Preface refers to sex as the reproductive instinct, there is scarcely any further indication in the book that sex has any connection with propagation. Yet clearly all things still follow where she leads, and somewhere in the authors' assumptions is buried the genial belief that still without her "nothing comes forth into the shining borders of light, nothing joyous and lovely is made." Her pandemic quality is still here—it is one of the great points of the Report how much of every kind of desire there is, how early it begins, how late it lasts. Her well-known jealousy is not abated, and prodigality is still her characteristic virtue: the Report assures us that those who respond to her earliest continue latest. The Lucretian flocks and herds are here too. Professor Kinsey is a zoologist and he keeps us always in mind of our animal kinship, although he draws some very illogical conclusions from it; and those who are honest will have to admit that their old repulsion by the idea of human-animal contacts is somewhat abated by the chapter on this subject, which is, oddly, the tenderest chapter in the book. This large, recognizing, Lucretian sweep of the Report is the best thing about it and it makes up for much that is deficient and confused in its ideas.

But the Report is something more than a public and symbolic act of cultural revision in which, while the Heavenly Twins brood benignly over the scene in the form of the National Research Council and the Rockefeller Foundation, Professor Kinsey and his coadjutors drag forth into the light all the hidden actualities of sex so that they may lose their dark power and become domesticated among us. It is also an early example of science undertaking to deal head-on with a uniquely difficult matter that has traditionally been involved in valuation and morality. We must ask the question very seriously, How does science conduct itself in such an enterprise?

Certainly it does not conduct itself the way its says it does. I have already suggested that the Report overrates its own objectivity. The authors, who are enthusiastically committed to their method and to their principles, make the mistake of believing that, being scientists, they do not deal in assumptions, preferences, and conclusions. Nothing comes more easily to their pens than the criticism of the subjectivity of earlier writers on sex, yet their own subjectivity is sometimes extreme. In the nature of the enterprise, a degree of subjectivity was inevitable. Intellectual safety would then seem to lie not in increasing the number of mechanical checks or in more rigorously examining those assumptions which had been brought to conscious formulation, but rather in straightforwardly admitting that subjectivity was bound to appear and inviting the reader to be on the watch for it. This would not have guaranteed an absolute objectivity, but it would have made for a higher degree of relative objectivity. It would have done a thing even more important—it would have taught the readers of the Report something about the scientific processes to which they submit their thought.

The first failure of objectivity occurs in the title of the Report, *The Sexual Behavior of the Human Male*. That the behavior which is studied is not that of the human male but only that of certain North American males has no doubt been generally observed and does not need further comment.[3] But the intention of the word *behavior* requires notice. By *behavior* the Report means behavioristic behavior, only that behavior which is physical. "To a large degree the present study has been confined to securing a record of the individual's overt sexual experiences." This limitation is perhaps forced on the authors by considerations of method, because it will yield simpler data and more manageable statistics;

[3] The statistical method of the report lies, necessarily, outside my purview. Nor am I able to assess with any confidence the validity of the interviewing methods that were employed.

but it is also a limitation which suits their notion of reality and its effect is to be seen throughout the book.

The Report, then, is a study of sexual behavior insofar as it can be quantitatively measured. This is certainly very useful. But, as we might fear, the sexuality that is measured is taken to be the definition of sexuality itself. The authors are certainly not without interest in what they call attitudes but they believe that attitudes are best shown by "overt sexual experiences." We want to know, of course, what they mean by an experience and we want to know by what principles of evidence they draw their conclusions about attitudes.

We are led to see that their whole definition of a sexual experience is comprised by the physical act and that their principles of evidence are entirely quantitative. Quality is not integral to what they mean by experience. As I have suggested, the Report is partisan with sex, it wants people to have a good sexuality. But by good it means nothing else but frequent. "It seems safe to assume that daily orgasm would be within the capacity of the average human male and that the more than daily rates which have been observed for some primate species could be matched by a large portion of the human population if sexual activity were unrestricted." The Report never suggests that a sexual experience is anything but the discharge of specifically sexual tension and therefore seems to conclude that frequency is always the sign of a robust sexuality. Yet masturbation in children may be and often is the expression not of sexuality only, but of anxiety. In the same way, adult intercourse may be the expression of anxiety, its frequency may not be so much robust as compulsive.

The Report is by no means unaware of the psychic conditions of sexuality, yet it uses the concept almost always under the influence of its quantitative assumption. In a summary passage (p. 159) it describes the different intensities of orgasm and the various degrees of satisfaction, but disclaims any intention of taking these variations into account in its record of behavior. The Report holds out the hope to respectable males that they might be as frequent in performance as underworld characters if they were as unrestrained as this group. But before the respectable

males aspire to this unwonted freedom they had better ascertain
in how far the underworld characters are ridden by anxiety and in
how far their sexuality is to be correlated with other ways of dealing with anxiety, such as dope, and in how far it is actually en-
joyable. The Report's own data suggest that there may be no direct connection between, on the one hand, lack of restraint and
frequency, and, on the other hand, psychic health; they tell us of
men in the lower social levels who in their sexual careers have
intercourse with many hundreds of girls but who despise their
sexual partners and cannot endure relations with the same girl
more than once.

But the Report, as we shall see, is most resistant to the possibility of making any connection between the sexual life and the
psychic structure. This strongly formulated attitude of the Report is based on the assumption that the real reality of sex is
anatomical and physiological; the emotions are dealt with very
much as if they were a "superstructure." "The subject's awareness of the [erotic] situation is summed up by this statement that
he is 'emotionally' aroused; but the material sources of the emotional disturbance are rarely recognized, either by laymen or
scientists, both of whom are inclined to think in terms of passion, or natural drive, or a libido, which partakes of the mystic [4]
more than it does of solid anatomy and physiologic function."
Now there is of course a clear instrumental advantage in being
able to talk about psychic or emotional phenomena in terms of
physiology, but to make a disjunction between the two descriptions of the same event, to make the anatomical and physiological
description the "source" of the emotional and then to consider it
as the more real of the two is simply to commit not only the

[4] We must observe how the scientific scorn of the "mystic" quite
abates when the "mystic" suits the scientist's purpose. The Report is explaining why the interviews were not checked by means of narcosynthe-
sis, lie-detectors, etc.: "In any such study which needs to secure quantities of data from human subjects, there is no way except to win their
voluntary cooperation through the establishment of that intangible
thing known as rapport." This intangible thing is established by looking
the respondent squarely in the eye. It might be asked why a thing which
is intangible but real enough to assure scientific accuracy should not be
real enough to be considered as having an effect in sexual behavior.

Reductive Fallacy but also what William James called the Psychologist's Fallacy. It must bring under suspicion any subsequent generalization which the Report makes about the nature of sexuality.[5]

The emphasis on the anatomical and physiologic nature of sexuality is connected with the Report's strong reliance on animal behavior as a norm. The italics in the following quotation are mine. *"For those who like the term* it is clear that there is a sexual drive which cannot be set aside for any large portion of the population, by any sort of social convention. *For those who prefer to think in simpler terms of action and reaction,* it is a picture of an animal who, however civilized or cultured, continues to respond to the constantly present sexual stimuli, albeit with some social and physical restraints." The Report obviously finds the second formulation to be superior to the first.

Now there are several advantages in keeping in mind our own animal nature and our family connection with the other animals. The advantages are instrumental, moral, and poetic—I use the last word for want of a better to suggest the mere pleasure in finding kinship with some of the animals. But perhaps no idea is more difficult to use than this one. In the Report it is used to establish a dominating principle of judgment, which is the Natural. As a concept of judgment this is notoriously deceptive and has been belabored for generations, but the Report knows nothing of its dangerous reputation and uses it with the naivest confidence. And although the Report directs the harshest language toward the

[5] The implications of the Reductive Fallacy may be seen by means of a paraphrase of the sentence: "Professor Kinsey's awareness of the [intellectual] situation is summed up by his statement that he 'has had an idea' or 'has come to a conclusion'; but the material sources of his intellecual disturbances are rarely recognized, either by laymen or scientists, both of whom are inclined to think in terms of 'thought' or 'intellection' or 'cognition,' which partakes of the mystic more than it does of solid anatomy or physiologic function." The Psychologist's Fallacy is what James calls "the confusion of his own standpoint with that of the mental fact about which he is making a report." "Another variety of the psychologist's fallacy is the assumption that the mental fact studied must be conscious of itself as the psychologist is conscious of it." *Principles of Psychology*, vol. I, pp. 196–7.

idea of the Normal, saying that it has stood in the way of any true scientific knowledge of sex, it is itself by no means averse to letting the idea of the Natural develop quietly into the idea of the Normal. The Report has in mind both a physical normality—as suggested by its belief that under optimal conditions men should be able to achieve the orgasmic frequency of the primates—and a moral normality, the acceptability, on the authority of animal behavior, of certain usually taboo practices.

It is inevitable that the concept of the Natural should haunt any discussion of sex. It is inevitable that it should make trouble, but most of all for a scientific discussion that bars judgments of value. Thus, in order to show that homosexuality is not a neurotic manifestation, as the Freudians say it is, the Report adduces the homosexual behavior of rats. But the argument *de animalibus* must surely stand by its ability to be inverted and extended. Thus, in having lost sexual periodicity, has the human animal lost naturalness? Again, the female mink, we learn, fiercely resists intercourse and must be actually coerced into submission. Is it she who is unnatural or is her defense of her chastity to be taken as a comment on the females, animal or human, who willingly submit or who merely play at escape? Professor Kinsey is like no one so much as Sir Percival in Malory who, seeing a lion and a serpent in battle with each other, decided to help the lion, "for he was the more natural beast of the two."

This awkwardness in the handling of ideas is characteristic of the Report. It is ill at ease with any idea that is in the least complex and it often tries to get rid of such an idea in favor of another that has the appearance of not going beyond the statement of physical fact. We see this especially in the handling of certain Freudian ideas. The Report acknowledges its debt to Freud with the generosity of spirit that marks it in other connections and it often makes use of Freudian concepts in a very direct and sensible way. Yet nothing could be clumsier than its handling of Freud's idea of pre-genital generalized infantile sexuality. Because the Report can show, what is interesting and significant, that infants are capable of actual orgasm, although without ejaculation, it concludes that infantile sexuality is not generalized but specifically genital. But actually it has long been known, though the fact of orgasm had not been established, that infants can respond erotically to direct genital stimulation; and this knowledge does not contradict the Freudian idea that there is a stage in infant development in which sexuality is generalized throughout the body rather than specifically centered in the genital area—the fact of infant orgasm must be interpreted in conjunction with other and more complex manifestations of infant sexuality.[6]

The Report, we may say, has an extravagant fear of all ideas that do not seem to it to be, as it were, immediately dictated by simple physical fact. Another way of saying this is that the Report is resistant to any idea that seems to refer to a specifically human situation. An example is the position it takes on the matter of male potency. The folk feeling, where it is formulated on the question, and certainly where it is formulated by women, holds that male potency is not to be measured, as the Report measures it, merely by frequency, but by the ability to withhold orgasm long enough to bring the woman to climax. This is also the psychoanalytic view, which holds further that the inability to sustain intercourse is the result of unconscious fear. This view is very strongly controverted by the Report. The denial is based on mammalian behavior—"in many species" (but not in all?) ejaculation follows almost immediately upon intromission; in chimpanzees ejaculation occurs in ten to twenty seconds. The Report therefore concludes that the human male who ejaculates immediately upon intromission "is quite normal [here the word becomes suddenly permissible] among mammals and usual among his own species." Indeed, the Report finds it odd that the term "impotent" should be applied to such rapid responses. "It would be difficult to find another situation in which an individual who was quick and intense in his responses was labeled anything but superior, and that in most instances is exactly what the rapidly ejaculating male probably is, however inconvenient and unfortunate his qualities may be from the standpoint of the wife in the relationship."

[6] The Report also handles the idea of sublimation in a very clumsy way. It does not represent accurately what the Freudian theory of sublimation is. For this, however, there is some excuse in the change of emphasis and even of meaning in Freud's use of the word.

But by such reasoning the human male who is quick and intense in his leap to the lifeboat is natural and superior, however inconvenient and unfortunate his speed and intensity may be to the wife he leaves standing on the deck, as is also the man who makes a snap judgment, who bites his dentist's finger, who kicks the child who annoys him, who bolts his—or another's—food, who is incontinent of his feces. Surely the problem of the natural in the human was solved four centuries ago by Rabelais, and in the simplest naturalistic terms; and it is sad to have the issue all confused again by the naivety of men of science. Rabelais' solution lay in the simple perception of the *natural* ability and tendency of man to grow in the direction of organization and control. The young Gargantua in his natural infancy had all the quick and intense responses just enumerated; had his teachers confused the traits of his natural infancy with those of his natural manhood, he would not have been the more natural but the less; he would have been a monster.

In considering the Report as a major cultural document, we must not underestimate the significance of its petulant protest against the inconvenience to the male of the unjust demand that is made upon him. This protest is tantamount to saying that sexuality is not to be involved in specifically human situations or to be connected with desirable aims that are conceived of in specifically human terms. We may leave out of account any ideal reasons which would lead a man to solve the human situation of the discrepancy—arising from conditions of biology or of culture or of both—between his own orgasmic speed and that of his mate, and we can consider only that it might be hedonistically desirable for him to do so, for advantages presumably accrue to him in the woman's accessibility and responsiveness. Advantages of this kind, however, are precisely the matters of quality in experience that the Report does not consider.[7]

[7] It is hard not to make a connection between the Report's strong stand against any delay in the male orgasm and its equally strong insistence that there is no difference for the woman between a clitoral and vaginal orgasm, a view which surely needs more investigation before it is as flatly put as the Report puts it. The conjunction of the two ideas suggests the desirability of a sexuality which uses a minimum of sexual apparatus.

And its attitude on the question of male potency is but one example of the Report's insistence on drawing sexuality apart from the general human context. It is striking how small a role woman plays in *The Sexual Behavior of the Human Male*. We learn nothing about the connection of sex and reproduction; the connection, from the sexual point of view, is certainly not constant yet it is of great interest. The pregnancy or possibility of pregnancy of his mate has a considerable effect, sometimes one way, sometimes the other, on the sexual behavior of the male; yet the index gives but one entry under *Pregnancy—"fear of."* Again, the contraceptive devices which *Pregnancy, fear of* requires have a notable influence on male sexuality; but the index lists only *Contraception, techniques.* Or again, menstruation has an elaborate mythos which men take very seriously; but the two indexed passages which refer to menstruation give no information about its relation to sexual conduct.

Then too the Report explicitly and stubbornly resists the idea that sexual behavior is involved with the whole of the individual's character. In this it is strangely inconsistent. In the conclusion of its chapter on masturbation, after saying that masturbation does no physical harm and, if there are no conflicts, no mental harm, it goes on to raise the question of the effect of adult masturbation on the ultimate personality of the individual. With a certain confusion of cause and effect which we need not dwell on, it says: "It is now clear that masturbation is relied upon by the upper [social] level primarily because it has insufficient outlet through heterosexual coitus. This is, to a degree, an escape from reality, and the effect upon the ultimate personality of the individual is something that needs consideration." The question is of course a real one, yet the Report strenuously refuses to extend the principle of it to any other sexual activity. It summarily rejects the conclusions of psychoanalysis which make the sexual conduct an important clue to, even the crux of, character. It finds the psychoanalytical view unacceptable for two reasons: (1) The psychiatric practitioner misconceives the relation between sexual aberrancy and psychic illness because only those sexually aberrant people who are ill seek out the practitioner, who never learns about the large incidence of health among the aberrant. (2) The emotional illness which sends the sexually aberrant person to find psychiatric help is the result of no flaw in the psyche itself that is connected with the aberrancy, but is only the result of the fear of social disapproval of his sexual conduct. And the Report instances the many men who are well adjusted socially and who yet show, among them, the whole range of taboo conduct.

The quality of the argument which the Report advances is as significant as the wrong conclusions it reaches. "It is not possible," the Report says, "to insist that any departure from the sexual mores, or any participation in socially taboo activities, always, or even usually, involves a neurosis or psychosis, for the case histories abundantly demonstrate that most individuals who engage in taboo activities make satisfactory social adjustments." In this context either "neuroses and psychoses" are too loosely used to stand for all psychic maladjustment, or "social adjustment" is too loosely used to stand for emotional peace and psychic stability. When the Report goes on to cite the "socially and intellectually significant persons," the "successful scientists, educators, physicians," etc., who have among them "accepted the whole range of the so-called abnormalities," we must keep in mind that very intense emotional disturbance, known only to the sufferer, can go along with the efficient discharge of social duties; and that the psychoanalyst could counter with as long a list of distinguished and efficient people who consult him.

Then no one except a straw man would insist that *any* departure from sexual mores, or *any* participation in sexually taboo activities, involves a neurosis or a psychosis. It is just at this point that distinctions are needed of a sort which the Report seems not to want to make. For example: the Report comes out in a bold and simple way for the naturalness and normality and therefore the desirability of mouth-genital contacts in heterosexual love-making. This is a form of sexual expression which is officially taboo enough, yet to say that its practice indicated a neurosis or psychosis would be impossible to any psychoanalyst. But a person who disliked or was unable to practice any other form of contact would justify the conclusion that there was a neurotic streak in his psychic constitution. His social adjustment, in the rather crude terms which the Report conceives of it, might not be impaired, but certainly the chances are that his psychic life would show signs of disturbance, not from the practice itself but from the psychic needs which make him insist on it. It is not the breaking of the taboo but the emotional circumstance of the breaking of the taboo that is significant.

The Report handles in the same oversimplified way and with the same confusing use of absolute concepts the sexual aberrancy which is, I suppose, the most complex and the most important in our cultural life, homosexuality. It rejects the view that homosexuality is innate and that "no modification of it may be expected." But then it goes on also to reject the view that homosexuality provides evidence of a "psychopathic personality." "Psychopathic personality" is a very strong term which perhaps few analysts would wish to use in this connection. Perhaps even the term "neurotic" would be extreme in a discussion which takes "social adjustment," as indicated by status, to be the limit of its analysis of character. But this does not leave the discussion where the Report seems to want to leave it—at the idea that homosexuality is to be accepted as a form of sexuality like another and that it is as "natural" as heterosexuality, a judgment to which the Report is led in part because of the surprisingly large incidence of homosexuality it finds in the population. Nor does the practice of "an increasing proportion of the most skilled psychiatrists who make no attempt to redirect behavior, but who devote their attention to helping an individual accept himself" imply what the Report seems to want it to, that these psychiatrists have thereby judged homosexuality to be an unexceptionable form of sexuality; it is rather that, in many cases, they are able to effect no change in the psychic disposition and therefore do the sensible and humane next best thing. Their opinion of the etiology of homosexuality as lying in some warp—as our culture judges it—of the psychic structure has not, I believe, changed. And I think that they would say that the condition that produced the homosexuality also produces other character traits on which judgment could be passed. This judgment need by no means be totally adverse; as passed upon individuals it need not be adverse at all; but there can be no doubt that a society in which homosexuality was dominant or even accepted would be different in the nature and quality of its life from a society in which homosexuality was censured.

The refusal of the Report to hold such a view leads us at this point to take into account what seem to be certain motives that animate the work. And when we do, we see how very characteristically American a document it is.

In speaking of its motives, I have in mind chiefly the impulse toward acceptance and liberation, the broad and generous desire for others not to be harshly judged. Much in the Report is to be understood as a recoil from the crude and often brutal rejection which society has made of the persons it calls aberrant. The Report has the intention of habituating its readers to the idea of sexuality in all its manifestations, to establish, as it were, a democratic pluralism of sexuality.

This good impulse shows itself very clearly in certain parts of our intellectual life, often in the more or less official parts. It is, for example, far more established in the universities than most of us, with our habits of criticism of America, particularly of American universities, easily admit. This generosity of mind is to be much admired, yet it is often associated with an almost willed intellectual weakness, with a preference for not making intellectual distinctions, perhaps out of fear that they may turn out to be social discriminations. Somehow the democratic virtues are inclined, in the intellectual life, to lead from the large acceptance of the facts of society to the belief that any use of these facts which perceives values and demonstrates consequences is dangerous.

One result of this set of mind is the worship of the factuality of the fact. There seem to be two criteria for factuality. One is the material physicality of the fact and its relative removal from idea and ideal, from complication and modification. The other is the numerical strength of the fact. As the first criterion is used in the Report it has the effect, ironic in a work that is so clearly directed to democratic values, of removing the human subject from its human implications. As the second criterion is used in the Report it has the effect, equally ironic in a democratic and instrumental document, of preventing the consideration of the consequences of certain forms of human conduct. The two criteria taken together have the effect of suggesting a most ineffectual standard of social behavior—that is, social behavior as it exists. Yet this is contradicted at any number of points and the Report is quite willing to judge among behaviors by various manipulations of its factual criteria. It is impossible to say of the Report that it does not bring light, and necessary to say of it that it spreads confusion.

Popular Taste and
"The Caine Mutiny"
by Harvey Swados

IN the months that have passed since the publication of Herman Wouk's *The Caine Mutiny*, it has become something of a phenomenon in the publishing business by climbing slowly to the top of the best-seller lists without fanfare or ballyhoo, and then staying there week after week, month after month, until it begins to look now like another *Gone With The Wind*. Why?

I should like to suggest that the answer will reveal a good deal about the changes that have recently taken place in the reading taste of the American public as well as in what is known as popular culture. The best-seller, unlike the movie or even the musical comedy, is still the work of one man, a creative craftsman of greater or lesser skill responding directly to his sense of the public taste. In the case of Mr. Wouk, this skill is pressed into the service of a mythmaking that more or less corresponds to certain ideas currently dominant in American middle-class life. *The Caine Mutiny* is in every aspect a faithful reflection of the morals, fears, and intellectual aspirations of the new middle class, that proliferant white collar segment of the American community that is basically responsible for "progressive" movies praised because they deal—no matter how—with the problems of minorities, musical comedies praised because their songs are filled with "social significance," and radio programs praised because in the recent past, before television, they evolved a kind of rhetorical statement that passed for poetry.

This new middle class, many of its members the successful sons and daughters of struggling and bewildered immigrants, is yearly producing larger and more avid audiences of high school and (increasingly) college graduates with more leisure time than working people ever had before. Impatient with traditional pulp stories, Western movies, and show-girl musical comedies, they want to feel that their intelligences are engaged by the programs they hear, the movies they see, the books they read; and they take it as an act of social piety and, by extension, of artistic integrity, when these media feature favorable stereotypes of minorities once represented by unfavorable caricatures. At the same time they participate in a kind of mass snobbery of which they are all but unaware, on the one hand rejecting in angry frustration those whom they instinctively fear and admire—aristocrats, millionaires and serious-minded intellectuals, and on the other hand patronizing the underlying population with pseudo-democratic verbiage about the "average Joe" and the "common man." To a large extent they are responsible for the new trends in popular taste because they are themselves the very begetters of our leading practitioners of popular culture, the Dore Scharys, the Stanley Kramers, the Irwin Shaws.

Consider how *The Caine Mutiny* meets the needs of this great audience. The American wartime experience is refracted through the eyes of Willie Keith, who might be described as the average American rich boy whom we have come to know from the writings of J. P. Marquand and even F. Scott Fitzgerald (there is in some ways a remarkable similarity between Amory Blaine or Anthony Patch and Willie): a home on Long Island, another house in Palm Beach, four years at Princeton, a small talent for versifying and piano playing, a domineering mother, a love affair with a poor but honest Italian night club singer, and finally a leap into navy officers' school to avoid the draft. In the navy, however, he is simply a reserve officer, a member of that middle segment of wartime society that lords it over the enlisted man and lives in fear, admiration and bewilderment of the regular navy career officer. Willie accepts assignment to a rusty old minesweeper, the *Caine*, which is commanded by Captain Queeg, an Annapolis man. It is soon apparent to everyone that Queeg is at best a tyrannical martinet and at worst a psychopath. A series of small but nasty incidents, described in lengthy and convincing detail, persuades Willie and his fellow reserve officers that Queeg is a coward, an unbalanced disciplinarian, and finally a madman.

In some of the most interesting pages of the book, the officers

of the *Caine* discuss Captain Queeg in an attempt to decide
whether he is mad or simply vicious. It is Lieutenant Thomas Keefer, intellectual, playwright, and budding war novelist, who first discovers the obscure naval regulations providing for the replacement
of mentally or physically incapacitated commanding officers
through a kind of legal mutiny. He plants in the mind of Lieutenant Maryk, a stolid and competent peacetime fisherman, the seed
that grows into a conviction of Queeg's insanity. But when Maryk
gets Keefer to accompany him to Admiral Halsey's office to plead
for Queeg's replacement, Keefer begs off at the last possible moment with the explanation that their proof is insufficient and subject to misinterpretation. Neither Willie nor any of his fellow
reserve officers from whose point of view Captain Queeg is observed can think of him apart from his role as navy officer. A fine
line divides them from Queeg and his Annapolis clubmates, who
are described as either fantastically tyrannical (Queeg) or infinitely
wise, experienced and compassionate (Queeg's superiors).

No effort is made to portray the enlisted men of the *Caine*,
except insofar as they advance the story and play their little super-
numerary roles in the mutiny. We see them vaguely, through a
veil of sympathy, although a good deal of the action takes place
in the confined quarters of the *Caine*. As for the messmen, who
appear only to pour coffee, they are simply good-humored, yassuh-
ing Rastuses. Not that there is anything of vulgar anti-Negro prejudice in this. Here is a different kind of vulgarity, not unlike the
blind "liberalism" of the Hollywood moviemakers who attempt to
represent a cross section of America by showing us army companies composed of bragging Texans, tough but sentimental
Brooklyn Jews, quiet and brave Westerners, oversensitive but essentially courageous rich mens' sons, and Negro boys who are
almost like everybody else. . . .

When the *Caine* is caught in a violent storm and seems
doomed, Queeg freezes on the bridge, unable to issue the orders
that would save the ship. At this crucial point Maryk takes command and does save the ship, with the passive consent of Keefer,
Willie and the other officers. After the storm the ship returns to
the United States and Maryk is court-martialed for his unprecedented behavior; and Willie, knowing that he, too, must stand

trial if Maryk is convicted, supports his fellow officer to the best of his ability. Keefer protects his own career by equivocating and refusing to swear to Queeg's madness. But Maryk is finally acquitted thanks to the brilliant courtroom tactics of his counsel, Lieutenant Commander Barney Greenwald, a crack Jewish lawyer from Albuquerque, who is recuperating from severe burns received on active duty as a carrier fighter pilot. Greenwald is convinced that Maryk and his mates are guilty, but he is equally convinced that he can get Maryk off, and he finally succeeds, by harping on Queeg's instability and by appealing to the navy's pride in its officer caste.

Keefer throws a champagne party to celebrate the sale of his novel together with Maryk's acquittal. Greenwald is invited, comes in drunk, and stays just long enough to deliver an impassioned speech to the shocked officers of the *Caine* and to throw his champagne in Keefer's face. In his speech Greenwald indicates that for him the war has been a struggle to save his grandmother from being melted down into soap like the Jewish grandmothers of Europe; in that struggle the Queegs—regardless of their brutality or stupidity—have played an essential role by contributing their skill to the maintenance of a vital core of defense in the years when military people and military expenses were belittled. The Keefers have sabotaged these defenders of freedom with their mocking cynicism, says Greenwald, and in Captain Queeg's case, Tom Keefer not only incited Maryk to an irresponsible, if well-meant, act of disloyalty (for he could simply have covered up for Queeg during the storm and then returned the ship's command to him), but compounded his guilt by his cowardly testimony at Maryk's court-martial.

Here we must be struck by the correspondence between what Mr. Wouk is saying and what the public wants to hear. It is his thesis that the Second World War was worthwhile if only because it put a stop to the enemy's slaughters; that it was won by a devoted and previously trained officer caste, despite the incompetence of individual members; and that the most insidious enemy is the man who works to destroy confidence in his country's military leadership.

It must be noted first that this is a thesis which can be—and

has been—upheld by fascist as easily as by democratic theorists.
Second, and perhaps even more important, is the identification of
the intellectual as the villain of the piece, with his cowardice and
his shameful sniping at the regular officer class. Here again it is
necessary to point out that the middle-class reading public would
almost certainly reject such a brutal assault on the intellectual
(against which one might have expected intellectuals to rally, just
as undertakers or chiropodists rally to meet unfair representations
of their professions in the movies) if it were made by a boor or an
obvious philistine. It is symptomatic of Mr. Wouk's shrewdness
that he puts his assault on the intellectual in the mouth of Barney
Greenwald, who speaks with the voice of authority, from the "inside." For in addition to embodying civic virtue as a wounded
hero, he gained enormous financial success in the law, a field popularly associated with the regular exercise of the higher faculties; he
is also a member and fighting representative of a minority group,
and a passionate defender of an even smaller minority, the American Indian! And it follows, therefore, that Greenwald's opposite
number, the cowardly intellectual who conceals his inadequacy
beneath a surface charm that temporarily captivates the susceptible
Willie Keith, should not be a shabby Greenwich Village Jewish
bohemian but a handsome and successful playwright named
Thomas Keefer.

If we reverse the roles, conceiving of a clean-cut Tom Keefer
charging a degenerate and decadent Barney Greenwald with being
an irresponsible intellectual whose writing and preachings have had
a devastating effect on American youth, we can imagine the justified protest that *The Caine Mutiny* would have aroused.

After he returns to the *Caine*, Willie, who had admired
Keefer, is forced to concede that Greenwald was right. Keefer is
now captain of the *Caine* and Willie his executive officer. In the
closing weeks of the war, the ship is hit by a Kamikaze, and
Keefer, to his own shame and disgust, hastily abandons ship, leaving Willie to save the *Caine* and the men who have remained
aboard, and returns only when the danger is past. Willie is given
command of the *Caine* after Keefer leaves the ship in Japan, and
he sails home to New York a man, a hero, prepared to cut loose

from his mother and to fight for the hand of the Italian girl who had seemed beneath him at the beginning of the war.

It must be noted that Mr. Wouk is an exceptionally good story-teller. Willie Keith's adventures, travails and loves are handled with a directness and a swiftness that bear the mark of the practiced professional writer. But this is true of a good many other novels, even novels dealing with the Second World War, that have not had a tenth the success of this book. What we must consider is the special quality that has made *The Caine Mutiny* seem important to so many people.

It is a quality not to be found in many best-sellers that depended for their popularity simply on romance, sword-play, décolletages and civil wars. For those books, despite obvious attractions, cannot possibly involve the modern middle-class reader's deepest feelings about sex, war and society, in a way that flatters him into the belief that he is participating in a thoughtful intellectual experience.

Let us turn to Willie's love affair. It is one of the novel's main themes and also serves technically both as counterpoint and relief. When Willie first meets Marie Minotti they fall in love, but are kept from intimacy by the bitter-sweet realization that their social backgrounds are worlds apart, for he is still under his mother's domination and she is only the daughter of a Bronx immigrant. So far their relation has a certain comfortable familiarity—tragedies have been written on just this theme and innumerable soap operas, too. There is, to be sure, a certain flavor of the archaic in tracing the difficulties of a love affair between two young people who come from utterly different milieux; when J. P. Marquand treats it, as he does so often, he removes the love affair a generation or two from current reality, presenting it as part of the recollections of an aging man. Furthermore, the liberal-minded middle-class reader is well aware of the impediments that have been removed from the path of true love by the withering away of the uppermost and nethermost classes in American society and the consequent expansion of the middle sector. Nevertheless he is also reminded by his parents and by columnists, whose sensible advice to the lovelorn is increasingly spiced with modern psychiatric lingo, of the dangers inherent in romance between young people whose family backgrounds are "incompatible."

In any case, Willie cannot bring himself to break off with Marie, and when he returns to the West Coast from his first Pacific cruise, he impetuously goes to bed with her. Here the reader is brought from the world of impossible romance into a world that he knows perfectly well exists. The author makes it quite clear that the couple have transgressed, although they are young, healthy and heedless; thus the reader has the double advantage of feeling that the love affair is realistic while protecting his moral sense. Marie, however, refuses to repeat the experience with Willie, who appreciates her new-found reserve, but begins to wonder if he can possibly love a girl who has given herself to him so easily, even if only once.

Although the reader knows that Willie is still rationalizing his snobbishness, Willie goes on torturing himself until his naval experiences bring him maturity and the need for permanent companionship. When he returns to New York in command of the *Caine* at the end of the war, he finds Marie singing for a prominent dance-band leader, and apparently living with him too. But now Willie is no longer a boy. He stands his ground and announces to Marie that he is going to take her away from the bandleader and marry her; she, fearing that Willie is simply feeling sorry for her, reveals that she has not *really* been sleeping with the bandleader, although everyone thinks so. At the close of the book it seems fairly certain that Willie will win the girl.

Here I think is an almost perfect correspondence between current sexual morality and the realities of the American experience. For a reading public caught between Sunday School training and exposure to the *Kinsey Report*, the dilemma of Willie Keith, although it can add no new dimension to their lives or depth to their experience, must seem completely "true to life" and overwhelmingly poignant. Even the falsity of his hard-won "maturity," which enables him to assert his love by suddenly disregarding the profound social differences between himself and Marie, is accepted by an audience eager for a description of love more meaningful than moonlight and roses but which still does not deprive them of the consolation of a happy ending. Virtue must still be rewarded; it is only that the rules defining virtue have been modified by the economic necessity for delayed marriages and by the back seats of forty million automobiles. Willie's virtue in loving Marie despite her affair with the bandleader is rewarded with the revelation that she has not *really* slept with the man. It is as though Mr. Wouk were subconsciously attuned to the precise degree of sexual liberation which the popular mind is ready to grant to American youth, as well as to the exact amount of traditional romance with which the depiction of the liberation must be leavened.

Indeed, any analysis of the most successful components of popular culture would compel us to refer to the ability of men like Mr. Wouk to let us have our cake and eat it, to stimulate us without unduly provoking us, to make us feel that we are thinking without really forcing us to think.

Just as Willie's virtue is rewarded with the revelation of his girl's purity, so are his heroism and his steadfast support of Maryk rewarded with a medal, a command, and a hero's return. Keefer, on the other hand, is punished for his sophistry, irresponsibility and cowardice, not by official action, but—what is worse for him— by the consciousness of his ineradicable inadequacy despite his literary success. And Maryk, in what is perhaps the neatest touch of all, is formally acquitted of the "mutiny," thanks to the brilliant defense of Greenwald, but suffers for his presumption in deposing Queeg by being deprived forever of the possibility of realizing his life's ambition—a career as an officer in the regular navy. Thus, the lives of all the principals are composed in accordance with their just deserts, i.e., with accepted standards of reward and retribution.

What the new middle class wanted—and found in *The Caine Mutiny*—was an assurance that its years of discomfort and hardship in the Second World War were not in vain, and that its sacrifices in a permanent war economy and its gradual accommodation to the emergence of the military as a dominant element in civil life have been not only necessary but praiseworthy. More than this, it requires such assurance in a sophisticated form, allowing it to feel that alternatives have been thoughtfully considered before being rejected: in *The Caine Mutiny* ample space is given over

to consideration of "psychoanalytic" motivations in Queeg and in
Keefer too, and even the Cain-Abel analogy is mentioned as evidence that the title is not an unmotivated slip of the pen.

The taste of the middle-class reading public is conditioned by
an increasing prosperousness in a military economy, tending to reinforce conservative moral concepts and to strengthen a traditional
envy and distrust of intellectuals and dissidents. But its taste is
modified by an indebtedness to its European forebears, New Deal
heritage, and continuously higher level of education. Thus it is inclined toward a sophisticated and hospitable acceptance of those
entertainments of the vanished European aristocracy which have
flowed into the mainstream of Western liberal culture through
the channels of mass production and distribution. Witness the
phenomenal increase of ballet audiences and the number of people
buying "classical" records. Writers like Herman Wouk will inevitably arise directly from this class to verbalize its inchoate and
often contradictory attitudes. Indeed Mr. Wouk's background—he
has combined a faithful adherence to Orthodox Judaism and a
career as a radio gag writer with no apparent discomfort—has prepared him admirably for his task as a practitioner of popular culture.

The Psychopathology
of "Time" & "Life"
by Marshall McLuhan

IT would seem a very good time to take stock of the performance of his trio now that Mr. Luce has begun to think seriously of adding a fourth star to his stable. The fourth member is to be definitely highbrow, as it appears. And in passing from glorified spot-news (*Time*) to nursery entertainment (*Life*) to managerial grand opera (*Fortune*) to high-brow criticism, Mr. Luce must still have an eye on *Der Verlag Ullstein* from whose activities and methods his own are so largely derivative. Thus Ullstein's *Querschnitt* printed Pirandello, Proust, Cocteau, Woolf, Mann, and others in their original languages, and aimed to be "a monthly for the literary gourmet" and for "the intellectually indulgent, the well read, the erudite, who sometimes preferred to smile superciliously than laugh outright."

Something between Mr. Eliot's *Criterion* and *The New Yorker* with, of course, an opulent lacquered finish would be the general character of such a magazine. Whether its somber sanity would be harmful or beneficial to present intellectual and artistic activity would be hard to predict. Benefits resulting would be wholly accidental, at any rate. Mr. Luce favors anonymous hack-work in his magazines for the reason that he has conceived each one within the co-ordinates of very simple stereotypes. And the men he would need for his new magazine would be less tractable to Luce cliché than the hackmen of *Time*, *Life*, and *Fortune*. Perhaps not utterly intractable. But the problem for Mr. Luce is first to reduce the present role of art and letters to a simple pattern which could be reproduced monthly without disturbing the existing affinities between his other three magazines. That problem solved, he could probably buy up quite a crowd of *clercs* for his new job.

I may as well say at once that I don't think the Luce brain can do it. Mr. Luce has a passion for glossy mediocrity and stereotypical order which derives from his obsession with mechanism. Even as a young man he must have been very fatigued, because he seems to have felt very strongly all the senescent and servile appeal of the brittle and lifeless perfection of machined thoughts and feelings. Mr. Luce wants the best imitation of thought and feeling that the machine can produce. But like Northcliffe he succeeds not so much by cynical innerdetachment from his Punch and Judy show as by irremediable identity with the weary vacuum of his reader-mass. He loves to show off the machine as much as any Hollywood director glories in camera show-off. But the machine as show-off is megalomaniac. And nobody will find either human dimensions, human order, or human complexity in *Time, Life,* or *Fortune.* These magazines are heavily farced mechanistic fantasies of a megalomaniac kind. And should Mr. Luce venture into the last sphere of human spontaneity and free intelligence he would inevitably feel urged to reduce that world to the kind of sub-human order he does understand. In a word, he would attempt to annihilate it for its own good.

For the independent artist and intellectual, the stereotype or insubordinate mechanism is death. The loss of perception and the abeyance of judgment. But because the areas in which perception is cultivated or even tolerated have been ever more rapidly circumscribed, the artist and intellectual have had to turn to unmasking clichés and the mass mechanisms of sensibility as part of the business of survival. Even in this role of the enemy of bloated inanities and glossy fakes the artist and intellectual find the ultimate enemies of the human to be extremely elusive. The centers of political initiative today are as inaccessible as the accusers of a Kafka character.

In this respect *Time, Life,* and *Fortune* appear at first in an ambiguous light. On one hand they affect the role of spectators of events. And they make no bones about being omniscient and alert spectators of the March of Time. But on the other hand they are always recommending their own spectator role and penny-arcade vision to millions of readers. Vigorously thrusting an emotionally-charged spectator role on their readers by every device of popularized snob-appeal and the big stick of scientific know-how is surely taking political initiative. Basically, therefore, the Luce triumvirate is carefully engineered political action. Sub-doctrinaire and sub-rational action, it's true. But still much the strongest and most definite political action to be discerned in England or America.

Time, Life, and Fortune represent three levels of irresponsible politics in much the same sense as Hollywood is willy-nilly a political force. That is, neither T.L.F. nor Hollywood attempts to hold up any kind of object or program for detached observation or appraisal. But both arrange their exhibits in suchwise as to manipulate the standardized reflexes of a semi-hypnotized and mentally helpless audience. So that the art of the movie is not to be judged by the invention and arrangement of images but by the effect which those images have on the contents of the mind or guts of a spectator. Likewise with T.L.F. It isn't the worth or character of the image or statement presented which is of any political significance but the effect which it is observed to have on a sharply focussed reader. Needless to say, the reader is not the one to do the focussing. He is held in position.

One of the most obvious facts, then, about T.L.F. is their tempo. They insist that the reader move rapidly. Pictures and ads produce an aura of sentimental awe for the sub-rational reception of rapid-fire prose, so that the mental situation of the reader is very nearly as low as that of a news-reel audience. Emphasizing the value of the movie medium for South America, R. S. Carr of the Rockefeller Agency wrote:

> The propaganda value of this simultaneous audio-visual impression is very high, for it standardizes thought by supplying the spectator with a ready-made visual image before he has time to conjure up an interpretation of his own.

This commonplace of press, radio, and screen receives the utmost stress in T.L.F. and will get closer attention further on.

Perhaps the most persistently risible feature of T.L.F. is the assumption of "god-like heights of observation." It is an inseparable feature of paranoid megalomania shared by every Dagwood who dreams of flying his own plane or leading an expedition to the top of Mount Everest. In the March of Time the extremely ado-

lescent emotionalism of this Olympian pose is obvious in the
phoney dramaturgy and the Zeus-like resonance of the announcer's
voice: "Who walks the bridge tonight, O King?" This god-like elevation sometimes assumes the air of god-like condescension, as in
Time's comic boast that it answers every letter received. It is seen
also in *Time's* arid assumption that "people are funny" which
Fortune, of course, strives to hide with well-heeled sobriety. Most
of all, this ludicrously facile and unearned elevation (contrast
Swift's Lilliput) of *Superman* naiveté, is observable in the inevitable mockery accorded both by *Time* and *Life* to major talent.

Perhaps this last remark should be documented at once since
nothing is more popularly accredited to these magazines than an
enlightened awareness and appraisal of events and figures of significance. The August 12, 1946, issue of *Life* devotes a page of pictures
and eight double columns of *Time* prose to Frank Lloyd Wright:
"The titan of modern architecture still flings his houses and his
insults at backward colleagues by Winthrop Sargeant." Under his
photograph we read: "After 77 flamboyant years Wright is hale."
And the first paragraph concludes after placing Wright's "bio-
graphical melodrama" in the company of Cellini and Casanova:

> Fellow architects have hailed and damned him as
> everything from a great poet and visionary to an insup-
> portable windbag. The clergy has deplored his morals.
> Creditors have deplored his financial habits, writers his
> literary style, wives his infidelities, politicians his opinions.

In this wise-guy tone and vein Sargeant parades the flamboyant
bear for an audience assumed to be at once Philistine and cre-
tinous. Wright is good for a thrill or two. Especially since he is a
clear case of genius who must be debagged and reduced to the
impotent condition of the *T.L.F.* public. Emasculation is necessarily the senescent *Time* process monotonously applied to every
game-cock. Only a fake virility can be tolerated. As one *Time* ad in
Life put it, under the head of "A nose for news and a stomach for
whiskey," the veteran reporter "knew bishops and gunmen, politicians and pickpockets, and treated both the great and the sham
with the same casual impertinence." Thus to flaunt as a virtue
one's resentful impercipience is the final degree of contempt for

the mental impotence of the deluded reader. But the ad is true enough to the facts. The tough-guy pose, the self-dramatization of sentimental despair is the familiar persona of the reporter. Hemingway hadn't far to look for his protagonist—the dumb-ox, the baleful and abbreviated member of the herd. Therefore it is quite possible that Sargeant himself admires Wright. He may even understand him. But, with the lethal weapon of *Time* prose in his hand, friend and foe alike are brought down:

> "An incurable esthete, Wright approaches his buildings as though they were poems or symphonies instead of mere houses. . . ." And the contents of his books:
> "provocative, poetic and preposterous by turns, include everything from house designing to morals and Utopian politics and read like rumblings of Old Testament prophecy."

That is the way in which Wright is interpreted and "placed" for what *Life* clearly regards as the "cretin crew." Let nobody dare to be as virile as the monkey-glandular hackmen of *Time* or he will soon have his manly parts thrown in his face as a reminder of his undemocratic stature. For that is the symbolic sense of the snide phrases under the candid camera shots in *Time* and the dissonant juxtapositions of *Life*.

In fact the shadow of the *artiste manqué* has hovered over these publications from the beginning. *Time* offers the free of its hand to big and small while affecting a mannered prose. The result is not unlike opera à la Spike Jones or Alec Templeton. The positive effects have to be good enough to convince the crowd that: "This is a darned smart bunch. Bet they could do the real thing if they wanted to. They can cut capers all around these bigwigs in the news, for my money." *Time* made its debut not long after *Ulysses* had made young Harvard sedulously apish. The prim, as well as the encyclopedic, arrogance of Stephen Daedalus offered an easily adaptable pose for the restless young journalist. A pose which could also be called the Harvard version of *Variety*.

In a word, *Time*, *Life*, and *Fortune* (*The New Yorker* can be tossed in with them) are the American Bloomsbury, our psychological bureaucracy, inhabited by well-paid artist-apes. In America art must pay off before it can be respectable or even interesting. And the artist-ape must here assume the air of executive or engineer in order to circulate or prosper.

The "sophisticated" tone of *Time*, then, arises from nothing more than queasiness about the main march of the human affections, which issues as hard-boiled flippancy. And it is the whole world, of course, which is dear dirty Dublin to the omnivorous hackmen of *T.L.F.* The world of popular science, of *homo boobiens*. That is, man is always homo boobiens in *T.L.F.* focus. But lest the parallel between Joyce and *T.L.F.* should be thought creditable to the Luce trio, it needs only to be pointed out that whereas Joyce developed a variety of techniques as means to presenting a vision of the world, *T.L.F.* are merely esthetish in exploiting these attitudes and techniques as exhibitionist devices which prove, after all, to be a personal indulgence, a narcissistic aggrandizement in which the reader is invited to share for less than $00.01 a day.

One would seek in vain, therefore, to discover any sort of hearty self-deprecation or any sense of unfitness for the highest tasks in the *T.L.F.* ranks. Readers and writers alike seem to enjoy a mood of self-congratulatory elation and robot-like unanimity as they keep briskly abreast of the *Zeitgeist*. They are encouraged to nurse a self-image of tweedy decorum and contented aplomb such as the "Men of Distinction" ads exhibit. So that altogether *T.L.F.* constitute the Hollywood of the East Coast enfolding their reader-mass in an hallucination appropriately more pretentious than that of the frontier. But Hollywood and *T.L.F.* are one in their dedication to the garish rhetoric of the machine.

Time is certainly a very forcible expression of what Sorokin calls the "deterioration of sensate culture by a host of scholars united in big research corporations led by social science managers and committees. Industriously they cultivate either misleading preciseness or scholarly emptiness, with all the Alexandrian thoroughness of 'trained incapacity.'" This applies even more forcibly to *Life* and *Fortune*, where a total absence of social and political thought is itself the major political fact. Hedonism or a self-indulgent nihilism is the reigning appetite which evokes the wonders of camera and laboratory as anodynes for trapped little men.

The "Letters" department then is always arranged as a nose-gay for *Time*. But not too obviously so. Soreheads are given free rein since they could never be identified with *Time* readers. They are simply funny. Like the people in the news. But the true *Time* addict wears a relic of the mantle of Stephen Daedalus, which raises him above those who could possibly be bitten by a *Time* notice. Perhaps most common of all are letters from *Time* readers who are bona fide "inside men at the skunk works." The little nobody can then say: "Ah, he's one of us." And how *Time* loves to admit small factual error: "We archly acknowledge our occasional limitations. But this should serve to remind you of our really super-human encyclopedism."

Across from the letters stretches the enormous masthead. And beside the masthead is a plug for *Time* in the form of a description of its Morgue: "Now presided over by 55 librarians and helpers. . . . They get about 5000 requests a month . . . to determine (among other things) . . . the form of poetry most similar to the rhumba rhythm . . . the Moslem stand on birth control." Obviously the Morgue is the driving-shaft which whirls the big Mother Goose Windmill and provides that raucously musical breeze in *Time*'s waggish pages.

Time's Morgue is the precise image of the graduate research futility we imported from Germany in the nineteenth century. When it goes "serious" it becomes the Morgue of *Fortune*, which strives to emulate the geopolitik Morgues built up for the German General Staff in recent decades. The form of the activity and the appetites it serves are the same whether it is the Disney mind stunting cinematically or Disney providing identity symbols for B-29's. However, the Anglo-Saxon will pay any price to pursue a destructive appetite with a benign countenance. And woe to the cad who undeceives him.

Across from "U.S. Affairs," dwarfing an inset of Truman, Connally, and Byrnes, is a full page Boeing ad. Country club comfort in the air. The sleek studio photography underscores the seedy shot of the statesman. As though this weren't plain enough we are given a heavy dig in the ribs by the inscription: "Behind the tawdriness, a moral force?" The whole *Time* credo is in the crude counterpoint of this situation. It is the creed of savage simplicity contained in the concept of Technocracy. The engineer (plastic, mechanical, chemical, social) is god. The politico is stooge. This stylized theme really exhausts the entire political and social philosophy of *T.L.F.* senility. For between the extremes of engineer and politico lie the human playthings of these two figures. And they are also the playthings of the wondrous nursery world presided over by *T.L.F.*

To an eye with any human light in it the Boeing ad is "the air-conditioned nightmare" of human evisceration—the dream of the hollow men. To such an eye there appears much more to admire in the Erskine Caldwell "corner" on p. 9 than in the Barmecide feast of current technical virtuosity. Technics are the opium of the commuters. Candid camera shots of murder and mutilation, their signal to "wake up and live."

"Mr. Byrnes, just before flying eastward in the *Sacred Cow*, said hopefully: 'Peace must come from the hearts of men.'" That is the concluding item in the survey of "The Nation." Apart from the gratuitous mention of the ludicrous *Sacred Cow*, the *Time* word in this is "hopefully." Byrnes was probably grim rather than hopeful. But "hopefully" is true *Time* clack, giving a hefty tweak to the noses of Byrnes and the dozing public for the bright *Time* reader. All *Time* reporting is heavily loaded with superfluous emotion in this way. But most of the loading is done by juxtaposition of items, pseudo-honorifics, counterpointed inscriptions, and salience of rampant adjectives.

Of course, any critical reader can find some use for *T.L.F.* Quite apart from the political importance of the phenomenon for the analyst, some utility is to be found in its coverage. But there are better means of "keeping up." However, most intelligent people say: "I like *Time's* book reviews anyway." And occasionally *Time* will plug a good book. But in order to do this the review has to be written straight. The flip *Time* style is dropped even at the risk of frightening the bulk of its nursery charges. It's as though a big voice were to come over the P.A. system. "All play will now stop. Something serious has happened." Obviously this sort of thing can't be permitted too often. But the regulation *Time* review, on the other hand, is always the signal for heavy chortles, as with that of Gertude Stein's *Brewsie and Willie* on page 51. The Mama of

Dada is given the works, and the smug reader is left feeling that he is master of Stein stutter and credo alike. The present number features "Montreal's Mayor Houde Bingo!" as cover man and follows up inside with "Montreal's Café Au Lutin Qui Bouffe" and waggish reminiscence of the "sacred past" of churches and bordellos: "Gone was Madame Baby's. . . . Gone also was Madame Cesar's . . . Only a memory was Madame Alice's where employees and customers alike had been required to wear evening dress." Typically, the entire scene is presented as very light opera indeed. Strictly musical politics again. George Gershwin's *American in Paris* is just about the level of *Time's* dealings with our world. Emotionally, a cut or two above *Winnie the Pooh*. A self-satisfied reverie in a warm tub.

It is this omnipresent aura of narcissistic exhibitionism which, it must be clear, levels all human events in the *Time* mill. That is the *Time* stereotype. On page 16 the "International" section gets under way: "DESIGN or PROVIDENCE? This week on the banks of the River Meuse, France's ex-President Charles de Gaulle broke a long silence." The first phrase sets the stock sneer in position. The next sentence wheezes with broken-winded rhetoric originally culled from Guedalla and Strachey. This, by way of training reader-sights on De Tocqueville. Unintentionally adolescent bathos. In this trick context, the towering De Tocqueville gets trimmed into a smart but small potato.

Life magazine needs much less attention, for it is written *down* from the *Time* level just as *Fortune* is written *up*. In place of the dry crackle and monotonous rhetorical clack of *Time*, the reader-mass is paraded through a richly scented seraglio. The cicerone oozes mock earnestness. The August 12, 1946 issue will serve here since the Frank Lloyd Wright item has already been drawn from it. Cover item: "Loretta Young models a decade of nightgowns and pajamas." One ploughs through a good many ads before reaching the "Contents" column, but the ads are worth it, of course. The "best brains in America" snap their synopses in those ads to make your heart (and purse) go pit-a-pat with wonder and awe. Thus the contents column is flanked on the left (p. 18) by a huge close-up of the most exciting legs in the sheerest black silk. It is as obvious as in *Vogue* that even voluptuous figures are given a definite narcissistic patina and abstraction. On the right, with tight breasties simply popping, is a saucy little semi-clad: "That blouse will catch more than the eye, chick!"

That is not only the theme but the inevitable accompaniment to *Life's* whirl through the week's events. "Blood Runs In Palestine Violence," (p. 21) and Sex. "Boss Crump Rides a Roller Coaster" (p. 27) and Sex. "Bolivian Dictator Villarroel Hangs From a Lamp Post Outside His Palace" (p. 29) and Sex. "Baker Day at Bikini" (p. 30–31) and Sex. "Midsummer at Jones Beach" (p. 32–34) and Sex. "Ten Years of Nightgowns" (p. 41–42) in technicolor, sex's own proper hue. "Confidence Games" (p. 45–52) heavily flanked by Sex. But especially *The Razor's Edge* (p. 75–84) and Sex. In this last item occurs the great meeting ground of technology and eroticism, the mysterious wedding between which is consummated in every issue of *Life*. A pox on the fuddy-duddy ethos of our age which has so long frustrated the natural development of *Life* and Hollywood. These agencies have been panting from their inception to turn the camera loose on the great drama of the ages. A close-up of the sexual act given from every angle, during every stage, and as effected by every variety of insect, animal, and *homo boobiens*. Where is the freedom of the press?

Meantime, there are many compromises to be made, as here with the scene from *The Razor's Edge*. "To explain the enormously complicated process of making such a movie, *Life* has selected a single sequence. . . . It shows the near-seduction of the hero, Tyrone Power, by the heroine, Gene Tierney." It all concludes with the great technological achievement: "Small Army Helps Shoot Final Kiss."

The *Life* stereotype, therefore, is technology and sex. Stress on eroticism, nudism, and primitivism being only too obviously the futile efforts of the mechanized slave to get the machine out of his guts. The child of these twain, in thriller and comic-strip as well, is death. And death romps through *Life's* every issue. In this issue it is Palestine violence with detail of human hand still in coat-cuff, etc. Close-up of Villarroel hanging from lamp post. How a rattler strikes. A *Life* camera man can't let an agonized woman be carried out of a burning theater without licking his candid

chops over her writhing thighs and backside. (Dec. 7, '42, p. 44)
The common touch?

But the feature item in this department consists of three pages of pictures: "As part of a six-week photographic seminar at Chicago's Institute of Design, the stubby, untidy, cigar-chewing Manhattan photographer who calls himself Weegee and who is famous for his pictures of mayhem and murder recently enlivened his course in spot-news photography by showing students how to photograph a corpse."

Back in tender-minded 1938 under pictures of a corpse-strewn battlefield, the Jan. 24 editor felt an *apologia* was necessary for *Life*'s obsession with mayhem and murder:

> Once again *Life* prints grim pictures of War, well-knowing once again they will dismay and outrage thousands and thousands of readers. . . . The important thing that happens in a prize fight is that one man hits another. Only a picture of a blow shows a fight. The important thing that happens in a war is that something or somebody gets destroyed. Victory comes to the side that destroys the greatest number of somebodies and somethings. . . . But even the best pictures . . . leave unrecorded the terrible will to kill, the even more terrible will to live. . . .

Let anybody spend ten minutes with this document of selfless dedication to truth and welfare if he would find all the perfect images of lethal sentimentality. Rationally, of course, the prose moves well below the level of sophistry. Another candid shot of *Life*'s editorial feeling for what it starkly insists is *homo boobiens* occurs under the headline *This Great Moment* in Oct. 21, 1940:

> Paradoxically, therefore, the readers of *Life*, as I understand them, want their Editor to talk with them in deepest sincerity about this election; but they don't want him to tell them how to vote. It is a difficult assignment. Here goes.

Self-immolation is a curious feint for a psychological butcher, but it is perhaps the only way to reserve for the reader-ox his last proud and defiant gesture of licking the butcher behind the ear. But what about the splendid pages of art reproduction in *Life?* Nothing can be said against them. They correspond to the occasional good book reviews of *Time.* They are to be described simply by their incongruity. Sterilized by context. And they serve to remind the dubious reader that after all these boys know "a good thing when they see it."

Everybody talks about the return of *panem et circenses. Life* is just that. Technology and sex and blood. The yellow press has ratted. Instead of prodding the public to the barricades it sends it to the newsstands. By sending *Life* to a party each week the dream-fast readers are given a share in the exotic fooleries of their economic superiors. Thus does *Life* draw the teeth of democratic envy of the rich by representing the rich as unbelievably moronic. And *Time* achieves the same end on a different level by its nihilistic stereotype.

It is easy to see where *Fortune* fits into this scheme. It is simply *Life* minus the sex and blood. The bureaucracy behind the *panem et circenses* is presumed to be dedicated austerely to know-how. Public opinion processes and industrial processes are *Fortune's* stereotype. How to gauge and manage the public. How to gauge and manage production and distribution. The economic and psychologic strata of the nation are frankly viewed as a reservoir of raw power to be analyzed and put to work. And the rhetorical music accompanying this libretto is fittingly Wagnerian. From engulfing sentiment to wild brassy bombast, the scale of both obliterates the human dimension. The two can't co-exist. Whether *Fortune* is taken seriously as a consultative aid in industrial and bureaucratic quarters is doubtful. But it is also unimportant. For the magazine is dedicated solely to self-heroics which must be at least gratifying to the tired tycoon. It is the pattern of drunken power that is significant. Going Gatsby one better. The success of success. The world is my milk-shake.

There is surely no reason to suppose that the actions of scientists and tycoons at this moment are less trance-like than those of the Dagwood commuter. Physics is now, directly, politics. But the physicist can't any more get reasonableness and order into atomic politics than a university president can get them into mass education. The sort of rationalism and order which finally recommends itself to these men is that which *Fortune* pumps for. The rationalism of the machine. It is a pseudo-order. But, they say, "it's the best we can get now." And it's quite true that once the bulk of society has been pulped into passivity by brainless routines imposed from above by industrial logic, then the greatest philosopher-king would be a tyrant such as Priscus Tarquin.

So the process of renewal can't come from above. It can only take the form of reawakened critical faculties. The untrancing of millions of individuals by millions of individual acts of the will. Psychological decentralization. A merely provisional image of how it might (not how it should) occur could be formed by supposing every mechanical agency of communication in the world to be suspended for six months. No press. No radio. No movies. Just people finding out who lived near them. Forming small communities within big cities. It would be agony. All psychological drugs cut off. No capsulated thoughts or melodies. To say that anything like this could never happen, or that it should never be allowed to happen is a remark worthy of those mesmerized practical men who are efficiently arranging for the obsequies of our world's mind and body alike. If something like this doesn't happen it is quite plain what will happen.

The only practical problem which remains today is that of restoring human dimensions so that a merely human order can become relevant and practical once more. It is obvious that, humbly envisaged, the machine could have helped to do this. But any rational hope in that quarter is now gone. The machine is power. And practical politics mean quite simply that the machine must assume increasingly its most powerful form. The shape and rational form of man is now irrelevant. The will of all society has persisted in this direction for more than a century. Enthusiastic abdication on behalf of the machine. Eager embrace of man when deloused of his humanity by technics. That is the impatient wish, the wider hope imbedded in the Luce publications examined here.

Thus, announcing *Life* as "America's most potent editorial force" in the January 1940 issue, *Fortune* tells us that after 20,000 interviews it is possible now "to replace undependable conjecture with dependable knowledge," and also that *Life* has 19,800,000 readers. Such absurd knowledge is a type of the dependable bomb-proof coffins which are now ready for all of us. The abject ant-like industry by which this "knowledge" is acquired is worthy of the mortician-like smile with which it is communicated and employed. Wherever this kind of certitude is sought or valued will be found a socially destructive force and hatred of man. It is time we knew how to recognize the universal new flunkeyism. That of the human beings who, contemptuous of their own humanity, professedly look for a serial number and hope to get a hair of the dog that bit them.

Why Americans Feel Insecure
by *Arnold W. Green*

MANY contributors to *Commentary* have examined what they regard to be the psychological plight of the modern Jew. He is generally seen as an atomized individual, deeply uneasy as to his status in society, with no firm roots anywhere in a complex, kaleidoscopic modern world. Thus, Irving Howe ("The Lost Young Intellectual," October 1946) anatomizes today's lower-middle-class intellectual in his bereaved alienation: having sloughed off his religion and traditional law, having been spoiled and petted by his mother and supported by his father, while being educated toward "success," he absorbs new values that further alienate him. Robert Warshow ("Poet of the Jewish Middle Class," May 1946) claims that the New York lower-middle-class Jewish family, having renounced age-old standards to accept "capitalism without sugar," is bereft of the dignity and purposefulness which upheld the European Jew in the face of all adversity. And Jean-Paul Sartre in his series "Reflections on the Jewish Question" paints a picture of the "inauthentic Jew" as a lone, lost individual who can call neither his soul nor his body his own.

Is the plight these writers outline the problem peculiarly characteristic of Jews? Perhaps it is. But perhaps it is more widely shared by the rest of the population than we customarily think. Perhaps all modern human beings are suffering from a sudden and dramatic historical break with traditional social values and structure, cutting vertically and horizontally through the entire warp and woof of our society, and focused in the disintegration of family and home as we have known them in the past.

This is not to say that there are no specific ethnic-group problems; rather it is a warning against the possibility of misplaced emphasis. Indeed, one can make a strong argument to the effect that even in a crumbling Jewish family life there appears to be more stability and unity than can be found in the Gentile family in the modern metropolis. Perhaps it is not the Jew at all, but the average white, native Protestant who is the typically alienated man of our age.

In a recent wail of pain, E. E. Cummings complained that the world is all a-leak, and life preservers there are none. In other words, we are all in the same boat.

Historically, from the ancient Hebrews, Greeks, and Romans, through the Middle Ages, and down to recent decades, a basic family tradition has been preserved in the West: the patriarchal, rural-familistic system.[1] Within that system, the person lived out his life, rooted to the land and to a way of life that encompassed all his activities. Unquestioned duties and obligations were enforced, but there was financial and emotional security, intimate emotional ties, and close identification with one's fellows.

The division of labor was familial, all working together toward a common goal of family maintenance and perpetuation. The family circle and the local community comprised a complete and virtually isolated social world. Economic life, recreation, education, religious observances, were all a matter of intimate association among a small group of life-long relatives and friends. While the pressures to comformity were overwhelming, the individual nevertheless controlled his fate in ways denied to modern man.

He, in his family, owned or had equity in his own land and tools of production. He was not swept hither and thither by the vagaries of a market economy. Many of the important economic and political issues were local ones, and he could directly affect their development. In this isolated world, social action did not ramify out in unanticipated ways to produce incalculable results. There was an obvious and close relationship between social cause and effect, reward and punishment. As one moved from childhood into adolescence, courtship, and marriage, and the assumption of adult responsibilities, the blueprint for behavior was stable, consistent, unquestioned. Finally, the individual possessed a single status in all of the intimate groups of which he was an important part.

Over against this description—made extreme for the sake of contrast—of the traditional family, another can be placed: the mod-

[1] Although cities have always existed in the West, the vast majority of people have until recent decades been rural dwellers, and rural values have dominated even urban areas.

ern, secular, individualized conjugal unit, composed of a restricted unit of husband, wife, and one or two offspring, living in an urban apartment. It finds itself in an impersonal world, in which personal relationships are scattered, partial, specialized. The old familial functions are no longer home-centered: the husband works away from home, among strangers; the children are educated outside the home by hired specialists; religious observances have waned; and each member of the family goes his own way in seeking recreation, which is today highly specialized for each age group.

Rights and duties are no longer rigidly defined. The demands of shifting and specialized groups with which the individual is associated in home, office, social and professional contacts, require specialized conformities, and not the total personality, but different parts of it, are involved. Emotional security has diminished. The roles assigned the person at different stages in his life history within the family are inconsistent and contradictory; similarly, one's status ebbs and flows as one moves rapidly from one association to another, one career situation to another. Under the impact of the competing needs and value of the various individuals in the unit, the family's solidarity is destroyed, leaving in its wake dissatisfaction, frustration, and intra-familial conflict.

This description is by now commonplace. Far less commonplace is the understanding of why all this happened. One might, like Philip Wylie, utter a roar of indignation, and demand a return to old-fashioned virtues. But the fact would remain that the entire structural basis for the rural-familistic system, to which we still pay ideological obeisance, has been undermined by gargantuan changes that no individual or group has directly planned or instituted.

To gain insight into what has happened to the family, it is necessary to grasp the fact that the industrial revolution has been a *continuing* process which is constantly accelerating, making of all Americans an uprooted people.[2] The accelerating rate of techno-

[2] For this and other generalizations in this section, a great debt is owed to the lectures of Dr. James H. S. Bossard, of the University of Pennsylvania, on the subject of "Social Change and Personal Adjustment."

logical invention and industrial expansion has meant the burgeoning of new industries and the falling off of old; sudden demands for new skills and the discarding of old ones. Individual and family fate are decided at a distance. Some unknown technician synchronizes film and sound, and hundreds of professional actors are out of a job. Rail rates are readjusted by a Washington bureau in favor of the South and thousands of mill workers in New Bedford must either migrate or learn a new trade. Factories in the fields dispossess the independent farmer. War orders pour into one area and depopulate neighboring ones; peace revises the process. Change has been so rapid, so cumulative, that it is becoming the hallmark of the American way of life. The continuity of generations is being shattered. Between 1920 and 1934 in excess of 46 million Americans moved from country to city or city to country; and during World War II, it has been estimated, 30 million Americans changed residence.

Up to 1820, more than 90 per cent of the working population in America was engaged in agriculture. By 1940, farm owners and tenants comprised only 10.1 per cent of the working population. From 1870 to 1940, the proportions employed in the manufacturing and mechanical industries shifted very little; but there was a tremendous increase in the size of the "white-collar" group—professionals, clerical workers, businessmen, and public service workers.

In other words, the dominant trend in American economic life is toward an increase in the proportion of *those who manipulate personalities* instead of tools to gain their livelihood. Alba M. Edwards of the Census Bureau (*Comparative Occupation Statistics for the United States, 1870 to 1940*) points out that since 1910 there has been an increasing *rate* of shift from "hand workers" to "head workers," and expresses the opinion that the trend will continue to increase.

Thus, in a few short decades a predominantly rural people has become an urban people. In 1860, 19.8 per cent of the population was urban; in 1946, 56.5 per cent. But this is not the whole story, for there is also the process by which the city dominates the hinterland with its values, commercialized recreation, styles, manners, for half of the rural population now lives within an hour's journey of a city of 100,000 or more. Even the physical activity of rural areas is becoming urbanized: according to the 1940 census, almost half the gainfully employed who lived on farms in Connecticut were employed in typical urban occupations: clerks, bookkeepers, salesmen, etc. The personal dislocation that has taken place is indicated by the fact that the *majority* of our urban residents were not born in the city, but migrated to it from rural areas.

But perhaps the most important and dramatic change, leading to a growing powerlessness on the part of the individual in directing his own and his family's life, is the centralization of power and control in our society. Eighty-eight percent of the working population, excepting agricultural workers, is no longer self-employed. Economic reality is no longer familial employment on familial holdings, but a series of stations in vast, bureaucratically-organized industrial, business, and governmental structures. And this is being accompanied by a steady concentration of wealth and savings (see David Lynch, *The Concentration of Economic Power*, 1946). Instead of a world in which the family directly controls its common economic endeavors, we find ourselves in a world where a growing rapprochement of big business and big government hires atomized individuals to fit pre-determined bureaucratic stations and functions under "directives." Very quietly, behind the ideological facade of verbal conflicts over "socialism," "fascism," and "democracy," this unlabelled trend has been taking place.

What does this mean psychologically? Since the family is no longer empowered to make plans and decisions and direct its own operations to anywhere near the extent that once was possible, the *individuals* who make it up are pushed and pulled by forces of which they are only dimly aware, and which they can neither control nor stop. A new technological development, a bank failure in Austria, an unidentifiable bureaucrat's decision, the rise to power of a fanatic across the Atlantic, any and all of these may blast and ruin. And all the individual citizen can do is read about it. The concrete world of reality in which he, his family, his associates operate becomes less real than the "paper world" which informs him what "they" are doing, what "they" are planning, what decisions "they" have made, what new scientific discoveries "they" have blessed him with.

Can the laborer find out whether his union leaders are taking him out on strike only to secure a higher wage for him, as they may claim, instead of political advantage for themselves? Can the citizen actually find out what is going on in one of the federal agencies, or the stockholder how the affairs of "his" corporations are being administered? How much control does the voter have over either of the two political machines he has the political right to help into office? As bureaucracy extends, power and responsibility become more and more hidden, with greater possibilities of setting off forces that will ramify out to change, disrupt, control, and manipulate individual lives. The average American scorns the average German's plea that he had no responsibility for the concentration camps, but the average American knows that *he* had nothing to do with the development of the atomic bomb. And, indeed, he did not.

The individual finds himself in a world in which personal and business ethics increasingly go by the board as personal long-range planning becomes more difficult, and life-long residence in one location is no longer the pattern. It is a world of insecurity and uncertainty, blaring headlines and sudden shocks, in which the accumulation of experience is insufficient preparation for the next, unforeseen stimulus. And meanwhile a tremendous discharge of nervous energy runs into a hundred deviant channels. Bitterness, despondency, dependency spread like a pall, along with the belief that all is chance. We are still oriented, in terms of thought pattern and emotional pattern, to the slow, stable rhythms of family life on the farm. But the structure that created this basic ideology of living is gone.

Together with the loss of its base in the economy and social organization, the modern family now finds itself supporting competitive values at a far remove from personal stability. The primacy of such disruptive "values" as individual success and romantic love in modern motivations is amply testified to by Hollywood and the advertising pages of any slick magazine.

Modern success-striving does not constitute an altogether radical break with America's past. Sanctification of success exaggerated one tradition while destroying another. In America, the tradition of mutual obligations within rural-familism ran parallel with that of frontier self-help and individualism. Destroying the former, corporate industrialism, with its demands for an urban, mobile, rational, fast-moving personnel, merely exploited self-help and individualism for its own purposes.

But success-striving became an end in itself, separate from all considerations of familial or community welfare, except that the successful, like all other members of society, had to be good to their parents—a matter of largesse, not of common enjoyment and control of newly won wealth and power—and that they were expected to dispense charity and endow foundations, often as devoid of the real sense of community as a business deal.

Each man became his own cause, and the heroes he admired were those who had pushed their way to wealth and power. The new gospel was preached to all classes. In fact, the very essence of success-striving is the refusal to accept any given station or position; instead, to hurl oneself up the class ladder, regardless of the consequences to oneself or others. Class levels became not so much fixed points of social position as a series of temporary vantage points, from which one either laboriously inched forward, or was forcibly dislodged.

The stability of rural-familism—at least in America—was not founded on cultural *prohibitions* against bettering one's station. Rather the system of rights and duties founded in the family and community, enjoining effort toward attainment of common goals, acted as a brake against physical or psychological freedom of movement. This system was virtually demolished by the new economy and its ideology of success-striving for all. The social changes accompanying the rapid rise of the new economy piled up with such pellmell haste that no new system of rights and duties had time to develop, with the result that each man's relations with other men remained poorly defined. State after state, for example, was forced to pass laws compelling legally adult children to contribute to the support of their parents. Mutual aid within the community broke down; specialized and impersonal agencies were forced to assume responsibility for the destitute and unfortunate.

And what are the *techniques* of success-striving? Modern bureaucratic structures sell, promote, manage; in other words, as business, governmental, or service agencies they manipulate publics instead of things. And within these vast bureaucratic structures, each man manipulates the personalities of those above and below him, guesses the other's ego wants and needs, and adjusts his overt responses toward gaining the good will of others. To "get ahead" one must feign interest in the activities of these others when one has no such interest, defer when one wishes to be aggressive, participate when one wants to withdraw. And, in a contracting economy, all this with the gnawing fear that it may go for naught.

Abraham Kardiner has said that success has become modern man's substitute for salvation. Poverty is as reprehensible today as sin was yesterday. Under the frantic pressure for cash and glory, the moral order has cracked. Double-dealing may be kept hidden from the world, but not *failure*. And yet ours is still ideologically, in large measure, a rural-familistic culture embodying the old Protestant values. The majority of our city dwellers were either brought up in rural areas, or are the children of parents raised in the country. Our children's toys and books deal with farm life and animals. Our patriotic songs extol coastlines, rocks and rills and templed hills. Our modern metropolis is inhabited by partially assimilated peasants. Hence our high verbal sanctification of honesty, integrity, and good-fellowship in personal relations, an emphasis that puzzles Continental Europeans and prompts them to accuse all Americans of being hypocritical Babbitts. In any event, to the extent that rural ideals still persist emotionally, they are at war with the drives of the city.

We have already spoken of the confusion of statuses in the new way of life. At one time, status, taken over from the family, was relatively fixed and definitive. Today, the person interacts within a plethora of groups, and will be accorded a *different* status as he steps from one to another: the moral religious adolescent may be praised at home and vilified in school; the liberal may be appreciated by his college professor and scoffed at later by his business associates. Under the dispensation of modern success-striving, social approbation and a sense of security must be constantly reaffirmed, and this pressure is aggravated by the fact that one is really not in control of one's economic fortunes, the chief determinant of status. Thus it happens that anxiety and conviction of personal failure are endemic in our society.

The Protestant ethic demanded that you work hard, save your money, praise God, pay your debts, and uphold monogamous marriage. At any given time one *knew* whether one was a worthwhile person or not; here, as well as in the strictly economic realm, there was a large measure of personal control. Today, this is no longer possible, for modern "success" is registered only through externals: bank account, clothes, mannerisms, automobile, club memberships; what counts is how these compare with what others have, and, more important, how *others* view what you have in comparison with what they have. Thus Karen Horney's suggestion that it becomes more important that others fail than that you succeed.

The fact that modern trends place the career in a bureaucratic structure gives a general cultural explanation of that loss of "spontaneity" to which Mr. Howe, cited above, refers. Station in a bureaucracy requires self-discipline: a systematic suppression of impulse in order to insure that the channels of success remain open. Exactly with whom is one's behavior to be spontaneous? With one's employer? With one's army officer? With one's clients? By acting spontaneously now, one may be insuring the loss of opportunity in the future. The bureaucratic control of the functionary's career through that all-important document, the recommendation, forces an attempt to preserve carefully one's relations with a long line of superiors, any one of whom is in a position to endanger the ultimate goal.

The psychological pressures thus created impinge directly upon the life of the family, since they divert energy, time, and talent away from the home. And the new economic order, with its demands for rationality, its dividing-up of the personality, its schooling of impulses, combined with the constant threat of sheer job insecurity as well as ultimate failure, places a tremendous emotional overload on the modern family. Within it love relationships must compensate for all the shocks, frustrations, and damming up of impulse that success-striving demands.

The function of "love" in modern society is peculiarly complex. With the partial disintegration of the rural-familistic system, the actual day-by-day involvement of personal relations—both in work and play—disappeared, and the improvisation and demonstration of a total *emotional* involvement became doubly important as an ideal. The emphasis on such emotional involvement was stepped up as codes of proper conduct with various kinds of persons became increasingly vague. When the behavior of husband and wife, for example, became more and more a matter to be settled in each marriage, rather than by reference to convention, the answer of the culture was to jazz up the tempo of romantic love.

The concept of romantic love rests on a myth. Two young persons arrive at an indeterminate age, meet, and a mysterious cosmic process informs each that this is the "one." They marry, and live happily ever after, constantly fulfilling in every act their *unique* relationship. Marriage becomes, then, not so much an institutional arrangement as a device by which each can secure his or her *individual* desire for personal happiness. Sadly enough, the very fact of basing marriage on romance operates to create a well-nigh universal frustration of the prized sentiment.

In the first place, romantic love is a highly stylized drama that demands some modicum of natural physical endowment and fitting surroundings. But the majority of men are not handsome, the majority of women are not beautiful, and the majority of both are poor. Frustration is inevitable.

Second, success and love, particularly for that segment of the population known as the "middle class," work at cross-purposes. Marriage is still the woman's chief career. The middle-class girl hopes to marry not only a man but a bank balance, so that she may combine the two major goals of her career in a single activity—courtship. But when a man is striving toward success, early marriage seriously interferes with his career. In the rural-familistic system a man's wife was a necessary adjunct to his economic activity; today, a wife is an unproductive luxury that an ambitious young man cannot afford. He needs time, energy, and his available funds for education and to get started in his individual career, a career that is no longer integrated with family life. Thus, at the very time when the culture demands the intensive idealization of courtship, the stage is set for a battle of the sexes, often involving sexual exploitation, in a context of what Dr. Willard Waller has called "pluralistic ignorance of each other's motives," where pre-marital relations are no longer supervised closely by family and community.

Third, the romantic concept of love in marriage must carry a tremendous overload of emotion engendered through success-striving. With marriage less "practical," there tends to arise a constant questioning of the extent to which one is receiving the expected emotional service: a ceaseless seeking-out of the other's motivations, with the feeling of betrayal if the other does not conform to expectations. While the shocks to success-aspiration dealt by our contracting economy make the psychic necessity of the other's fulfilling the ideal more acute, the tensions engendered outside the home make that fulfillment all the more uncertain.

Fourth, while romantic love appears to be needed in modern society in order to get people married, serving as an emotional drive that smashes past individualistic considerations of success, it cannot be depended upon to keep a marriage together through the years. The family remains, in however truncated a form, an *institution* with a certain minimum of obligations that must be met in a certain way regardless of the present emotional tone of relations between husband and wife. The tragedy of love, as Somerset Maugham has so honestly observed, is that it does not last. Marriage, as sexual-emotional interaction, in time inevitably seeks a lower level of habitual expression, and the aging mate no longer fulfills the romantic ideal. Sociologists in the field of marriage and the family have been somewhat dishonest in this regard, writing confidently of "another kind of love" which replaces the erotic euphoria of the honeymoon. Perhaps there is such a love, but it most certainly is not the kind of love that moderns have been specifically conditioned to expect in their marriage—an effortless, timeless ecstasy. And so we have the phenomenon of "romantic divorce"—if this other person no longer fits the romantic ideal, I will retain my ideal intact, and seek another love-object. That the same failure will only be repeated with another partner is not considered, and so, in 1946, there was one divorce for every three marriages.

It is questionable whether the new freedom in marriage has appreciably raised the general level of happiness. In most cultures, and in our own historical perspective, people have not married for individual happiness or the development of their personalities, but to form a necessary basic economic unit, and the necessity of maintaining it was as unquestioned as it was unquestionable.

Interestingly enough, various schools of psychotherapy have recently been soft-pedalling the neo-Freudian injunction to allow children to develop their egos without restriction, in favor of pointing out the valuable psychological security that can derive from a child's knowledge of absolute limits to "freedom." A similar formulation has yet to be devised for the child's parents. Paradoxically, "freedom" for the individual has value, or even meaning, only in terms of some indeterminate authoritarian framework. The divorce rate does not begin to measure the amount of dissatisfaction, the wistful longing for escape, that is generated by the mere knowledge that the back door of divorce is swinging wider. (No advocacy of restricting divorce legislation is implied here. To do so would be to mistake effect for cause.) It may be that the Victorian, with all his "repressions," had the better of the argument. His marriage and family were buttressed by a no-nonsense set of community, family, and religious exactions. He was not at the same time forced to uphold an institution and impelled to "develop his own personality," i.e., fulfill individualistic cravings at the expense of that institutional structure.

Mental health or emotional stability (the term used is not a critical matter, being imprecise in any case) in a sociological framework, depends upon a continuity of conditioning and group expectation: either personal roles, goals, and self-conceptions remain fairly uniform throughout the life history or undergo a series of easy transpositions. The typical modern family, which contains the majority of the population and embodies the dominant social trends, rips that continuity to shreds.

Let us consider what happens in such a family—let us say, a family of the Protestant, urban, college-educated, lower-middle income group. (The training of children born to parents who can thus be characterized is so consistent as to permit prediction, in a certain range.)

The father's primary goal is success; yet he cannot use his *child* to this end. The child, far from being an economic asset as he was under rural-familistic conditions, has become a serious liability: the sheer dollar outlay for medical care, diets, lengthening schooling, etc., represents a diversion of energy as well as funds at the very time when the father's career is in its early, crucial stages. This is made more painful by the feeling that the child will in all probability never contribute to his father's support.

The child also interferes with pleasures. Modern recreation is no longer designed for family-wide participation: rather, whether in the form of movies, sports events, plays, golf, bridge, tennis, dinner parties, it is designed for individual or couple participation.

And what is the role of so-called scientific child care in this complex? The child must not be spanked, parents must be patient, the child's ego development must not be curbed. The assumption of much of the literature on child rearing seems to be that the parents have a combined culinary, nursing, and psychiatric function, and nothing more. But note that in a commercial, industrial, specialized job-world, cooks, nurses, and psychiatrists are paid for what they do.

In other words, the father's duties and obligations constantly increase, while his rights diminish. An ambivalence toward his child emerges, which is more or less widespread, though very rarely admitted, even to confidants.

The child's mother also feels somewhat ambivalent toward him. Nurtured on the romantic concept of love, possessing a success-drive only slightly less intensive than her husband's, having embarked upon a career of her own prior to marriage, or at least dallied in fantasy with the idea of a career, she is left ill-fitted for the drudgery of housecleaning, child care, and the preparation of meals. The freedom that modern household conveniences have brought her has been commonly misinterpreted as well as exaggerated. While the housewife in the past had more work to do, that work was part of a well-integrated system of household and community activities. The modern housewife, with more leisure time, still must work at a number of household tasks for which she has not been trained, for which she has no respect, and which are isolated from her social activities.

Having little to do, in or out of the home, she is her child's constant companion. So-called scientific child care enforces a ubiquitous supervision and diffused worrying over the child's health, diet, and ego development; this is complicated by the expenditure of much energy aimed at forcing early walking, toilet-training, talking, because in an intensively competitive milieu the parents are constantly comparing their own child's development with that of the neighbor's children.

Under constant supervision, with limited play area in a house touching other homes on all sides, or in an apartment, and lacking companions, the child's physiological expansiveness, fed by his boredom, persists in getting him into trouble. Similar behavior was not so likely to occur in the rural-familistic household, and even when it did, it did not constitute so much of a crisis.

Already the parents have made "love" of supreme importance in their relation to their child, theirs for him and his for them, partly because of the love complex of our time, and partly as a compensation for the many sacrifices they have made for the child, long debated before and after its arrival. The child, in turn, comes to need love desperately, precisely because he has been conditioned to need it. Now, the more ambivalent the parents are towards the child, the more seriously is the "trouble" he causes them interpreted. He should not act in such a way because of the sacrifices they have made on his behalf, and the least he can do is show his gratitude by "loving" them in turn, i.e., keeping out of "trouble." When the trouble inevitably occurs, the most effective punishment imaginable is the threat to withdraw love from him. To the extent that the child's personality has been absorbed and blanketed by lack of companionship other than with his parents, he will be thrown into a panic, and will develop guilt feelings to help keep him from getting into further trouble.

But obedience and propitiation are not enough. The modern child, particularly the boy, having tried to escape from anxiety and guilt by blind obedience and "love" for his parents, finds he cannot stabilize his relationships with others on that basis. His play group, which may be denied him until he has reached school age, makes him feel a certain shame and inadequacy in approaching its members with his accustomed techniques. He also discovers that he is involved in competition with others—as an individual with his contemporaries, and as a representative of his family unit with other families. Before he has developed a real self-awareness he becomes part of a process of invidious comparison with other families.

But effective competition demands a certain degree of independence, firmness of purpose, perhaps aggressiveness. His earliest conditioning was toward obedience, dependence, and love, and he is still expected to exhibit these virtues within the home, but he must "do things" outside the home. In the case of the boy, the father, as the representative of the outside male world, makes this demand uncompromisingly—this, incidentally, may be one of the unsuspected sources of the so-called Oedipus complex. In any event, contradictory demands are made on the child, and an integration of the conflicting roles is virtually impossible. Thus is laid the basis for so many self-blocking drives in modern society, and the widespread feeling of frustration and inadequacy.

In the earlier years, the girl's training tends to be not so traumatic as the boy's. Girls are still for the most part being prepared for marriage as an ultimate goal. Girls are not subjected to so much familial pressure to assume early roles of independent, aggressive action. For both sexes, however, but perhaps especially in the case of the boy, adolescence is a period of "storm and stress," not so much because of the biological changes taking place at that period, but rather because the parents received their basic life orientation as children in a milieu that was radically different from the one the modern adolescent encounters outside the home. Thus the parents attempt to impose on the child a life organization that is out of gear with the adolescent's outside experience. Also, the period of dependence upon parents is steadily lengthening.

The adolescent of either sex must defer sexual satisfaction and the assumption of responsible adult activities until long after the period when he is biologically and intellectually (if not emotionally) mature. This is complicated by the fact that the culture has not worked out guides for the gradual relinquishment of parental authority over children, so that a conflict tends to arise: the parents attempting to lengthen the period of parental authority, the adolescent attempting to cut it short. Since the job world has no place for the adolescent, and age at marriage is on the average increasing, he must fight out the battle on minor personal issues, such as when he must get home from the dance, the use of the family automobile, the right to "express" himself. Postponement of adult roles slows the process of emotional maturity, and represents malpreparation for marriage.

The girl's childhood may not be beset by so many contradictory familial demands as the boy's, but as she grows older, the inchoate values of "female emancipation" involve her. Perhaps she won't get married. There is always the possibility of a career. In any event, she also has been caught up in the new values of individualism and success and is no longer willing to accept the subordinate role in marriage that once was unchallenged. If marriage can be used to secure a high standard of living, she "succeeds," otherwise she may be assailed by doubts. The writer has traced, in case records taken over a period of years in a university psychological clinic, the educated woman's reluctance to accept *any* marriage as a way out.

A new role is emerging for the woman in marriage, the role of equal partner, which is more acceptable to her than the traditional housewife-and-mother role. Yet, despite the growing tendency to regard marriage not as an institutional complex but as an opportunity to get something for herself, to fulfill the romantic ideal, to develop her own personality, there remains a widespread reluctance to renounce the protection and security of the older role. At the same time the bearing of children, and the domestic service performed for the husband, are unacceptable. And her husband hardly simplifies her problem. He was raised in a home which had its chronological setting two decades ago, but centuries ago in terms of social change. His recollection of his own father's role is strikingly patriarchal compared to his wife's expectations of him. He is not ready to forego the rights accruing to the patriarch though he may be perfectly willing that his wife work, assume equal responsibility in making decisions, manage family finances. And so the stage is set for a conflict of expectations.

The acute problems of old age have belatedly received attention in modern society.[3] Old age was usually no problem in the rural-familistic system. The aged *gradually* relinquished activity and control in the home or on the farm. Food and space were abundant, and they could continue until bed-ridden to perform some useful activity. Furthermore, community and religious sanctions were so uncompromising that any alternative to the aged parents living with their children was unthinkable.

But the modern job world is neither rural nor agricultural; the aging can no longer continue to be productive (a drive that is inherent in the Protestant ethic), with only a gradual decrease in work activity. In some lines of endeavor, men are now considered "old" at forty, and are haunted by the fear of being discarded. Further, the value complex has so shifted that young people no longer feel an unequivocal sense of obligation toward aged parents. Governmental agencies are planning their old-age security programs on the assumption that a growing number of persons will be unwilling to assume responsibility for their parents. Meanwhile the number entering homes for the aged mounts year by year.

This value change can partly be explained by the life situation of the married children. No longer resident on the family holding, they typically move to a city far from the parental home. They live in a small apartment where space is restricted and where there is no productive activity available for their parents. The costs of maintenance are paid with money, not by direct production on the home site, and the costs are heavy. Add to this the fact that recreational activities are no longer a matter of family-wide participation, but highly specialized in terms of narrow age groupings.

No matter what is done, the children feel either that they are making an uncalled-for sacrifice, or are guilty of ingratitude, or both. They are caught between their individualistic strivings and a set of obligations stemming from a fading tradition. And the parents, if placed in an old folks' home, feel discarded; if a common home is established, the two generations trample upon one another's toes psychologically. Under the old dispensation, the parents typically held title to family holdings until their death, and thus had a bar-

[3] The present writer is deeply indebted to Dr. Otto Pollack, who has allowed him to borrow generously from an unpublished manuscript.

gaining position from which they could retain some measure of authority. But the economic activity of the son, or son-in-law, bears no relationship whatsoever to the old people today. Yet, as is common with the old, they tend to regard their grown children as still their wards and subordinates; from the point of view of their children, on the other hand, they are expected to accept a reversal of roles, and to become the children's subordinates.

It is questionable that moral exhortation will change this whole picture. Family stability in the modern world (as Lewis M. Terman thoroughly demonstrated in his *Psychological Factors in Marital Happiness*, 1939), as well as individual adjustment within it, are dependent upon the preservation of older patterns, since no new bases for the family have taken their place. At the same time, the socio-economic structure which was the underpinning of the older values has been too greatly modified to support an effective demand that a generation of vipers cease chasing its strange new gods. We may well have to reconcile ourselves to the fact that we will have to live, for some time to come, in a society increasingly made up of persons subjected to the process we have described.

The effect of this modern personality on social life can scarcely be imagined or contained. Politics becomes less and less the rational response of responsible individuals, and more and more a field in which some individuals attempt to discharge crippling conflicts. Political programs, fascist and otherwise, lose their rational character and become illusions appropriate to seizing the imagination of sick individuals. Psychiatrists clamor for individual therapy—but this therapy is either an effort to restore the earlier, steadily weakening authoritarian norms in one form or another, or creates an individual who sees himself as a single soul saved, in a hell where almost everyone else is damned. In any case, changes in significant numbers of individuals can only come from social changes which are as yet in no way obvious.

To return to the Jewish group. It may be, as the writers referred to at the beginning of this article have claimed, that unique pressures have been created which reverberate in the personality of the modern Jew. Nevertheless, there are two reasons for questioning the specifically Jewish character of the problems they pose.

First, if the analysis presented above has any validity, we are dealing not with an ethnic-group phenomenon but a general cultural one.

Second, there are a number of factors that would appear to mitigate the effect these changes have had for recent immigrant groups in general and Jews in particular.

The Jews, historically, have been an urban and commercial people. The culture-wide trend in this direction does not seem as radical a break with the traditional past as it does for the Protestant, rural majority. On the other hand, observation tempts one to the generalization that the majority of middle-income Jewish family heads are spared the bureaucratic pressures described above, working as independent professional men and as small retail shop proprietors and businessmen. Most important, perhaps, Jews, despite the changes they feel so painfully, may well have been more successful in maintaining the patriarchal family through generations of urban living, and may be more successful in maintaining the old psychological patterns governing the behavior of fathers and mothers, husbands and wives, parents and children.

The evidence would seem to justify the conclusion that the prototype of the "alienated" person of our age is really the rural Protestant in the modern metropolis.

Dashiell Hammett's "Private Eye"

by David T. Bazelon

THE figure of the rough and tough private detective—or the "private eye," as we have come to call him with our circulating-library knowingness—is one of the key creations of American popular culture. He haunts the 25-cent thrillers on the newsstands, he looks out at us grimly from the moving-picture screen, his masterful gutter-voice echoes from a million radios: it is hard to remember when he was not with us. But he is only some twenty years old. His discoverer—his prophet—is Dashiell Hammett.

In the chief critical history of the detective story written by a fellow-believer—Howard Haycraft's *Murder for Pleasure* (1941) —Dashiell Hammett is placed centrally in "the American Renaissance of the late twenties and early thirties." Except for the fact that this "Renaissance" started a bit late and ended a bit soon, it coincides with a much larger cultural and social impulse that (except for the depression and the consequent preparation for war) was the most significant feature of the inter-war period. Culturally, this impulse would include, defined in the most general way, the productions of Hemingway, Faulkner, Dos Passos, Farrell; the critical work of Edmund Wilson; the "brain trust" aspect of the New Deal; and the whole complex of expression connected with the diffusion of Marxist ideas and the growth of political consciousness.

But what began as a revolt of the individual sensibility against the whole ideological pattern allied with American participation in the First World War (the great "debunking") ended in bureaucracy, Stalinism, proletarian literature, lots and lots of advertising-Hollywood-radio-popular-magazine jobs, and—another war.

The relation between Popular Frontism and popular culture is not accidental; the kind of mind that is able to construct commercial myths without believing in them is the same kind of mind that needs to construct one great myth in which it can believe, whether it is the myth of Abraham Lincoln-Franklin Roosevelt-Walt Whitman-John Henry, or the myth of the Socialist Fatherland, or some incongruous mixture of the two. And the tenacity with which the creator of popular culture holds to this myth—in the face of all the facts which precisely his "sophisticated" mind might be expected to understand—is the measure of the corruption that this one great "ideal" is supposed to cover. Nor is it accidental that these members of the "working class," when threatened with the loss of their fantastically lucrative jobs, should be able to speak in all sincerity of being threatened with starvation because of their political convictions. For what holds this uneasy psychic structure together for the living individual is that American Nirvana—the Well-Paying Job. In America a good job is expected to be an adequate substitute for almost anything; in an industrial society, the job is the first and last necessity of life. And American society is not only more industrialized than any other, it also embodies fewer traditional elements that might contradict the industrial way of life.

The ascendancy of the job in the lives of Americans—just this is the chief concern of Dashiell Hammett's art. When tuberculosis forced him to return to writing, it was his job experience that he drew upon; his knowledge of the life of detectives could fit easily into a literary form that had at least as much in common with a production plan as with art. As soon as he got a "better" job, he stopped writing. And, as we shall see, the Job determines the behavior of his fictional characters just as much as it has set the course of his own life.

The most important fact in Samuel Dashiell Hammett's biography is that he worked off and on for eight years as an operative for the Pinkerton detective agency. Hammett claims that he was pretty good as a detective. (He was involved in several "big" cases, including those of Nicky Arnstein and "Fatty" Arbuckle.) We may take him at his word, since detective work is the only job—including his writing—at which he ever persevered.

Hammett seems to have come from a farm—his place of birth is specified only as St. Mary's County, Maryland, and the date is May 25, 1894. But he received his slight education in Baltimore, leaving school—the Baltimore Polytechnic Institute—at the age

of thirteen. His jobs, in more or less chronological order, were:
newsboy, messenger boy, freight clerk, stevedore, railroad laborer,
detective. During the First World War, he served in Europe as a
sergeant in the Ambulance Corps and contracted tuberculosis. He
spent two years in hospitals; and his disease finally forced him to
abandon his career as a private investigator. Until he began to write
in 1922, he worked as advertising manager for a small store in San
Francisco.

Apart from one tubercular hero and one dipsomaniac (both of
whom are also investigators), Hammett's fictional characters are
derived almost entirely from his own experience as a detective.

His first detective stories, built around the nameless figure
of the "Continental Op," were published in pulp magazines—*Black
Mask, Sunset,* and the like. Hammett was one of a group of detective-story writers who had begun producing violent, realistic
material in opposition to the refined puzzles of such old hands as
S. S. Van Dine. These postwar stories signified a sharp turn from
the genteel English tradition toward the creation of a "lean, dynamic, unsentimental" American style (although, as George Orwell
has demonstrated, the English too were solving imaginary crimes
in new ways and in new settings). Hammett took the lead in this
development.

He published five novels between 1929 and 1933. Together
with short stories written concurrently and earlier, these novels
constitute almost the total body of his work. He has been phe-
nomenally successful: his books are still being reprinted and most
of his old stories have been dug up and republished. But he has
written almost nothing in the last fifteen years. Since 1932 he has
wanted to write a play, to begin with, and then go on to "straight"
novels; he has said that he does not admire his detective stories.
Hammett has been in Hollywood off and on since the early 30's.

There is an obvious coincidence between the beginning of
Hammett's sojourn in Hollywood and the *de facto* end of his
literary effort. Moreover, his job in the West Coast magic factories
(at a reported fifteen hundred dollars a week) is not strictly a writing one; he is employed as a trouble-shooter, patching up scripts
and expediting stories, often when the film is already before the
cameras. Until 1938 Hammett seems to have been exclusively oc-

cupied with his joy-ride on the Hollywood gravytrain, but in that year—it was the height of the Popular Front period—he was seized by "political consciousness." Already forty-four, he had spent six of his best years in Hollywood instead of writing his play, and thus was more or less ready for religion.

Unlike many victims of the Popular Front, Hammett went on following the Communists—up hill and down dale: Popular Front—No Front—Second Front. We can only assume that his need is great. During the war he was president of the League of American Writers and as such occupied himself lining up talent behind war activities in general and the second front in particular. He also joined the army. At present he serves as head of the New York branch of the Civil Rights Congress, a Stalinist "front" organization; most recently his name turned up as a sponsor of the Cultural and Scientific Conference for World Peace, held in New York in March.

The core of Hammett's art is his version of the masculine figure in American society. The Continental Op constitutes the basic pattern for this figure, which in the body of Hammett's work undergoes a revealing development.

The older detectives of literature—exemplified most unequivocally by the figure of Sherlock Holmes—stood on a firm social and moral basis, and won their triumphs through the exercise of reason. Holmes, despite his eccentricities, is essentially an English gentleman acting to preserve a moral way of life. The question of his motives never arises, simply because it is answered in advance: he is one of the great army of good men fighting, each in his own way, against evil. Who needs a "motive" for doing his duty? (Holmes' love for his profession is never contaminated by any moral ambiguity: he is not fascinated by evil, but only by the intellectual problem of overcoming evil.) With Hammett, the moral and social base is gone; his detectives would only be amused, if not embarrassed, by any suggestion that they are "doing their duty"— they are merely *doing*.

The Op is primarily a job-holder: all the stories in which he appears begin with an assignment and end when he has completed it. To an extent, *competence* replaces moral stature as the criterion of an individual's worth. The only persons who gain any respect from the Op are those who behave competently—and all such, criminal or otherwise, are accorded some respect. This attitude is applied to women as well as men. In *The Dain Curse*, the Op is attracted deeply only to the woman who has capacity and realism —and he fears her for the same reason. So Woman enters the Hammett picture as desirable not merely for her beauty, but also for her ability to live independently, capably—unmarried, in other words.

But the moral question is not disposed of so easily. Hammett's masculine figures are continually running up against a certain basic situation in which their relation to evil must be defined. In *Red Harvest*, for instance, the detective doing his job is confronted with a condition of evil much bigger than himself. He cannot ignore it since his job is to deal with it. On the other hand, he cannot act morally in any full sense because his particular relation, as a paid agent, to crime and its attendant evils gives him no logical justification for overstepping the bounds of his "job." Through some clever prompting by the Continental Op, the gangsters—whose rule is the evil in *Red Harvest*—destroy each other in their own ways. But it becomes a very bloody business, as the title suggests. And the Op's lost alternative, of perhaps having resolved the situation—and performed his job—with less bloodshed, grows in poignancy. He begins to doubt his own motivation: perhaps the means by which a job is done matters as much as the actual accomplishment of the job.

One of the most suggestive aspects of this situation is that the Op's client hinders rather than aids him in resolving the evil. For the client is the capitalist who opened the city to the gangsters in the first place, to break a strike. (This ambiguous relation to the client is characteristic in that it further isolates the detectives; suspicion is imbedded like a muscle in Hammett's characters, and lying is the primary form of communication between them. In two of the novels, the murderer is an old friend of the detective.) If the Op were not simply *employed*—that is, if he were really concerned with combating evil—he would have to fight against his client directly, to get at the evil's source. As it is, he confines his attention to his "job," which he carries out with an almost blood-thirsty determination that proceeds from an unwillingness to go beyond it. This relation to the job is perhaps typically American.

What is wrong with the character of the Op—this American—is that he almost never wrestles with personal motives of his own. The private eye has no private life. He simply wants to do his job well. One might think he was in it for the money—but his salary is never made known, is apparently not large, and he isn't even *tempted* to steal. Each story contains at least one fabulously beautiful woman—but the Op goes marching on. If he is a philosopher of some peculiarly American *acte gratuit*, a connoisseur of crime and violence, we never know it, since we are never permitted to know his thoughts. So, while this character often holds a strong primitive fascination because he represents an attempt at a realistic image of a human being who succeeds (survives not too painfully) in an environment of modern anxiety, he is, ultimately, too disinterested—too little involved—to be real.

It is interesting, in view of the importance of job doing to the detective, to remark the reasons for this lack of personal motivation. What the Op has as a substitute for motives is a more or less total projection of himself into the violent environment of crime and death. And by "projection" I mean that he surrenders his emotions to the world outside while dissociating them from his own purposeful, responsible self; he becomes a kind of sensation-seeker. So, despite all the *Sturm und Drang* of his life, it remains an essentially vicarious one, because the *moral* problem—the matter of individual responsibility or decision making in a situation where society has defaulted morally—is never even faced, much less resolved. The question of doing or not doing a job competently seems to have replaced the whole larger question of good and evil. The Op catches criminals because it is his job to do so, not because they are criminals. At the same time, it is still important that his job is to catch criminals; just any job will not do: the Op has the same relation to the experience of his job, its violence and excitement, the catharsis it affords, as has the ordinary consumer of mass culture to the detective stories and movies he bolts down with such regularity and in such abundance. His satisfactions require a rejection of moral responsibility—but this in itself requires that he be involved in a situation charged with moral significance—which exists for him solely that it may be rejected.

Hammett must have felt the lacks in the Op, for the detective figures that follow—Sam Spade in *The Maltese Falcon*, Ned Beaumont in *The Glass Key*, and Nick Charles in *The Thin Man*—all represent attempts to give his character a more genuine human motivation. And this attempt to intensify the meaning of his detective was also, naturally, an effort on Hammett's own part to express himself more deeply.

"Spade had no original. He is a dream man in the sense that he is what most of the private detectives I worked with would like to have been and what quite a few of them in their cockier moments thought they approached. For your private detective does not—or did not ten years ago when he was my colleague—want to be an erudite solver of riddles in the Sherlock Holmes manner; he wants to be a hard and shifty fellow, able to take care of himself in any situation, able to get the best of anybody he comes in contact with, whether criminal, innocent bystander or client." This statement of Hammett's in his 1934 introduction to *The Maltese Falcon* could have applied equally to the Op, except that Spade is more fully realized.

Spade differs from the Op primarily in the fact that he has a more active sexual motive of his own. This sexual susceptibility serves to heighten, by contrast, his basic job-doing orientation. So when Spade, in conflict, chooses to do his job instead of indulging in romantic sex, he takes on more dramatic meaning than does the hero of the Op stories. That is, a new, definite motive has been admitted to the public world, and its relations to that world explored dramatically. But Spade *always* chooses to be faithful to his job—because this means being faithful to his own individuality, his masculine self. The point of the character is clear: to be manly is to love and distrust a woman at the same time. To one woman, Spade says, "You're so beautiful you make me sick!"

The very center of Spade's relation to women resides in a situation where the woman uses her sex, and the anachronistic mores attached to it, to fulfill a non-sexual purpose of her own, usually criminal. It is this situation in *The Maltese Falcon*, coming as the climax of Spade's relation to Brigid O'Shaughnessy, that is the supreme scene of all Hammett's fiction. Its essence is stated very simply by Spade as he answers Brigid's—the woman's eternal—"If you loved me you would. . . ." "I don't care who loves who," he says. "I'm not going to play the sap for you."

In his great struggle with Brigid, Spade must either deny or destroy himself. Because of the great distance between his *self* (summed up in a masculine code grounded in a job) and *others* whom he loves and does things for (women or clients), Spade is seldom able to act "normally" in significant situations. His choice is usually between being masochistic or sadistic—unless he simply withdraws his inner sentient self from the objective situation. It is his job that so alienates him from life—and yet it is his job also that gives him his real contact with life, his focus. If his emotions released their hold on his job, he would find himself adrift, without pattern or purpose. On the other hand, the job is obviously a form of—not a substitute for—living. This dissociation of the form of one's life from the content of actual life gratifications is symbolized excellently by the fact that the Maltese Falcon—around which so much life has been expended and disrupted—turns out to be merely a lead bird of no intrinsic interest or value.

Ned Beaumont of *The Glass Key* is Hammett's closest, most serious projection, and the author himself prefers *The Glass Key* to all his other books—probably because it was his chief attempt at a genuine novel.

Loyalty is the substitute for job in *The Glass Key*. And the factors of masculinity are a little more evenly distributed among the several characters than in Hammett's more purely detective-story writing. Beaumont is not a professional sleuth, although he occupies himself with getting to the bottom of a murder. Furthermore, the book ends not in the completing of a job but with the hero and heroine planning marriage. We never know whether Beaumont's motive in solving the murder is loyalty, job-doing, or love. However, because the motivation is more complex, though confused, it is superior to that in Hammett's other work.

Beaumont is Hammett's only *weak* hero. He gambles irrationally, gets nervous in a crisis, and seems to be tubercular. The issue of the masculine code is therefore presented in him more sharply and realistically. Unlike the Op, Beaumont is directly involved in evil since he is sidekick to a political racketeer. His relation to the woman involved is ignored over long stretches of the novel, and when Beaumont ends up with Janet Henry we are surprised because unprepared emotionally—although the development is logical in the abstract. It makes sense as consequence rather than as conscious purpose. All in all, *The Glass Key* is an expressive but very ambiguous novel. And this ambiguity reflects, I think, Hammett's difficulty in consciously writing an unformularized novel—that is, one in which an analysis of motives is fundamental.

The ambiguity is also reflected in the style, which is almost completely behavioristic. "He put thoughtfulness on his face"—and one doesn't know whether he is thoughtful or not. We are given various minute descriptions of the hero's breathing process, the condition of his eyes, etc. Hammett employs the technique, I presume, as expertly as it can be. But it is a poor one to begin with, being too often a substitute for an analysis of consciousness—being, that is, the *distortion* of such an analysis. (There is only one story in which Hammett shows us the processes of thought in his characters—*Ruffian's Wife*—and it is an embarrassing failure.) But just as consciousness is a weakness for Hammett the man (his conscious mind has been dominated by mere formulas—Stalinism, the detective story, etc.), so analysis of consciousness would appear the same for Hammett the artist. And, of course, he is not wrong. Consciousness is either accepted as an essential, growing factor in the structure of one's life, or else it suffers continual distortion—not by accident, but inevitably.

Beaumont's friend, Paul Madvig, is also his boss and his superior in strength and manliness—almost, indeed, a homosexual love-object. The factors that make Beaumont succeed where Madvig fails—in getting Janet Henry—are therefore extremely important: Beaumont has more awareness of the pretensions of higher society; he banks more on cunning than on pure power; he prefers silence to lying; he does not protect the girl's father-murderer but fights him. Beginning with more weakness than Madvig, with defects in his male armor, he is eventually a more successful male because of his capacity to approach the objects of his desire indirectly—to work upon their relations in the real world rather than remaining fixed on the intrinsic qualities that his desire attributes to them. This factor of cunning and restraint, of knowing when to talk and when to shut up, when to fight, when to run, appears, then, as the final fruit of Hammett's brief but not unrewarding engagement in literature. The private investigator's shrewdness emerges finally as more important—more reliable in a pinch—than his toughness (which in Ned Beaumont is reduced to the power to endure rather than the power to act aggressively).

Now such an indirect road to satisfaction must be supplemented by consciousness—by which I mean a comprehensive hypothesis as to the nature of real life, based on as accurate as possible an understanding of the environment—or else it is likely to become frustrating beyond endurance. We can assume this alliance between our deep desires and a carefully defined world *on paper*, intellectually; but can it be *lived*? Or, a less ambitious question, can it subserve the creation of an aesthetically unified novel?

In the case of Hammett, the answer apparently is no—not without great distortion. For Hammett, in *The Glass Key*, got only as far as the experience of the vital need of knowing (beyond the horizon of the job). He then collapsed—quite completely. Instead of following his literary problem where it was leading him, he preferred to follow his new-found Hollywoodism down whatever paths of pleasure *it* might take him. He postponed the attempt to resolve those problems with which life had presented him. But it was, it could be, only a postponement, and after a few years he came upon Stalinism—that fake consciousness, fake resolution, perfect opposite of Hollywoodism—and crossed the t's of his lost art.

Nick Charles, the hero of *The Thin Man*, spends more time drinking than solving crimes. If he does his job at all, it is only because Nora, his wife, eggs him on for the sake of her own excitement. Nick is as indulgent of his wife's whims as he is of the bottle's contents. Ned Beaumont's weakness, which was at least to some degree a product of moral consciousness, becomes in Nick Charles the weakness of mere self-indulgence, the weakness of deliberate *unconsciousness*; thus literal drunkenness becomes a symbol of that more fundamental drunkenness that submerges the individual in commercialized culture and formularized "progressive" politics. *The Thin Man* was very successful, as I have noted. It is a very amusing detective comedy. But whatever the book was publicly, to Hammett himself it must surely have been an avowal of defeat. He had to give up Ned Beaumont, because Ned Beaumont was almost a human being and *The Glass Key* was almost a novel. It is Nick Charles who survives best in the atmosphere in which Hammett has stifled his talent.

The Liberal Conscience
in "The Crucible"
by Robert Warshow

O NE of the things that have been said of *The Crucible*, Arthur Miller's new play about the Salem witchcraft trials, is that we must not be misled by its obvious contemporary relevance: it is a drama of universal significance. This statement, which has usually a somewhat apologetic tone, seems to be made most often by those who do not fail to place great stress on the play's "timeliness." I believe it means something very different from what it appears to say, almost the contrary, in fact, and yet not quite the contrary either. It means: do not be misled by the play's historical theme into forgetting the main point, which is that "witch trials" are always with us, and especially today; but on the other hand do not hold Mr. Miller responsible either for the inadequacies of his presentation of the Salem trials or for the many undeniable and important differences between those trials and the "witch trials" that are going on now. It is quite true, nevertheless, that the play is, at least in one sense, of "universal significance." Only we must ask what this phrase has come to mean, and whether the quality it denotes is a virtue.

The Puritan tradition, the greatest and most persistent formulator of American simplifications, has itself always contained elements disturbingly resistant to ideological—or even simply rational —understanding. The great debate in American Calvinism over "good works" versus the total arbitrariness of the divine will was won, fortunately and no doubt inevitably, by those who held that an actively virtuous life must be at least the outward sign of "election." But this interpretation was entirely pragmatic; it was made only because it had to be made, because in the most literal sense one could not survive in a universe of absolute predestination. The central contradiction of Calvinism remained unresolved, and the awful confusions of the Puritan mind still embarrass our efforts to see the early history of New England as a clear stage in the progress of American enlightenment. Only Hawthorne among American writers has seriously tried to deal with these confusions as part of the "given" material of literature, taking the Puritans in their own terms as among the real possibilities of life, and the admiration we accord to his tense and brittle artistry is almost as distant as our admiration of the early New Englanders themselves; it is curious how rarely Hawthorne has been mentioned beside Melville and James even in recent explorations of the "anti-liberal" side of our literature.

The Salem witch trials represent how far the Puritans were ready to go in taking their doctrines seriously. Leaving aside the slavery question and what has flowed from it, those trials are perhaps the most disconcerting single episode in our history: the occurrence of the unthinkable on American soil, and in what our schools have rather successfully taught us to think of as the very "cradle of Americanism." Of Europe's witch trials, we have our opinion. But these witch trials are "ours"; where do they belong in the "tradition"?

For Americans, a problem of this sort demands to be resolved, and there have been two main ways of resolving it. The first is to regard the trials as a historical curiosity; a curiosity by definition requires no explanation. In this way the trials are placed among the "vagaries" of the Puritan mind and can even offer a kind of amusement, like the amusement we have surprisingly agreed to find in the so-called "rough justice" of the Western frontier in the last century. But the more usual and more deceptive way of dealing with the Salem trials has been to assimilate them to the history of progress in civil rights. This brings them into the world of politics, where, even if our minds are not always made up, at least we think we know what the issues are. Arthur Miller, I need hardly say, has adopted this latter view.

Inevitably, I suppose, we will find in history what we need to find. But in this particular "interpretation" of the facts there seems to be a special injustice. The Salem trials were not political and had nothing whatever to do with civil rights, unless it is a violation of civil rights to hang a murderer. Nor were the "witches" being "persecuted"—as the Puritans did persecute Quakers, for instance. The actual conduct of the trials, to be sure, was outrageous, but no more outrageous than the conduct of ordinary criminal trials in England at the time. In any case, it is a little absurd to make the whole matter rest on the question of fair trial: how can there be a "fair trial" for a crime which not only has not been committed, but is impossible? The Salem "witches" suffered something that may be worse than persecution: they were hanged because of a metaphysical error. And they chose to die—for all could have saved themselves by "confession"—not for a cause, not for "civil rights," not even to defeat the error that hanged them, but for their own credit on earth and in heaven: they would not say they were witches when they were not. They lived in a universe where each man was saved or damned by himself, and what happened to them was personal. Certainly their fate is not lacking in universal significance; it was a human fate. But its universality—if we must have the word—is of that true kind which begins and ends in a time and a place. One need not believe in witches, or even in God, to understand the events in Salem, but it is mere provinciality to ignore the fact that both those ideas had a reality for the people of Salem that they do not have for us.

The "universality" of Mr. Miller's play belongs neither to literature nor to history, but to that journalism of limp erudition which assumes that events are to be understood by referring them to categories, and which is therefore never at a loss for a comment. Just as in *Death of a Salesman* Mr. Miller sought to present "the American" by eliminating so far as possible the "non-essential" facts which might have made his protagonist a particular American, so in *The Crucible* he reveals at every turn his almost contemptuous lack of interest in the particularities—which is to say, the reality —of the Salem trials. The character and motives of all the actors in this drama are for him both simple and clear. The girls who raised the accusation of witchcraft were merely trying to cover up their own misbehavior. The Reverend Samuel Parris found in the investigation of witchcraft a convenient means of consolidating his shaky position in a parish that was murmuring against his "undemocratic" conduct of the church. The Reverend John Hale, a conscientious and troubled minister who, given the premises, must have represented something like the best that Puritan New England had to offer, and whose agonies of doubt might have been expected to call forth the highest talents of a serious playwright, appears in *The Crucible* as a kind of idiotic "liberal" scoutmaster, at first cheerfully confident of his ability to cope with the Devil's wiles and in the last act babbling hysterically in an almost comic contrast to the assured dignity of the main characters. Deputy Governor Danforth, presented as the virtual embodiment of early New England, never becomes more than a pompous, unimaginative politician of the better sort.

As for the victims themselves, the most significant fact is Miller's choice of John Proctor for his leading character: Proctor can be seen as one of the more "modern" figures in the trials, hardheaded, skeptical, a voice of common sense (he thought the accusing girls could be cured of their "spells" by a sound whipping); also, according to Mr. Miller, no great churchgoer. It is all too easy to make Proctor into the "common man"—and then, of course, we know where we are: Proctor wavers a good deal, fails to understand what is happening, wants only to be left alone with his wife and his farm, considers making a false confession, but in the end goes to his death for reasons that he finds a little hard to define but that are clearly good reasons—mainly, it seems, he does not want to implicate others. You will never learn from this John Proctor that Salem was a religious community, quite as ready to hang a Quaker as a witch. The saintly Rebecca Nurse is also there, to be sure, sketched in rapidly in the background, a quiet figure whose mere presence—there is little more of her than that—reminds us how far the dramatist has fallen short.

Nor has Mr. Miller hesitated to alter the facts to fit his constricted field of vision. Abigail Williams, one of the chief accusers in the trials, was about eleven years old in 1692; Miller makes her a young woman of eighteen or nineteen and invents an adulterous relation between her and John Proctor in order to motivate her denunciation of John and his wife Elizabeth. The point is not that this falsifies the facts of Proctor's life (though one remembers uneasily that he himself was willing to be hanged rather than confess to what was not true), but that it destroys the play, offering an easy theatrical motive that even in theatrical terms explains nothing, and deliberately casting away the element of religious and psychological complexity which gives the Salem trials their dramatic interest in the first place. In a similar way, Miller risks the whole point of *Death of a Salesman* by making his plot turn on the irrelevant discovery of Willy Loman's adultery. And in both plays the fact of adultery itself is slighted: it is brought in not as a human problem, but as a mere theatrical device, like the dropping of a letter; one cannot take an interest in Willy Loman's philandering, or believe in Abigail Williams' passion despite the barnyard analogies with which the playwright tries to make it "elemental."

Mr. Miller's steadfast, one might almost say selfless, refusal of complexity, the assured simplicity of his view of human behavior, may be the chief source of his ability to captivate the educated audience. He is an oddly depersonalized writer; one tries in vain to define his special quality, only to discover that it is perhaps not a quality at all, but something like a method, and even as a method strangely bare: his plays are as neatly put together and essentially empty as that skeleton of a house which made *Death of a Salesman* so impressively confusing. He is the playwright of an audience that believes the frightening complexities of history and experience are to be met with a few ideas, and yet does not even possess these ideas any longer but can only point significantly at the place where they were last seen and where it is hoped they might still be found to exist. What this audience demands of its artists above all is an intelligent narrowness of mind and vision and a generalized tone of affirmation, offering not any particular insights or any particular truths, but simply the assurance that insight and truth as qualities, the things in themselves, reside somehow in the various signals by which the artist and the audience have learned to recognize each other. For indeed very little remains except this recognition; the marriage of the liberal theater and the liberal audience has been for some time a marriage in name only, held together by habit and mutual interest, partly by sentimental memory, most of all by the fear of loneliness and the outside world; and yet the movements of love are still kept up—for the sake of the children, perhaps.

The hero of this audience is Clifford Odets. Among those who shouted "Bravo!" at the end of *The Crucible*—an exclamation, awkward on American lips, that is reserved for cultural achievements of the greatest importance—there must surely have been some who had stood up to shout "Strike!" at the end of *Waiting for Lefty*. But it is hard to believe that a second Odets, if that were possible, or the old Odets restored to youth, would be greeted with such enthusiasm as Arthur Miller calls forth. Odets's talent was too rich—in my opinion the richest ever to appear in the American theater—and his poetry and invention were constantly more important than what he conceived himself to be saying. In those days it didn't matter: the "message" at the end of the third act was so much taken for granted that there was room for Odets's exuberance, and he himself was never forced to learn how much his talent was superior to his "affirmations" (if he had learned, perhaps the talent might have survived the "affirmations"). Arthur Miller is the dramatist of a later time, when the "message" isn't there at all, but it has been agreed to pretend that it is. This pretense can be maintained only by the most rigid control, for there is no telling what small element of dramatic *élan* or simple reality may destroy the delicate rapport of a theater and an audience that have not yet acknowledged they have no more to say to each other. Arthur Miller is Odets without the poetry. Worst of all, one feels sometimes that he has suppressed the poetry deliberately, making himself by choice the anonymous dramatist of a fossilized audience. In *Death of a Salesman*, certainly, there were moments when reality seemed to force its way momentarily to the surface. And even at *The Crucible*—though here it was not Miller's suppressed talent that broke through, but the suppressed facts of the outside world —the thread that tied the audience to its dramatist must have been now and then under some strain: surely there were some in the audience to notice uneasily that these witch trials, with their quality of ritual and their insistent need for "confessions," were much more like the trial that had just ended in Prague than like any trial that has lately taken place in the United States. So much the better, perhaps, for the play's "universal significance"; I don't suppose Mr. Miller would defend the Prague trial. And yet I cannot believe it was for this particular implication that anyone shouted "Bravo!"

For let us indeed not be misled. Mr. Miller has nothing to say about the Salem trials and makes only the flimsiest pretense that he has. *The Crucible* was written to say something about Alger Hiss and Owen Lattimore, Julius and Ethel Rosenberg, Senator McCarthy, the actors who have lost their jobs on radio and television, in short the whole complex that is spoken of, with a certain lowering of the voice, as the "present atmosphere." And yet not to say anything about that either, but only to suggest that a great deal might be said, oh an infinitely great deal, if it were not that—what? Well, perhaps if it were not that the "present atmosphere" itself makes such plain speaking impossible. As it is, there is nothing for it but to write plays of "universal significance"—and, after all, that's what a serious dramatist is supposed to do anyway.

What, then, *is* Mr. Miller trying to say to us? It's hard to tell. In *The Crucible* innocent people are accused and convicted of witchcraft on the most absurd testimony—in fact, the testimony of those who themselves have meddled in witchcraft and are therefore doubly to be distrusted. Decent citizens who sign petitions attesting to the good character of their accused friends and neighbors are thrown into prison as suspects. Anyone who tries to introduce into court the voice of reason is likely to be held in contempt. One of the accused refuses to plead and is pressed to death. No one is acquitted; the only way out for the accused is to make false confessions and themselves join the accusers. Seeing all this on the stage, we are free to reflect that something very like these trials has been going on in recent years in the United States. How much like? Mr. Miller does not say. But *very* like, allowing of course for some superficial differences: no one has been pressed to death in recent years, for instance. Still, people have lost their jobs for refusing to say under oath whether or not they are Communists. The essential pattern is the same, isn't it? And when we speak of "universal significance," we mean sticking to the essential pattern, don't we? Mr. Miller is under no obligation to tell us whether he thinks the trial of Alger Hiss, let us say, was a "witch trial"; he is writing about the Salem trials.

Or, again, the play reaches its climax with John and Elizabeth Proctor facing the problem of whether John should save himself from execution by making a false confession; he elects finally to accept death, for his tormentors will not be satisfied with his mere admission of guilt: he would be required to implicate others, thus betraying his innocent friends, and his confession would of course be used to justify the hanging of the other convicted witches in the face of growing community unrest. Now it is very hard to watch this scene without thinking of Julius and Ethel Rosenberg, who might also save their lives by confessing. Does Mr. Miller believe that the only confession possible for them would be a false one, implicating innocent people? Naturally, there is no way for him to let us know; perhaps he was not even thinking of the Rosenbergs at all. How can he be held responsible for what comes into my head while I watch his play? And if I think of the Rosenbergs and somebody else thinks of Alger Hiss, and still another thinks of the Prague trial, doesn't that simply prove all over again that the play has universal significance?

One remembers also, as John Proctor wrestles with his conscience, that a former close associate of Mr. Miller's decided some time ago, no doubt after serious and painful consideration, to tell the truth about his past membership in the Communist party, that he mentioned some others who had been in the party with him, and that he then became known in certain theatrical circles as an "informer" and a "rat." Is it possible that this is what Mr. Miller was thinking about when he came to write his last scene? And is he trying to tell us that no one who has been a member of the Communist party should admit it? Or that if he does admit it he should not implicate anyone else? Or that all such "confessions" may be assumed to be false? If he were trying to tell us any of these things, perhaps we might have some arguments to raise. But of course he isn't; he's only writing about the Salem trials, and who wants to maintain that John Proctor was guilty of witchcraft?

But if Mr. Miller isn't saying anything about the Salem trials, and can't be caught saying anything about anything else, what did

the audience think he was saying? That too is hard to tell. A couple
of the newspaper critics wrote about how timely the play was, and
then took it back in the Sunday editions, putting a little more
weight on the "universal significance"; but perhaps they didn't
quite take it back as much as they seemed to want to: the final
verdict appeared to be merely that *The Crucible* is not so great a
play as *Death of a Salesman*. As for the rest of the audience, it
was clear that they felt themselves to be participating in an event
of great meaning: that is what is meant by "Bravo!" Does "Bravo!"
mean anything else? I think it means: we agree with Arthur Miller;
he has set forth brilliantly and courageously what has been weigh-
ing on all our minds; at last someone has had the courage to
answer Senator McCarthy.

I don't believe this audience was likely to ask itself what it
was agreeing to. Enough that someone had said something, anything, to dispel for a couple of hours that undefined but very real
sense of frustration which oppresses these "liberals"—who believe
in their innermost being that salvation comes from saying something, and who yet find themselves somehow without anything very
relevant to say. They tell themselves, of course, that Senator Mc-
Carthy has made it "impossible" to speak; but one can hardly believe they are satisfied with this explanation. Where are the heroic
voices that will refuse to be stilled?

Well, last season there was *The Male Animal*, a play written
twelve or thirteen years ago about a college professor who gets in
trouble for reading one of Vanzetti's letters to his English composition class. In the audience at that play one felt also the sense of
communal excitement; it was a little like a secret meeting of early
Christians—or even, one might say, witches—where everything
had an extra dimension of meaning experienced only by the com-
municants. And this year there has been a revival of *The Children's
Hour*, a play of even more universal significance than *The Crucible*
since it doesn't have anything to do with any trials but just shows
how people can be hurt by having lies told about them. But these
were old plays, the voices of an older generation. It remained for
Arthur Miller to write a new play that really speaks out.

What does he say when he speaks out?

Never mind. He speaks out.

One question remains to be asked. If Mr. Miller was unable to write directly about what he apparently (one can only guess) feels to be going on in American life today, why did he choose the particular evasion of the Salem trials? After all, violations of civil rights have been not infrequent in our history, and the Salem trials have the disadvantage that they must be distorted in order to be fitted into the framework of civil rights in the first place. Why is it just the image of a "witch trial" or a "witch hunt" that best expresses the sense of oppression which weighs on Mr. Miller and those who feel—I do not say think—as he does?

The answer, I would suppose, is precisely that those accused of witchcraft did *not* die for a cause or an idea, that they represented nothing; they were totally innocent, accused of a crime that does not even exist, the arbitrary victims of a fantastic error. Sacco and Vanzetti, for instance, were able to interpret what was happening to them in a way that the Salem victims could not; they knew that they actually stood for certain ideas that were abhorrent to those who were sending them to death. But the men and women hanged in Salem were not upholding witchcraft against the true church; they were upholding their own personal integrity against an insanely mistaken community.

This offers us a revealing glimpse of the way the Communists and their fellow-travelers have come to regard themselves. The picture has a certain pathos. As it becomes increasingly difficult for any sane man of conscience to reconcile an adherence to the Communist party with any conceivable political principles, the Communist—who is still, let us remember, very much a man of conscience—must gradually divest his political allegiance of all actual content, until he stands bare to the now incomprehensible anger of his neighbors. What can they possibly have against him? —he knows quite well that he believes in nothing, certainly that he is no revolutionist; he is only a dissenter-in-general, a type of personality, a man frozen into an attitude.

From this comes the astonishing phenomenon of Communist innocence. It cannot be assumed that the guiltiest of Communist conspirators protesting his entire innocence may not have a certain belief in his own protest. If you say to a Communist that he is a Communist, he is likely to feel himself in the position of a man

who has been accused on no evidence of a crime that he has actually committed. He knows that he happens to be a Communist.
But he knows also that his opinions and behavior are only the
opinions and behavior of a "liberal," a "dissenter." You are therefore accusing him of being a Communist because he is a liberal,
because he is for peace and civil rights and everything good. By
some fantastic accident, your accusation happens to be true, but it
is *essentially* false.

Consider, for example, how the controversy over the Hiss
case reduced itself almost immediately to a question of personality,
the "good" Hiss against the "bad" Chambers, with the disturbing
evidence of handwriting and typewriters and automobiles somehow beside the point. Alger Hiss, for those who believe him innocent, wears his innocence on his face and his body, in his "essence," whereas Chambers by his own tortured behavior reveals
himself as one of the damned. Hiss's innocence, in fact, exists on
a plane entirely out of contact with whatever he may have done.
Perhaps most of those who take Hiss's "side" believe that he actually did transmit secret documents to Chambers. But they believe
also that this act was somehow transmuted into innocence by the
inherent virtue of Alger Hiss's being.

In a similar way, there has grown up around figures like Whit-
taker Chambers, Elizabeth Bentley, and Louis Budenz the falsest
of all false issues: the "question" of the ex-Communist. We are
asked to consider, not whether these people are telling the truth,
or whether their understanding of Communism is correct, but
whether in their "essence" as ex-Communists they are not irre-
deemably given over to falsehood and confusion. (It must be said
that some ex-Communists have themselves helped to raise this
absurd "question" by depicting Communism as something beyond
both error and immorality—a form of utter perdition.)

Or, finally, consider that most mystical element in the Communist propaganda about the Rosenberg case: the claim that Julius
and Ethel Rosenberg are being "persecuted" because they have
"fought for peace." Since the Rosenbergs had abstained entirely
from all political activity of any sort for a number of years before
their arrest, it follows that the only thing they could have been

doing which a Communist might interpret as "fighting for peace" must have been spying for the Soviet Union; but their being "persecuted" rests precisely on the claim that they are innocent of spying. The main element here, of course, is deliberate falsification. But it must be understood that for most partisans of the Rosenbergs such a falsification raises no problem; all lies and inconsistencies disappear in the enveloping cloud of the unspoken "essential" truth: the Rosenbergs are innocent *because* they are accused; they are innocent, one might say, by definition.

In however inchoate a fashion, those who sat thrilled in the dark theater watching *The Crucible* were celebrating a tradition and a community. No longer could they find any meaning in the cry of "Strike!" or "Revolt!" as they had done in their younger and more "primitive" age; let it be only "Bravo!"—a cry of celebration with no particular content. The important thing was that for a short time they could experience together the sense of their own being, their close community of right-mindedness in the orthodoxy of "dissent." Outside, there waited all kinds of agonizing and concrete problems: were the Rosenbergs actually guilty? was Stalin actually going to persecute the Jews? But in the theater they could know, immediately and confidently, their own innate and inalienable rightness.

The Salem trials are in fact more relevant than Arthur Miller can have suspected. For this community of "dissent," inexorably stripped of all principle and all specific belief, has retreated at last into a kind of extreme Calvinism of its own where political truth ceases to have any real connection with politics but becomes a property of the soul. Apart from all belief and all action, these people are "right" in themselves, and no longer need to prove themselves in the world of experience; the Revolution—or "liberalism," or "dissent"—has entered into them as the grace of God was once conceived to have entered into the "elect," and, like the grace of God, it is given irrevocably. Just as Alger Hiss bears witness to virtue even in his refusal to admit the very act wherein his "virtue" must reside if it resides anywhere, so these bear witness to "dissent" and "progress" in their mere existence.

For the Puritans themselves, the doctrine of absolute election was finally intolerable, and it cannot be believed that this new community of the elect finds its position comfortable. But it has yet to discover that its discomfort, like its election, comes from within.

Hail, Meeters! Greeters, Farewell!

by Reuel Denney

IN every American decade we say goodbye to a landmark or a character we had grown used to. A generation ago we said goodbye to the five-cent stein and the Uncle Tom Negro. Today we seem to be seeing the decline of the Greeter. The Greeter was a man masculine who always came to the Chicago conventions in a back-slapping mood. His literary portrait, by Sinclair Lewis, was completed while he was beginning to become extinct. What ever happened to the Greeters? Many died, some retired, and the rest are becoming Meeters.

Take my old friend George R. Waffletree, now in his fifties. When I saw him recently, after a lapse of years, I realized immediately that he had changed in many ways. He did not slap me on the back or shake my hand roughly, as in the past. This was not chilliness on his part; it was the sign of a general alteration in this once jolly Vice President in Charge of Rebates. I later learned that it was a new kind of warmth, the "group-participative" kind, that he was aiming for.

George was always a good mixer in high school days, and he was a pretty good golfer too. From the beginning of his career in business he rightly guessed that these gifts promised him a good future. He worked hard, he played hard, and he mixed hard, and all these activities were as inextricably blended together as the stuff in his tackle box. His idea of business was to get in there and make money and be friendly to anyone who would play fair. His idea of a good time was to spend his money mostly in the ways his neighbors and the people in the advertisements did. One of the liveliest events of his business year was the industry's convention in Chicago. Yet this is where his transformation began.

George tells me that he drifted into Chicago on the Zephyr, back in '47, feeling as good as ever. He had been with his firm long enough to feel quite at home at these big meetings. There were responsibilities, of course. He had to attend some meetings of his own company, including at least one at which some members of his board would be present. These prospects were nothing to fret about; ever since joining the firm, George had followed the lead of Tal Adams, who was a director as well as president. It was all routine. The fun consisted of standing in the lobby and comparing your kid's college with those of other men's kids. If any real problems came up, they were solved in small gatherings at the bar, out on Clark Street in a late conference in a honky-tonk, or up in Adams' room.

Early in the convention, George turned up at a meeting with a few drinks under his belt and slept through it with his eyes open. Toward the end of the meeting there was a vote about something, but George paid no attention to it. He figured that the basic decision had already been made up in Adams' room. After the meeting, Adams took George by the arm and asked him why he hadn't said anything, and why he hadn't voted. George protested that he never bothered to do anything of the kind in meetings on that level and asked Adams if everything was all right? Adams told him that a new expense account system for the salesmen had been voted in. "I thought you had that all cooked up before the meeting," said George. "Not at all," said Adams. "That would be autocratic—we discuss things out in the open now. And remember—participate."

George was simply paying up for his lack of acquaintance with the work of Kurt Lewin. Lewin, as he learned later, was a German émigré psychologist who came to America in 1932, did much of his work at Iowa State, and was head of the Research Center for Group Dynamics at the Massachusetts Institute of Technology when he died in 1947. Lewin, experimenting with groups of children at Iowa State, had learned that groups with more or less permissive and democratic forms of organization were both happier and more self-sustaining than other kinds. The other kinds of groups he studied were those with autocratic leadership, and those with little leadership at all.[1] Lewin, sometimes called the "father of topological psychology," was especially interested in the idea

[1] George read *Resolving Social Conflicts*, by Kurt Lewin, and *Training in Community Relations* by Ronald Lippitt.

206

The Scene Before You

that people in groups occupied something like magnetic fields in relation to each other. Feelings of attraction and repulsion, dominance and submission, could be charted like physical forces and barriers to forces. In summer sessions in Bethel, Maine, the group dynamists also discovered a number of ways to improve meetings.

George told me rather breathlessly that Lewin's student Bavelas [2] had extended Lewin's methods in order to study business and other executive groups. One of the things he did was to set up screened desks in two different patterns. In one pattern, call it the "circle" pattern, everybody could communicate with everyone else, while seeing no one. In the other pattern, call it the "line" pattern, each person could communicate only with a person "above" or "below" him, while seeing no one. Bavelas gave the people sitting at the two kinds of screened desks the same kind of task to do— something like sorting out order slips. The "line" group, in which the orders came from the "top" and went "down," got the job done faster; but the individual members didn't feel so good about the whole thing. "Just cogs," said George.

The "circle" group, in which everyone had to deal with everyone else until they figured out a scheme to unscramble themselves, got the sorting done very slowly, as you might expect. But they felt pretty good about their work together. The big test came when Bavelas gave the line group and the circle group an entirely new task to solve. This time, the circle group, having established a flexible group identity, swung into the new task very efficiently. The line group bungled around for a long time trapped in its order-taking habits. "Just like me, see?" said George.

This was not all. A month or so before the convention, George had called in Thompson the personnel man and asked him to look around in his magazines to see if he could find any good gimmicks for a sales meeting. Thompson came back with the suggestion that he be allowed to run a little demonstration about "Reality and Salesmanship." It sounded good to George, and he told him to go ahead.

[2] George made the mistake of trying to read Bavelas's "A Mathematical Model for Group Structures," in *Applied Anthropology* (1948). He later shifted to simpler works by Bavelas and others.

Well, after George, as chairman of the meeting, made his speech, "Purchasing Power Isn't Enough," Thompson put on his demonstration. He brought in some models from one of the advertising agencies and the idea of the demonstration skit was that these models were receptionists in Hades, and the salesmen were supposed to be trying to get to see the Devil and make a sale to him. In the first skit the receptionist, who was dressed in red flames, got the drop on the salesman. She acted as if to say: "What are *you* doing here?" The salesman got off into a long explanation of why he was in Hades and not at St. Peter's—forgetting all the time that the receptionist and the Devil might be proud of their own business locations! Of course, he didn't get in.

In the second skit, the salesman went out of his way to talk about the weather Down There, and what good night clubs they had. The receptionist agreed and made a date with him. But he didn't get in to see the Boss, either.

In the third skit, the salesman acted as if it was a matter of course to be selling in Hades, and he took the attitude that if the Boss was good enough for the receptionist to work for, then he was good enough to be sold. He got in.

George may have simplified all this in telling it to me, and I rather suspect that he did. But anyone listening to George would understand why he did so, after hearing the final chapter in this experience of his. As he tells it, he was sitting on the platform after the demonstration thinking that it was all over and done with, when Thompson asked for the privilege of saying another word. George gave Thompson the floor. The first thing that Thompson had to say was that he thought that perhaps George himself might like to play the part of the salesman in a re-enactment of the Hades scene. Thompson genially explained his suggestion by pointing out that this would give George a chance to directly experience the demonstration technique. It would also play down George's status as Vice President in Charge of Rebates, and make a wonderful climax of participation in the meeting.

George is a pretty fast thinker. The first thing he realized was that nobody was telling him whether the receptionist was going to treat him well or not. In other words, he was really going to have to sell her. George thought fast and remembered a girl in the

Pittston Iron Works who looked like the model, and decided to walk through it the way he treated her. He walked over and asked the receptionist how her friend in the navy was doing, and the girl gave him a funny look and smile, and handed him a picture out of a locket. It turned out she did have a correspondent in the navy. They got talking in such a friendly way that the sales audience yelled "Louder," and from that minute, George's demonstration of the first step in the sales interview was a success. George says that was just luck.

Afterwards, he learned that he had been "role-playing." It seems that an Austrian psychologist, J. L. Moreno, came to this country in the 1920's with a method he called "psychodrama." [3] The main idea is to ask people who are having emotional difficulties to "act out" their troubles. If they are children, you can have them dramatize the lives and deeds of dolls. They don't always realize until later that they have been making the dolls act out situations they themselves are worried about. With adults, as in the case of a man who loses all his confidence because he has been given a metal desk instead of a mahogany one, you can apply similar "psychodramatic" methods. George told me that the case of the man with the desk is real, by the way; it is reported in an article in *Fortune*.[4]

In a popularization of group methods, George read:

"Groups which are used in role-playing come to recognize, almost automatically, those moments when its use is indicated; others learn very soon, by trying it. If a problem, a decision, a situation touches or will touch the feelings and emotions of people, role-playing will provide a better answer than discussion. How can you judge this, however, the first time?

"Again we use the core of suggestions worked out by the National Training Laboratory Clinic group.

"1. The scene should reveal or deal with a valid problem in human relations.

"2. The problem should be clear, single, and specific; it should never include related problems.

[3] The scary title of Dr. Moreno's main work is *Who Shall Survive?*
[4] "Problem for the Front Office," May 1951.

"3. It should be one the group is capable of acting out; i.e., one in which the players can understand how the characters might feel.

"4. It must mean something not only to the people who are doing the role-playing, but to the people who are watching it. It should, if possible, mean approximately the same thing to all of them." (*New Ways to Better Meetings* by Bert and Frances Strauss.)

These two experiences, of course, convinced George that something was going on; during the next few days he asked Thompson to tell him a little about the new atmosphere of the convention. Thompson began by explaining that group action in the United States was not all that it could be. Certain students of meetings, for example, had discovered that in a two-hour meeting, the active members of the average group participate between thirty and forty times each.[5] However, most of them don't realize that they have; and most of them haven't participated effectively; and when the meeting is over, many inefficiencies have occurred. The result, they told George, was frustration. Frustration is interference with a goal (Jimmy asks for an ice cream cone, but isn't given one) and frustration leads to aggression (Jimmy kicks mother) or displacement of aggression (Jimmy kicks little brother). When George protested that much of this came out of Sigmund Freud [6] and that he had heard of it before, they said, yes, perhaps some of it did. But they wanted him to hear more about the science of meetings.

After that, George learned all he could about meetings, groups, and group leadership. Thompson told him about Frederick Taylor,[7] the efficiency expert who died with a stopwatch in his hand, and how Taylor had invented scientific management. He

[5] By now George found that he could drop *Applied Anthropology* and get some of his material from an excellent popularization of "group science" entitled *Roads to Agreement*, by Stuart Chase, in collaboration with Marian Tyler Chase.

[6] George had been forced by his college-age daughter to read the case of "Little Hans."

[7] George had not heard of Taylor's *Scientific Management*. He had once sat in on a talk by Efficiency Engineer Frank Gilbreth and his wife Lillian, and he liked the movie about them called *Cheaper by the Dozen*.

pointed out the bad old disregard of the employee's feelings in
Taylor's work, and then reviewed the Western Electric experiments reported by Elton Mayo. His tutor told him the famous
story about how they raised the lights in the General Electric wiring room, and got more work out of the girls; then how they low-
ered the lights in the wiring room—and got more work out of the
girls. That impressed George. He was quick to see that this study
showed that mere physical working conditions were not the sole
factors in morale and productivity. The attitude of management
was important, too. The girls worked well despite experimentally
decreased illumination because they knew they were an experimental group; and this meant to them that an interest was being
taken in them.

George learned a great deal about the new science of human
relations in the next few months, and he was soon convinced that
the democratic team-work approach could produce much more for
his firm than the old-fashioned back-stage maneuvers. He was impressed by the possibility that these new methods might even
throw new light on international relations. One of the populariza-
tions remarked that:

". . . listing all possible items of agreement between two bel-
ligerents sometimes helps to narrow the conflict. It is not improbable that most Americans and most Russians would subscribe to
the following list. . . ."

The list itself, besides including public health, conservation,
decent living standards, and other items as commonly agreed upon
goals in both countries, also noted that:

"Both want the narcotic trade controlled.

"Both peoples welcome an exchange of nonpolitical art, music, literature, films. . . .

"Both enjoy the Olympic games and other international sport-
ing events. The Russians are particularly keen on chess tourna-
ments. . . ." (*Roads to Agreement* by Stuart and Marian Tyler
Chase.)

By this time George had become sufficiently well acquainted
with the field to be able to develop a rather impressive after-dinner
talk employing the Boston Tea Party as an illustration of certain

group principles at work. George usually began his talk by recol-
lecting that he had recently read in a periodical an article entitled
"Don't Let Them Push You Around." The article emphasized
a "how to" approach to the problem of avoiding coercion by parliamentary procedures in a meeting—it didn't say anything directly
about the emotions of meanings. George contrasted with this approach the one he had found in the Strausses' helpful new digest
he had been reading. This digest didn't concern itself with the
rules of order, either in new forms, or in the form they acquired
when Roberts, a British engineer, first codified them. In fact, it
bowed to Roberts only to suggest that his followers were the fools
of order, as out of date as the 1925 edition of Emily Post. It suggested that parliamentary rules scare the voices out of more people
than the microphone, and that many a garden club [8] has almost
perished because of them. It favored the informal approach rather
than the formal, parliamentary approach.

To show why he agreed, he went on to argue that the heroes
of the Boston Tea Party undoubtedly used the informal approach.
As George imagined it, following the general scheme laid down in
his favored digest, the heroes of the Tea Party:

(1) Agreed that the average group judgment is superior to
most individual judgment—especially the individual judgment of
one George Hanover of Buckingham Palace.

(2) Agreed to agree that a group is more likely to accept good
suggestions than to reject them—for example, Revere's suggestion:
"One if by land, two if by sea."

At the same time, George argued, the meeting at the Boston
tavern in which much of the Tea Party was planned must have
undertaken a "problem census." They may even have used a black-
board, if there were any blackboards in the taverns. Their problem
census probably went as follows:

(a) What do you think is the reason for this group's existence? (Shouts: "The Stamp Tax!")

(b) What do you think the big problems are likely to be?
(Shouts: "Finding Indian suits. Slugging first mate on British

---

[8] On club parliamenteers, George had forgotten that he had ever
read the famous study by group-observer Robert Benchley, in *The Treas-
urer's Report.*

merchantmen. Getting permission from the wife to stay out all night.")

(c) How do you think we should go about solving them? (Shouts: "Committees!")

(d) What difficulties do you think we'll run into? (General laughter.)

George was especially vivid in his description of the whole American Revolution in terms of the discussion-blocking types of meeters described in his favorite manual. Was the Revolution slowed up for a while by "legalists" who said it was against the law? Of course—by the Tories. Were the colonists fortunate enough to have an "Explorer Type"? Sure, Paul Revere. Did they have to contend with a "Wise-cracking Talker"? Aaron Burr. With a "Fence Sitter"? Benedict Arnold. Then who were the "Expediters"? Madison and Washington. And "Resource Persons"? John Adams and Ben Franklin, no doubt. And so the job that the colonists faced got done. In the events known as the Tea Party, role-playing, too, played its part.

During the course of these studies, George changed. He lost some of his old color and back-slapping; he learned to participate in meetings; and when he went to meetings, he *went* to them. The change was not all for the best, for it turned George into a rather quiet and even troubled person who was constantly preoccupied with "mood." "How is the mood of the meeting?" he was often heard to say.

Meanwhile, some literary friends of George produced some confusion in his mind by arguing that psychodrama had been invented by a Norwegian named Henrik Ibsen, who wrote plays. In one of his works, a lady named Mrs. Alving spends a good deal of her time "playing out" roles with a pastor named Manders. In fact, this is about all that happens in the play, except toward the end, when a lot of things that happened twenty years before turn up again. Most of the people on the stage, especially Mrs. Alving and her friend the minister, affected the audiences of the time as if they were seeing themselves. Then there is another play of Ibsen's about a bitch that acts out being a bitch—name of Hedda.

Indeed, they even dispute the claims of the Norwegian as an

inventor of psychodrama by pointing to the *commedia dell' arte*. This Italian form of drama provided merely a set of characters, defined in advance by their traits and costume. The businessman Polcinello, Columbine and Harlequin, and others were the products of this drama,[9] which resembled group dynamics in its scriptlessness. Others told George that some of the *commedia dell' arte* idea turned up again in the Moscow Art Theater, when Stanislavski used the scriptless "situation" as a method of teaching the histrionic art. George stood back from this revelation for a while and then decided that even if the artistic entertainers had made a contribution, this meant that students of groups knew where to go for good ideas. And if some role-playing experiments in business and club life left things exactly where they were before, so did some dramas he had been subjected to.

Other friends were skeptical and forced him to think over his own experience in these new terms. He wondered whether he had learned as much as he thought he had. For example, if the Tea Party used advanced psychological methods without knowing that it had, would its members have been better off if they had known? Still other friends pointed out to George that these new techniques seemed to be concentrated only in certain kinds of meetings. Many corporations remained uninterested in them—the Brooklyn Dodgers Corporation, for example—and were nevertheless successful. When George thought this over he realized that he had never seen a Norman Rockwell magazine cover of a town meeting with a group-dynamic selectman in it, either.

By this time, however, George was no longer a Greeter. To be a Greeter smacked of unreal warmth, coercion, apathy, lots of other bad things. Above all it was not participative, in the real sense. George had become a Meeter. There was no going back to the old style.

George's most recent reflections, however, reveal a certain amount of residual puzzlement. He reminded me a month or two ago that he had gone through the whole 1947 convention watchful

---

[9] George somehow or other did not find time to read *Der Unterbau des Dramas* by K. T. Preuss, in "Kulturwissenschaftliche Bibliothek Warburg," Hamburg.

for the "private power group" that decided everything. He never found one. Everything was being decided in the open participative meetings. Last year, however, George went to a pre-convention conference with a group of people interested in groups. They had a meeting about the meetings that were to come up later in the day.

"Those fellows, I suddenly realized," said George, "were deciding a lot of things. Not that they knew it. But they were, for instance, planning a strategy to prevent the bright and talkative salesmen from intimidating the others at the convention; they were going to get participation even if they, in a nice way of course, had to slug somebody, and the role of slugger—not just a role-playing role, either—was assigned in advance. When I said, Let the bright group talk, I was told I was being undemocratic—and if that isn't a slug-word what is? Most surprising of all, the experts on meetings seemed to be running this meeting, with Adams taking a back seat as if he didn't quite know how he got there." Then George leaned over and said, "It occurred to me—don't get me wrong, please—that what I was in looked very much like a smoke-filled room."

National Nonsense

by William S. Poster

IT is because it is a democracy, I suppose, that the United States
manages to contain such a vast quantity of nonsense in its public life without anyone getting excited about it or making any
effort to eliminate it. Since there are millions of dollars and thousands of fine, dignified, well-paying offices lying about to reward
people for putting words into print, broadcasting them, or hurling
shovelsful at public gatherings, nobody condemns those who take
advantage of these opportunities and dream up all sorts of weird
phrases to express what they usually have on their minds—namely,
nothing. Since there is so much unavoidable nonsense about, a
strange, half-weary tolerance comes over most people. They put up
with it as they put up with smoke in the air, bad food, traffic
noises, or any of the myriad discomforts modern civilization foists
upon one.

As a result, nonsense has become one of the great public
deities of America and hardly anyone dares address himself to any
kind of audience without paying it tribute. Anybody who tries to
do otherwise is apt to feel all the fears and tremors of a religious
innovator. What right has he got to be different? he wonders, and
begins to worry about his sanity. Nobody likes him, he discovers,
and he isn't doing anybody any good or getting anywhere himself.
Then gradually he begins paying homage to the deity and makes
everybody around him happier, if a trifle confused.

It is my opinion that nearly every moderately intelligent person in America has a special, complex department in his brain to
take care of all the nonsense it receives. This department develops
early, when, in grammar school, he has to listen to, and repeat
back to the teacher, a bunch of axioms, evaluations, and beliefs
which are flatly contradicted by everything he witnesses the minute he hits the sidewalk. He can't get sympathy or even an explanation from his folks because they haven't got the time and pa-

tience. They just tell little Johnny to behave himself and get good marks if he doesn't want his allowance cut off. He goes back, gives all the required answers, and stoically endures his baptism in imbecility.

Slowly his brain begins to divide and adjust to circumstances. He keeps one part of it reserved for grownups, parents, relatives, schoolteachers, cops, etc. Honesty is the best policy, he agrees politely; home, mother, chastity, sportsmanship, fair play, the American way of life are all respectfully saluted by him with one section of his brain. Then he meets the kids down on the corner and the other sections take over. He discusses ways and means of clipping quarters from his mother's purse, kneeing his opponents in a fight, how to foul someone in a basketball game, and the chances of getting the crazy girl around the corner to take off her clothes.

Soon, the nonsense starts pouring in on him in floods and he learns that, if he wants to get along in the world, he has to accept it. A strange little mechanism something like a thermostat begins to function inside his head. At a certain point in a movie, book, newspaper, or radio program, infallible signs warn him that a nonsense period is beginning. There is a quick click, the normal receiving circuit goes out of action, and the nonsense department takes over. It keeps him patient, calm, and contained until signs tell him the ritual is over, then there is another click and he shifts into normal.

Of course, this description doesn't fit everybody. Either through occupational necessity, because every generation must have its quota of nonsense-purveyors, or through insufficient cranial capacity, in a large percentage of Americans the sense and nonsense departments slowly dissolve into each other. This process produces a respectable number of people who talk like radio commercials and newspaper editorials even to their wives and intimates. But they aren't normal Americans. They are too well unified. The normal American is a happy schizophrenic with two brains, two languages, and two ways of looking at life—one for the public and the other for his buddies.

To the normal American, 99 per cent of all political speeches fall into the nonsense category. If a politician tells a joke or in-

NATIONAL NONSENSE

217

dulges himself in a frenzied outburst of mud-slinging, he listens with the receptive part of his brain, but it isn't long before the nonsense-thermostat clicks, enabling him to contain his boredom and assume the necessary pious countenance. He doesn't bear too much of a grudge against the politician. He knows that nonsense is a hallowed part of the act. A politician cannot offend the innumerable pressure groups that function in his constituency or among the contributors to his campaign fund. A certain amount of noble rhetoric is also customary.

A very strange object is the reformist politician. I don't deny that some of them occasionally do good. If they didn't emerge now and then, graft and inefficiency would pile up so thickly on the machinery of government as to cause serious breakdowns. But there is something inherently comic about anybody who emerges from the intricate deals and shenanigans of major party politics standing up and righteously denouncing a bookie or a swindler.

I remember listening one morning to the late Fiorello La-Guardia fervidly excoriating "grifters, tinhorns, and gamblers." I then strolled downstairs and passed the local poolroom, where a bookmaker was raking in the morning bets while a uniformed patrolman sat next to him, helping the bookie make change while he figured up his cut. Was the late Mayor ignorant, helpless, or crooked? Not at all. He must have learned quickly that if he wanted to stay in office and clean up some city departments, he had to wink at considerable corruption in the others.

Sooner or later, all crime and corruption investigations in this country run up against the same insurmountable obstacles. Suppose a few small-time criminals are brought in and pressure is put on them to reveal how they stay in business. They give a certain amount of information about bigger criminals; the bigger criminals can then be made to yield information about small-time politicians who in turn can be made to explain how the bigger politicians allow them to function. Pretty soon, the investigators discover that if they continue they will be swatting themselves or their best friends right in the eye. It then becomes the object of the investigation to appease the public or to throw out the politicians and criminals who have lost their utility and allow a new set to take over. It also spreads a certain euphoria abroad. The nonsense departments of the newspapers are given some fresh exercise. Thousands of editorials are written expressing the belief that Investigation XYZ has started cleaning out the Augean stables and stating that the good work should continue until the job is done.

The Kefauver committee is, of course, somewhat unique. For one thing it has national power and it reaches the public directly through the very vivid medium of television. Now it seems to me that before embarking on such a sensational project, with the national spotlights shining full upon them, the members of the committee should have at least obtained in advance a general idea of the magnitude of the operation they entered into. It may be very noble but it is not practical to set about knocking over a skyscraper with a few axes and blowtorches. What will result is bound to be chiefly smoke, noise, ugly vapors, wasted labor, and some needless injuries.

Nobody knows just how much money was involved in the crime syndicate operations, but if you toy with some stray figures you may get an idea. A reliable newspaperman reported that in Senator Tobey's home state of New Hampshire, in one year, $30,000,000 was bet, outside the tracks, on horses. The population of New Hampshire is about half a million. Multiply the figure quoted above by two hundred plus for the population of the rest of the country and you have a very rough estimate of the bookie handle of horse money alone. To this must be added the revenues derived from other forms of gambling, the narcotics and protection rackets, and various other illicit enterprises. It is easy to see that crime and graft are among our bigger industries, if they are not actually the biggest.

Now I am just as anxious as the next man to see these vast pools of dirt scoured out of the national economy, but I don't think anyone but an incurable optimist can believe the job is going to be done with Congressional whiskbrooms or helped by such coy tactics as the Kefauver committee indulged in.

To begin with, it was not helpful to have Senators Tobey and Kefauver, grown-up men and politicians to boot, registering such blushing innocence and amazement every time a cop confessed to taking a fifty-dollar bribe. It strains the nonsense department of the American brain to the breaking point, particularly when it is revealed that these witnesses were previously questioned extensively in secret session. Also, there is no need for newspapers to pretend that these were new and shocking revelations. Quite a large number of people must have had some idea of what was going on —even multiple smoke-screens of nonsense can't hide operations of such size and complexity.

It is also an inescapable inference that every politician in the country, investigating or non-investigating, could have obtained some pretty good information about crime years ago if they wanted it. If they were not actually shaking hands with racketeers, then they were certainly and knowingly shaking hands and making deals with men who shook the hands of racketeers. And they did nothing about it. And you can't exactly blame them. The whole thing had gone too far and they had to join in. How could any one watching the Kefauver show refrain from asking himself how substantial the difference was between the questioners and the questioned?

Now perhaps I am sentimental but it also gives me considerable pain to watch the small operators get it in the neck while so many of the big, staid, respectable people who profit by their operations never get questioned, but even join the parade of outraged crusaders. The other day I was reading an account of a Brooklyn trial no doubt inspired by the Kefauver example. A small-time judge, his boilers apparently ready to burst with suppressed rhetoric, let go with a furiously eloquent denunciation of a captured public enemy—a cop with a wife and two kids who had been caught accepting bribes to the staggering total of a few hundred dollars a year. With millions being juggled by the RFC, with hundreds of illegal millions disappearing in front of the public eye and hardly a pilferer getting scratched, this unfortunate flatfoot caught a two-and-a-half to five year jail sentence and a deluge of juridical hogwash from a man who probably got appointed through the usual sacrosanct political channels. How nonsensical can you get?

A few more questions. If O'Dwyer and Moran got black eyes

and even Tom Dewey a slight smudge, how can we in all sense and conscience stop there? During the last decade has there been a single state or big town where a horse-player couldn't find someone to take his deuce or where a heroin addict couldn't get his daily shot? And where some public officials were not paid off for allowing these activities to go on? Then why not call every governor and important mayor up before the committee rather than taking it out on a few carefully selected goats? And while you are at it, why not call up a few of the businessmen who helped launch the hoods when they needed them to break strikes or knock off the competition?

I happen to believe that corruption, at least in the epic proportions that we have known it, can, should, and ultimately will be eliminated from the scene, but the current approaches to the problem contain too many traces of our national schizophrenia to make me have much faith in them. If we are going to eliminate crime and graft, we have to look at them historically and realistically and recognize that they have positive as well as negative social functions, else they would have ceased to exist long ago. American political life has simply grown in size and complexity beyond anything our constitutions and most of our laws take into account. The parties are composed of thousands of people, from small wardheelers to the big candidates, all of whom work hard at difficult and unpalatable tasks. We may not like the ways in which they have been rewarded, but it's no use trying to destroy these ways without finding substitutes.

Gambling and crime, too, function as outlets for the pent-up, restless, frustrated energies of the lower classes. If you want them eliminated, substitutes are likewise necessary. Then, there is the matter of police departments. It seems that any mayor of New York (and probably any other big town) who during the last thirty years seriously wanted to cut down corruption, soon found out that a rigorous application of his principles would leave him without a police force. Police are led into dishonesty not only by almost irresistible temptations, but also because excessive honesty and scrupulous law-enforcement would get them in trouble with their superiors. The entire police system of the country has to be studied with an eye to changing its controls and also perhaps the pay of the lower grade men and the opportunities open to them. And no matter how bitter a pill it is, it must be realized that any investigation into the grand orgy of illegality in the last twenty years has to be more in the spirit of a research project than a punitive expedition. The jails aren't big enough to hold all the criminals.

And, finally, it seems to me the last expression of the national nonsense cult to leave the investigation of crime and corruption in the hands of even our best and least besmirched politicians. They are obviously too close to what they are investigating and are apt to have friends and acquaintances who are even closer. If the Senate really wants something done, let them appoint a dozen or so sophisticated, intelligent individuals, who have lived as far from politics as possible, to spend a couple of years studying the problem without hullabaloo, headlines, or TV cameras. Then, perhaps, without trying vainly to catch up with all the mistakes of the past, we might do something to prevent their repetition in the future.

The Psychoanalysts and the Writer
by Harold Rosenberg

SPOUTING liquid fire at anyone who may dare disagree with them, two psychoanalytic doctors have gone over the top with books just published into an area of the human spirit which their master had declared a scientific No Man's Land. "Psychoanalysis must lay down its arms before the problem of the artist," Freud had concluded. He didn't really mean it, explain our savants, interpreting other Freudian quotations. Besides, Freud believed in scientific progress, and time has been passing. In the early days psychoanalysis had captured alive very few writers, Dr. Bergler in his *The Writer and Psychoanalysis* points out—he himself has "couched" thirty-six, and from this roundup derived enough data to dissolve all mysteries regarding what was to Freud "unanalyzable genius." For his part, Dr. Schneider, in his *The Psychoanalyst and the Artist*, putting in no claim that he is surpassing Freud on the basis of "clinical" experience, bounds past the front lines with a résumé of Freud's remarks on art, augmented with speculations of his own; on the other hand, he seems more interested in art and literature than Dr. Bergler.

To go beyond Freud in this field, our doctors would, you might imagine, need to be endowed with greater knowledge, a more precise theory, a deeper imagination, a superior experience of art and of artistic creation—above all, perhaps, to be better writers, thus proving their qualification for an introspective study of the phenomenon of composition. The magic of Bergler's Thirty-Six and Schneider's O[edipus]-Complex-Plus dispenses with these requirements. It will reveal not only what was hidden from Freud but from Poe, Goethe, Dickens, Delacroix, Picasso, Kafka. "It is vain," says Dr. Bergler, "to question the creative person himself about inspiration." It isn't that Goethe *et al*. didn't want to know or that they were so dumb. They suffered the historical handicap of lacking the "arms" of psychoanalysis by which they could have found out what was happening to them when they composed.

This, then, is strictly a question of scientific progress. Our
doctors do not rest on an "I have found" or "I think"; with them
it is always "psychoanalysis finds" or "psychoanalysis proves"
(though this does not cramp Bergler's bragging or Schneider's
omniscience). If these authors talked only for themselves one
could discuss their books in terms of the brutality of Dr. Bergler's
approach, the fantastic vulgarity of his style and thought, his indifference to self-contradiction, his abnormal repetitiveness (a
compulsion neurosis?), which includes quoting a half-page paragraph from Freud on page 235, then quoting it again to the same
effect on page 257. One could caution the reader that here is a
physician who slyly suggests that he solves his patients' literary
problems and who concludes his book with a "commercial" assur-
ing us that "the chances for 'unblocking' a blocked writer [Bergler's
specialty] are highly favorable . . . are, in fact, nearly 100 per
cent." The fee per hour is not stated, but we assume that the following is a money-back-if-not-satisfied guarantee: "We can make
the blocked writer write—we cannot make him a genius [a rotten
thing to be, anyway, from Bergler's point of view]. We can, however, definitely make him a better writer by giving his Ego power
to wrest more from his cruel Super-Ego."

There is a certain astringency in Bergler's barbarism from
which it is possible to derive a perverted pleasure. Schneider, who
goes in for "fine writing"—he is actually the author of a novel (why
under the pseudonym of "Taylor"?)—has a style so muffled in
platitudes that one cannot even enjoy his absurdities. His judgments are always in harmony with a heart that is in the right place:
you never saw a more respectable person nosing around these aro-
matic areas. He hates "formalists" and "abstractionists." He thinks
art ought to be healthy, social, universal, etc. The experience of
Oedipus, to the Greeks the ultimate tragedy, is for him a contribution to democracy and progress (page 41), a verification of the
Ten Commandments (page 40), and a warning about the atom
bomb (page 29). For him Kafka's *Metamorphosis* "expresses only
his condemnation of himself for his hatred of rival children and
his inability to love." Therefore *Metamorphosis* "becomes a monstrosity in a jar on the shelves of literary museums" (what are
"jars" doing in literary "museums"?). But that other account of

the death of a salesman, by Arthur Miller, that is an "enduring play," endlessly significant, no doubt because, as Dr. Schneider exclaims in italics: *"It is visualized psychoanalytic interpretation woven into reality"* (this I can believe).

If this were just a literary criticism one would know how to deal with it. But who wants to risk the diagnosis that he is "apoplectic at the psychoanalytic approach" because of his "guilt at having the source of aesthetic enjoyment revealed to him"? Since these truly incredible books are "science" the critic had better behave himself. When the truth itself is addressing you it is rash to carp about bad writing, muggy formulas, shrieky little *Daily Mirror*-style editorials against the narcissism and homosexuality of vanguard art movements.

The trouble is that here "science" has not even gotten together with itself on what it is talking about, nor on the method by which to approach it. Both Dr. Bergler and Dr. Schneider presumably are explaining the same thing, artistic creation, using a common jargon and the same sort of flights into sex-analysis. But while for Dr. Schneider creation is to be studied as a phenomenon of genius, for Dr. Bergler the process displays its laws in any kind of writer, even in a writer who doesn't write. "It is immaterial, for psychological evaluation, whether he is a 'good' or 'bad' writer . . . everyone who feels impelled to write . . . is, by the terms of the definition, *psychologically* a writer." (Though Bergler contradicts himself in order to mug Samuel Johnson with the concept of the *creative* writer: "Johnson himself was not a creative writer, as is well known.") Bergler is psychologizing a profession, Schneider a selection of unique individuals. In sum, our scientists have failed to agree on their subject or their data.

Bergler's approach to what Freud called "the pleasure of the artist in creation" consists in studying "blocked" writers, that is, people who are not creating and who certainly did not come to him with pleasure. The creator is simply the opposite of the man who has "dried up"—he is a self-milking, self-nourishing "mother-child shop" (a typical example of Berglerian eloquence). Hence literature springs from the "oral level of the unconscious." Writing is merely feeding oneself words instead of milk, as proved by all the references in poetry to the flowing of inspiration. "The 'fluid' phrase denotes directly the identification of the 'flowing' of talent with the lactitional precursor." Supplying his own milk, the writer is able to pretend to get along without his mother who once refused it to him, and thus to disguise his unconscious masochistic wish to be refused.

Is this a theory or a crudely extended metaphor (Bergler's whole thesis could be put down on one page) taken literally? It is unnecessary to decide, since in either case its central feature, "the artist's fear of unproductivity," is derived from data (the blocked thirty-six) that have no relation to the topic under discussion (the psychology of creation). In following the amazing procedure of describing the writer in terms of the man who can't write, Bergler obliges us to estimate his book as a piece of advertising copy promising to make the latter into the former. From this point of view, his bullying, his argot, his bouts with literary critics, begin to make sense.

Bergler doesn't guarantee to produce genius. The writer who wants to be a genius, or have his genius "saved," had better go see Dr. Schneider, who begins with the Oedipus complex, *sine qua non* of genius, and for whom van Gogh "stands as an arch example of the tortured neurotic whose life and genius might have been saved by psychoanalysis." But before he telephones for an appointment let him ponder this last warning from Dr. Bergler: ". . . if the analyst is not acquainted with the [oral-masochistic] theory and technique [i.e., is not Bergler or a Berglerian], he will treat the patient as an oedipal-hysterical case." Should this happen the writer may get unblocked anyway; frightened by the penetrating intellect of the analyst, the blocked writer will unconsciously hoax him and write like mad (no pun intended) in order to conceal his symptoms. But it won't last. Soon he'll be blocked again. Or something worse may happen. "The patient plays a diabolical joke on the innocent in the easy chair [careful, doctor] and becomes at once creatively sterile." (Some joke!) Anyway, you can see how important it is to decide whether the creative unconscious is oral or oedipal.

Though Dr. Schneider does us the honor of discussing Sophocles and Picasso instead of sublimated milk, he doesn't help us much. It is not that castration-anxiety is less inviting than playing the cow. Unless we are to be guided by our preferences in fluids, we need to know by what method and upon what foundation the limits of psychoanalysis set by Freud with regard to inspiration are to be exceeded. What has Dr. Schneider added to the method of psychoanalysis which, according to its founder, was only able "to take the inter-relations between the impressions of the artist's life, his chance experiences and his works, and from them to construct his constitution and the impulses at work in it—that is to say, that part of him which he shared with other men"? The answer is, Dr. Schneider has added Dr. Schneider—his metaphysics, tastes, political opinions, prejudices, fancies. For instance: "The beautiful is the result of a particular kind of transformation of the true; to beauty, truth imparts power and immutability, into truth, beauty diffuses the pleasures of pain and the pain of pleasure," and so on. It is this kind of terminology that permits Dr. Schneider, despite Freud, to deal with "the total nature of the artistic gift."

The Freudian kernel of Drs. Bergler and Schneider consists in their taking "the interrelations between the impressions" and "the chance experiences" and constructing a character—but as they damn please. Disagreeing on almost everything else, Drs. Bergler and Schneider have one point in common, that all artists, past and present, are but amateur psychoanalysts endowed with "writing technique"; that is, practitioners of an allied but inferior trade. Sophocles, Shakespeare, Dostoevsky were bringing out in an impure and primitive way what our doctors present consciously and systematically. The writer, to be sure, is a "self-analyst." But "there are grave narcissistic dangers in any kind of 'self-analysis'— grave pitfalls of illusion and delusion into which even the greatest artist, the most intuitive 'self-interpreting' man can slip" (Schneider). Understand that beyond analyzing himself in this slippery way no writer has ever had anything to say. "The writer is not objective, he is the infantile person having unconsciously only one aim in mind—to furnish his inner alibi" (Bergler). It follows that the content of all art and literature is now to be found, *corrected*, in psychoanalysis. "The artist, throughout human history,"

NALYSTS AND THE WRITER 227

says Dr. Schneider, "has been loved and revered by the less articulate, less analytic man. For centuries mankind had no other
analyst." Lucky fellow, you may now shift your love and reverence
where it belongs.

"The artist has a lesson to learn from the psychoanalyst"—
on this our Drs. Kronkheit also agree. Can it be that he needs to
be told by Dr. Schneider that "painting is visual; literature is
verbal"? Or is the following summary of Dr. Bergler's science indispensable to him: "He [the writer] must, first of all, have a
specific solution of his conflicts—oral, voyeuristic, the different
mechanisms of appeasement of inner guilt—and besides this he
must believe inherently in human dignity." (That human dignity
business is a surprise, isn't it? Well, it has to do with infantile
megalomania and Dr. Bergler ordinarily instills it as part of his
treatment.)

The danger in all this horseplay is that under the cover of
psychology an artistic norm is set up which corresponds exactly to
the most vulgar official views. Dr. Bergler, who boasts that "I see
no reason to take off my shoes when visiting the literary mecca,"
and Dr. Schneider, to whom Kafka's work is a "monstrosity," can
be readily imagined testifying *as scientists* that such and such an
artist is not an artist at all, or is a crippled one, that his work
simply expresses oral-this or anxiety-that, and that consequently it
would be just as well if instead of being allowed to continue with
his work he were sent off somewhere to be cured. In a sense these
books are just such a testimony *regarding the control of all future
art*, for had the analyst been present in the past he could have corrected van Gogh and Delacroix and gotten better and more work
out of them. On the other hand, the writer who, like Arthur
Miller, has accepted the guidance of psychoanalysis, is giving the
people the true, the good, and the beautiful.

Of course, this psychological norm has nothing whatsoever to
do with art. Why do our doctors want *more* van Gogh or Kafka?
("Franz Kafka is an example of an 'interesting' distorted writer
whose output was only a fragment of what he might have
achieved"—Schneider.) Because they have applied to art a concept of "success," and cannot comprehend that the so-called frag-

mentary work of the "neurotic" genius is precisely a qualitative whole that constitutes his particular unique creation and which modifies all subsequent artistic norms.

In that its scheme of symbolic readings has brought to the details of works of art the quiver of unexpected meanings related to the lusts, fantasies, terrors of human beings, psychoanalysis has contributed much to art appreciation. When Dr. Schneider evokes from Chagall's flying lovers or rampant poultry their classical Freudian references, or when he is struck by the absence of a principle of development in Picasso's shifts in style, psychoanalysis has led him to legitimate intuitions. Of course, neither Chagall nor Picasso has been ignorant of the power of childhood imagery. An outgrowth of the symbolist movement in literature, psychoanalysis has long ago entered into the consciousness of our epoch. All the more difficult to deal psychoanalytically with what springs spontaneously into a work of art from what is called the unconscious.

It is naive to imagine that in enlarging human experience psychoanalysis has all but bagged those invisibles that assemble together in the act of creation. With or without psychoanalysis, one who tried to explain the style of a single original sentence, even if he had written it himself, could not spend less than his whole lifetime becoming aware of that unique way of experiencing and composing. Yet even those who see at a glance that such books as Bergler's and Schneider's have no bearing on the problem of inspiration may continue to sustain illusions concerning psychoanalysis. Isn't it a question of the limitations of these authors? Isn't psychoanalysis itself capable of progressing until it has gotten to the bottom of all behavior, including the act of origination?

There seems no evidence that progress takes place within the so-called sciences of humanity, any more than it does in religions. The grand insights of their innovators tend to remain their greatest truths. And since anything less than the greatest truth with regard to man is a falsehood, the insights of the masters are also *the last truths*. Reality supports what Freud said, as it does what Marx said, in a much larger measure than it does the corrected systems of their followers. Here, too, is a problem of creation.

Nothing could be a greater obstacle to the understanding of the creative act than the notion that a method exists by which it can be finally described by others than those who have engaged in it. To convince the artist that there is someone else who knows better than he what is taking place within him as he is moved in his work is to undermine his confidence and induce an abnegation of his responsibility toward a research to which he alone can contribute. Freud's statement concerning the limits of analysis should be placed above the junk heap of all psychoanalytic marionettes of the artist: "It [psychoanalysis] can do nothing towards elucidating the nature of the artistic gift, nor can it explain the means by which the artist works—artistic technique."

Muskrat Ramble:
Popular and Unpopular Music

by Weldon Kees

*". . . in the ripe olives the very circumstances of their being
near to rottenness adds a peculiar beauty to the fruit."*

IT is midafternoon. I come away from the window and the roof-
tops and turn the knob on the radio that sends a thin line
cutting across the rows of numbers. I would like to hear, say,
Jelly Roll Morton playing "The Crave," but will settle for a Lee
Wiley record; except for a station on which a voice not easily
distinguishable from Miss Margaret Truman's is singing "At
Dawning" and another on which a program of "light classics" by
a feeble string group emerges oppressively distinct, all the other
stations are playing record after record by big dance bands. Claude
Thornhill, Kay Kyser, Tex Beneke, Charlie Spivak, Vaughn Mon-
roe. I switch off the radio and go into the other room to pour myself a drink.

We live in a time of triumphant demonstration of the three
laws Mr. Nock found so illuminating: Epstean's law (people
satisfy their needs and desires with the least possible exertion),
Gresham's (bad money drives out good money), and the law of
diminishing returns.

For the last ten years or more, a period that has been sufficiently dispiriting for both High and Popular Culture, it has still
been possible, though the occasions of possibility have been rare
enough, for some works of value to emerge. In High Culture, individual writers, painters, and composers, most of them isolated
as so many bears in winter, have gone on working, and in climates
colder than most bears care for. Although Gresham's law in particular has continued to function with the efficiency and drive of
a supercharged bonecrusher, it has had to cope with one factor

that alone has kept the world from becoming a cultural Nagasaki —the granitelike recalcitrance of these figures of High Culture. It is all that stands between what little we have left and a world completely at the mercy of the John Steinbecks, Eli Siegmeisters, Fibber McGees, Leon Krolls, and Henry Seidel Canbys.

High Culture, although it has been subject to the same accelerated tendencies toward decay that kept Henry Adams awake and put the world to sleep, still has a kind of life, however spasmodic its successes and however hemmed in by the all but completely victorious Middle Culture that takes what it can assimilate both from High and Popular Culture for the purpose of mashing them to death.

But Popular Culture is completely at the mercy of the laws hastening corruption and decay. Popular Culture must *go along*. No other road is open. Unlike High Art, it cannot fall back on attitudes of recalcitrance for survival. Lloyd Hamilton, W. C. Fields, Buster Keaton—comedians of wit, humanity, and situation, for instance, give way to verbalizing gagsters: Bob Hope, Milton Berle, Red Skelton.[1] The comic strip evolves into a series of continued stories that are linear replicas of soap operas and the pulps; and similar patterns tiredly repeat themselves in every field of Popular Culture.

If the laws of which I have spoken could themselves speak, however, their proudest boast would be reserved for the debasement of popular music. Here is total capitulation. The period from the end of the First World War to about 1936 was one of enormous productivity of first-rate tunes; month after month accounted for numbers that are still fresh after a decade of repetition. Even David Rose has done his worst and left them relatively untouched. The period represents a flowering that has few comparable examples in the Popular Arts. But after 1936 the drought set in. The last ten years, so far as popular music is concerned,

---

[1] Fields, toward the end of his life (like Chaplin today) became increasingly savage in his satire, and an audience that wanted nothing but reassurance could only respond uneasily, baffled and repelled; eventually it turned away from him. Along these lines, the reception of Chaplin's last film has been very instructive.

have been bleak. From around 1920 to 1936: Exactly Like You, Thou Swell, Tea for Two, My Fate is in Your Hands, Honeysuckle Rose, April in Paris, Avalon, Get Out of Town, I Never Knew, Nice Work if You Can Get It, Baby Won't You Please Come Home, Fascinatin' Rhythm, The Man I Love, Just One of Those Things, Yesterdays, On the Sunny Side of the Street, Cherry, It Had to Be You, There'll Be Some Changes Made, You Do Something to Me, Moanin' Low, I Know That You Know, Liza, My One and Only, Embraceable You, Someone to Watch Over Me, Memories of You, Lady Be Good, I Can't Get Started With You (written by Vernon Duke and Ira Gershwin in 1936—about the last gasp of the period), My Kinda Love, Time on My Hands, Concentratin' on You, Delilah, Rose Room, Body and Soul, After You've Gone, Old Fashioned Love, Keepin' Myself for You—a much-truncated list, but one that includes most of the tunes on which some jazz performers and everyone on down from there— including the large ponderously-stringed music-to-read-by *schmalz* combinations—have depended most heavily.

A handful of men wrote most of them: Gershwin, Spencer Williams, Fats Waller, Youmans, Cole Porter, Rodgers and Hart. Most of these men are dead; there have been no successors. (Out of an earlier jazz period that stretched into the twenties came such impressive and enduring hot classics as Wolverine Blues, King Porter Stomp, Ballin' the Jack, Shake That Thing, Dippermouth, Shreveport Stomp, Snag It, Mamie's Blues, Mabel's Dream, Gimme a Pigfoot, Original Rags, Euphonic Sounds, Steamboat Stomp, The Pearls, Snake Rag, among a great many more. Almost everything written by Jelly Roll Morton, King Oliver, Scott Joplin, Clarence Williams, Jimmy Blythe—most of them musicians and band leaders of a very high order—remains fresh and robust. Men of their quality belong to a time as enclosed and without continuance as that of the Ephrata Cloisters, Vorticism, or the demesne of Lord Timothy Dexter.) Today from the broken tap that Cole Porter turns on at widely spaced intervals leak repetitive imitations of his earlier smooth flow. Vernon Duke's more recent work—show tunes, largely—is not the sort of thing that interests recording directors, unfortunately. Duke Ellington interests himself in musical embroidery work. He has also recently become a disk jockey and plays some of the most richly debased stuff ever committed to wax. Richard Rodgers composes music for operettas like *Oklahoma* and *Allegro*, a very sad end. Harold Arlen, responsible for such unfaded period pieces as Fun To Be Fooled, You Said It, Moanin' in the Morning, and Down with Love, has eliminated from his work his early originality and spontaneity.

The general drift of songwriters to the West Coast since the introduction of sound films has had its effects. In Hollywood, Epstean's law finds its purest expression. Songwriters, malleable as margarine, easily made happy by residences convenient to a racetrack, have lived up to the pattern. Hollywood Hit Parade-juke box-Hooperized numbers tailored to blanket the country and ravel out in four weeks, become all-pervading models. Just as large sections of industry seem to be consciously aiming at the creation of over-priced jimcrack merchandise—expensive fountain pens that feed great blots on one's stationery, alarm clocks that fail to go off, shirts that turn to ribbons after three washings, toothpaste that brings on gingivitis, chinaware that disintegrates in the dishwater, so does the songwriting industry aggrandize the ephemeral as it ransacks the most barren and unserviceable ideas of the past. "Imitation diamonds," wrote Tocqueville over one hundred years ago, "are now made which easily may be mistaken for real ones; as soon as the art of fabricating false diamonds shall have reached so high a degree of perfection that they cannot be distinguished from real ones, it is probable that both one and the other will be abandoned, and become mere pebbles again." Tocqueville's prediction has yet to be realized; the relevance of his metaphor persists. Songwriters of late have attempted only the imitation of imitations.

The nervous, gay, compulsive music of the twenties gives way to a tastelessness streamlined beyond belief. Gershwin and some of his contemporaries were greatly gifted men *for what they were doing*, expressing simple emotions with a freshness of melodic and harmonic ideas and with a particular sense of joy that the thirties buried (enthralled Stalinist gravediggers wielding albums of Josh White and the Red Army Chorus under their arms; "folk" operettists; novelty swing combinations; exponents of calculated corn; floy-floy hysterics; the composers of the song "everyone" is whistling—Chi Baba Chi Baba, Chickory Chick, Open the Door Richard, Pistol Packin' Mama, People Will Say We're in Love, Jingle Jangle Jingle, Deep in the Heart of Texas, There'll Be Bluebirds Over the White Cliffs of Dover, I'll Dance at Your Wedding—an endless and unspeakable catalogue. There are few more dependable methods of obtaining a quick migraine than by merely reading over a list of the hit tunes of the last ten or twelve years.

Monolithic symbol of the whole period is the juke box: this permanent guest in public places that squats like some ominous and temporarily static beast, afoam with lights and tubes of colored water; it might have been built by André Breton in collaboration with some monstrously sick and divided opponent of industrialism who had spent a claustrophobic lifetime in Greek candy stores. There it sits, booming or silently awaiting a nickel, ready with "A Rainy Night in Rio" and Perry Como, where the piano player used to be, his cigarette turning the ivories of the upper register a sickly Mars yellow. He was not often a good pianist, but he knew more tunes than the twenty the juke box knows; and you could talk to him.

Compared with the music currently being written, musical performance is deceptively healthy. Even the best jazz today lacks the fresh originating intelligence at work in the late twenties; and the best musicians are now only extending and developing patterns of improvisation laid out during the early quarter of this century. There is an immense concern with mere preservation. The unearthing, several years ago, of Bunk Johnson, probably the oldest living pioneer of jazz, who had dropped out of music and had to be provided with a set of new teeth before his triumphant comeback, was a welcome act of antiquarian recovery. Johnson's long-buried and pure turn-of-the-century New Orleans style served as a landmark from which to view almost fifty years of jazz mutations and variants. Johnson's more impassioned admirers correctly placed great emphasis on his astonishing power and wide-open tone, alive with personal feeling. These almost compensated for an inventive deficiency that made for considerable monotony as chorus followed chorus.

It has been the practice of some later musicians to work intensively at the inventive, though feeling has often been buried in displays of virtuosity. Performers such as Tony Parenti, Don Ewell, Paul Lingle, Bob Helm, Wally Rose, Burt Bales, Turk Murphy, among others, continue to resist corruption; but their ranks are systematically being thinned out by desertions for cushier swing bands, by sudden collapses of talent, and the normal high death rate among jazz musicians, whose occupational hazards include heart attacks, malnutrition, and a recurrent pattern of drunkenness and sudden death of pneumonia in Middle Western cities.

More than a few go on playing well; the difficulties of hearing them continue to multiply. Manhattan's Fifty-Second Street, once as devoted to night clubs featuring jazz and jam sessions as Grand Street is to wedding gowns or Bleecker Street to salami, makes way for replacements in the form of office buildings, expensive clubs, business establishments, and tourist night spots with "intimate" singers and Hawaiian dancing girls. Four years ago there was at least one night club in New York that offered first-rate jazz, unwatered and nonpoisonous liquor at reasonable prices, and a quiet crowd that did not come there to have their photographs taken, their caricatures drawn, or to annoy the musicians. This was the Pied Piper, on Barrow Street, in the Village. For a brief period, when it first opened, it offered a memorable five-piece group that included Max Kaminsky, the late Rod Cless on clarinet, Frank Orchard on valve trombone, and, as intermission pianist and at the top of his form, the remarkable, vastly influential, and still underrated James J. Johnson. There is nothing remotely like the Pied Piper left in New York. Indifferent music, high prices, poor liquor, or combinations of this trinity have taken over everywhere. The rash of jazz "concerts" in such places as Town Hall have not been very satisfactory substitutes. The musicians, along with the more ravaged-looking members of the audience, wear expressions of strain brought on by the absence of a bar and by a milieu too little enclosed. At various times, attempts have been made to present regular programs of good jazz on the air—notably those conducted by Condon and by Rudi Blesh; but from the start their chances of commercial sponsorship were as remote as those of Wallace Stevens' appearing as a regular contributor in *Collier's*. The networks made short work of both programs.

While jazz persists on records and occasionally elsewhere, the best of it increasingly nostalgic, depending more and more on a cultist rather than on a popular base, it is almost drowned out by the racket of the large swing and popular bands. These have next to nothing to do with jazz, although they often contain remnants of rather gratuitous jazz in solo work (the best of these bands, Artie Shaw's and Benny Goodman's, are gone). Standard practice today in the search for trade-marks and novelty is the isolation of some rhythmic pattern, tonal element, or harmonic trickery to vulgarize and thus "build up" a "style." Hence "rippling rhythms," slinky piano effects, fixated use of a series of augmented chords, musical statements that are so surfacy that they beg the question of feeling at all. The Stan Kenton band is a good example of tremendous effort going into the creation of such a style, through echo chamber effects and hollow intimations of Debussy and Stravinsky.

Enormously popular just now are the relaxed Cream of Wheat-Gerber's Baby Food instrumental trios, usually piano, guitar, and string bass, with one man singing empty little jump tunes. There are dozens of these, all playing at a volume undeviating as a cat's purr. This music had its origin, I would guess, in the dimly lit night clubs of the East Fifties, where it served, and still serves, the purpose of covering up dead spots in the conversation. Like the music that dominated the period in the late 1700's just before the revolutionary music of Gluck, it was not originally intended to be listened to at all. Millions now follow it, over the air and on records.

And now, finally, we come to those who play in the latest and extravagantly-acclaimed manner variously labeled Be-Bob, bebop, and rebop. Here is a full-fledged cult. Its more orthodox devotees even model their appearance on that of Dizzy Gillespie, bebop's pioneer and bellwether, a goateed trumpet player who wears a beret, horn-rimmed glasses, and neckties with his own not very appealing countenance painted thereon. Iconoclastic and compulsive types, many bebop cultists extend their interests beyond music—to drug-addiction, abstract painting, and the theories (and for all I know the practice) of Wilhelm Reich, philosopher of the orgasm. Some beboppers are interested in the close textual critics of poetry; I learned from a friend whom I believe to be reliable that one such fan announced that Cleanth Brooks is "definitely hip"—a term of warm approval.

The beboppers or hipsters are, however, a great deal more interesting than bebop itself. Yet they offer the most insistent testimonies to bebop's superiority to other kinds of music. " 'Do you dig Dizzy?' is fast becoming the musician's counterpart to 'Do you speak English?' " writes Mr. Mort Schillinger in *Downbeat*, in the characteristic razmataz style of the swing magazines. "Never before in the history of Jazz has so dynamic a person as Dizzy Gillespie gained the spotlight of acclaim and idolization . . . from the humblest of the unknown to the heights of huzza at which he stands today. With the waxing of Hawk's [Coleman Hawkins'] *Body and Soul* . . . Jazz reached a pinnacle of development. The human imagination has its limitations, just as the human arm or leg, and Jazz had reached the point where the musician's imagination could no longer function effectively without the added stimulus of new horizons for exploitation. There were two alternatives: either Jazz could remain stagnant and in time lose its identity as a highly creative art, or it could develop new facets for the imagination, new stimuli to artistic fabrication. Fortunately it followed the latter course—chose it and assigned the task to Dizzy Gillespie." Mr. Schillinger goes on to remark Gillespie's "genius for substituting and extending chords in unorthodox but singularly thrilling ways and places [and] Dizzy's entirely original articulation and phrasing which is hardly describable through the medium of the printed word without recourse to highly technical terminology. . . ."

Mr. Rudi Blesh, in a recent piece in the *Herald Tribune*, is more controlled. "Seeming non-sequiturs can be artfully combined to express an integrated idea, and this method, a psychological one, is common in modern music and literature. But the irrelevant parts of bebop are exactly what they seem; they add up to no such unity. . . . A capricious and neurotically rhapsodic sequence of effects for their own sake, [bebop] comes perilously close to complete nonsense as a musical expression. . . . Far from a culmination of jazz, bebop is not jazz at all but an ultimately degenerated form of swing, exploiting the most fantastic rhythms and unrelated harmonies that it would seem possible to conceive."

I have been listening to bebop on occasion for several years now, and lately, as I started work on this piece, listening with more strict attention; and I can only report, very possibly because of some deeply buried strain of black reaction in me, that I have found this music uniformly thin, at once dilapidated and over-blown, and exhibiting a poverty of thematic development and a richness of affectation not only, apparently, intentional, but enormously self-satisfied. Whole-tone progressions and triple-tongued runs are worked relentlessly, far beyond the saturation point. There has been nothing like this in the way of an over-consciousness of stylistic idiosyncrasy, I should say, since the Gothic Revival. Although bebop's defenders reserve as their trump card this music's "element of the unexpected," it is precisely bebop's undeviating pattern of incoherence and limitation that makes it predictable in the extreme, and ultimately as boring as the projects of Gutzon Borglum.

In Paris, where Erskine Caldwell, Steinbeck, Henry Miller, and Horace McCoy are best sellers and "nobody reads Proust any more," where the post-Picasso painters have sunk into torpor and repetition, and where intellectuals are more cynically Stalinized than in any other city in the world, bebop is vastly admired. Evidently Gresham's and Epstean's laws work with equal severity in other countries besides the United States, although a lot of people are taking Christ's own time finding it out.[2]

[2] This was written in 1948. Since that time, my ideas on the subject have changed a good deal, and so has the music. Recording directors and engineers with stopwatches, publishers unable to read music who listen only to "demonstration" records of tunes (preferably high fidelity), A&R men who stress technical quality at the expense of music, are firmly in control at the large recording companies. Many small labels have made an appearance, and some of them—Riverside, Fantasy, Good Time Jazz, and "X," among others—have been markedly successful in marketing both reissues and some new material. A fresh interest in New Orleans revivalism is growing. Bebop has given way to "progressive" and "cool" music. And the hit parade king of tune has become even more vacuous than it was in 1948, stressing repetition, witless lyrics, and self-pity.

—W.K.

Notes on the
American Intelligentsia
by J. F. Wolpert

THOUGH the role and function of the intellectuals in the modern world has been much discussed of late, there has been surprisingly little analysis of the distinctiveness of this social group as it operates within the American culture. What studies we have are characterized by an impressionism not very useful for systematic analysis. The lack of such material is in itself sociologically significant, showing that the American intelligentsia has moved on the periphery rather than within the mainstream of our social life.

The category "intellectuals" has been amorphous and ill-defined. It has been taken to include, or exclude, a host of groups as befits the particular bias of the writer dealing with the problem. It is therefore incumbent upon us to formulate our definition as explicitly as possible. We may begin the characterization of this group—taken as a whole—by saying that its main concern is with the production and dissemination of ideas in their broadest connotations. Ideas we may define both as the stored body of knowledge from the past of which our colleges and universities are the official transmitters and the contributions of the humanities as well as the social and natural sciences not as yet sanctioned by tradition. The latter of course have their main source outside the academy. Further, it is important, when using our definition of ideas, to distinguish them from folk beliefs and the uncritically accepted assumptions and stereotypes of nonintellectual social strata.

What characterizes the intellectuals, then, is their need for a critical attitude lifting the type of knowledge they are concerned with to the level of ideas. This is an attitude shared by all divisions of intellectuals. Also, their concentration upon ideas, even those of the strident sort lately propounded by the Nazi intellectual apologists, tends toward universality. If the times are propitious for their acceptance, neither national frontiers nor ethnic background can prevent their finding wider and wider audiences.

The great German Sociologist, Max Weber, distinguished in his study of political structures between two types of politicians, those who lived for politics and those who lived off politics. The former have no emotional investment in particular ideologies which converts their job into a devotion to a calling, whereas the latter are in politics merely as a way of making a living. We may use this dichotomy broadly in subdividing types of intellectuals in America. Those who conceive of their role as a devotion to a calling live for ideas, even though they do live off their intellectual production in a psychological sense. This group formally includes members of the faculties of the universities and the few writers in the large cities who do independent critical work pitched beyond the level of commercialism. These find their outlet in the little magazines. In the latter group—those who live off ideas— would be included the journalists of the large city dailies and the writers of the organs of the public opinion on a mass scale such as the Luce publications.

There is another distinct group which fits into neither of these categories, whom we shall call the ideologists. They are, in America, the acolytes of Stalinism such as the contributors to the *New Masses,* also the writers on the staff of *PM* and the facile popularizers who disseminate the orthodox views of the party, sugar-pilled for mass consumption. The ideologists' attitude toward ideas is ruthlessly pragmatic. Their touchstone for the evaluation of an idea is whether or not it contributes to the realization of the party program. Thus every idea is judged in terms of its political manipulability. The ideologists also carry with them numerous dupes, intellectuals who because they want to be considered revolutionary or "progressive"—the word debased to party usage nowadays—support the Stalinist position with trivial reservations. In doing so they serve the useful function of making Stalinist propaganda respectable. This group has been aptly named the "totalitarian liberals" by such trenchant analysts of their social role as Sidney Hook.

In the historical tradition of Western culture the academic intellectuals are the direct descendants of the clerks who formed, in the medieval period, the nucleus of what was to become the modern university. Even in America this heritage, however much dissipated by the norms and practices of capitalist democracy, can be discerned in the academic attitude. In a secularized social frame this manifests itself in a cloistered disinterested pursuit of knowledge for its own sake. The secularized function of salvation is served by the contribution, however small, of a scrap of knowledge to the particular discipline. This procedure is institutionalized via the requirements for the Ph.D. degree in the graduate schools.

In America, however, the position of the university man is most ambiguous and the ideal set forth has been twisted out of easy recognition by the pressures of the American social structure. These pressures erode the formal devotion to a calling, turning, in the large universities, the monastic cell into a place more nearly resembling the assembly line. The bureaucratic structure of the university with its divorce of administration and scholarship, commented upon by Veblen, results in the dependence of the scholar upon the administration. Finally the authority vested in the boards of trustees gives them the power to withhold economic rewards in case of deviation from accepted norms. These trustees come from the most conservative segment of American society. They are businessmen of repute or their satraps in the state universities, the politicians who live off politics.

The psychological effect of this situation on the personality of the academic man is that of imposing unconscious, if not conscious, limits upon his categories of inquiry. There is a gradual shading in analysis from the patently innocuous to that which might call into question the basis of the existing order. The academic hierarchy, from instructor up to full professor, enforces caution on the imaginative or adventurous thinker. The graduate schools serve as training grounds for the inculcation of proper occupational norms. Here the aspiring scholar learns to conform to prescribed ways of doing his work. If there is no check upon inquiry because of its possible social effects, there is one set up by academic mediocrity itself which spurns a subject of signal interest or one marked by too much originality. Along with this goes the strange belief that finished writing is incompatible with thorough analysis.

Another form of academic self-regulation is the Ph.D. routine, which contributes to the frustration of the aspirant in embarking on an independent course of study. In order to hold a job he must get his Ph.D. union card or risk a precarious existence. By looking askance at any work which does not fit into the pattern the academic societies aid in disciplining recalcitrant academics. The organs of expression of these societies print material which concerns itself, for the most part, with some pulverized particle of knowledge without relevance to general problems. A perusal of such magazines as the *American Historical Review, American Sociological Review, American Economic Review,* or the *Modern Language Quarterly* will convince one of this fact. And since the audience for the material is strictly within the prescribed field, the result is intellectual incest.

The academic conventions reveal the plight of the scholars. These annual gatherings have a threefold function. Ostensibly, but of least importance for most, unfortunately, they provide an opportunity for the reading of papers and personal discussion of intellectual problems which the wide dispersion of academic centers does not ordinarily afford. The other two functions of the convention are derived from the over-all social structure. Established academicians from the various colleges converge upon the designated spot to investigate the chances of better jobs, and neophytes in search of careers sound out department heads for any possible openings. The departmental heads themselves are often there for the sole purpose of discovering a man to fill a vacant position. This aspect of the convention takes on the character of the market-place where the fine American art of the manipulation of personality comes to the fore. Here is a version of the businessman's club, in which the mores of American culture operate in a more subdued way. The other important function served by the convention is the chance it provides for the big shot in the field to bask in the limelight, to command deference from the lesser brethren and expand under the warmth of prestige made manifest. For the lesser fry there is the opportunity to exchange a few words with the great ones. Status relationships are brought sharply into focus by these gatherings so that after the initial forced cameraderie the great ones retire among themselves, and discussion is limited down the line by hierarchical criteria, reaching bottom with the proletariat of graduate students who, genially ignored, cringe self-consciously in the corners and corridors of the meeting place.

It must not be thought that there is perfect uniformity in the general personality-structure of the academic man. The variations in attitude, aside from individual idiosyncrasy, are the products of the different fields of interest. The economist, for instance, is, as a type, inclined to act as a man of affairs. Since orthodox classical economics still prevails, he displays many of the characteristics of the big businessman. He is in the way of being the businessman's ideologist, systematizing and refurbishing the economic beliefs of these American barons, making objective and highly abstract, in terms of the monetary calculus, the subjective valuations of the men of hard-headed action. In this respect the economist differs considerably from the philosophy teacher, who usually is inclined to underestimate the weight of social and economic conditions that bear down on him.

There is an accepted pattern for the academic man not only in his intellectual but also in his personal life. In the latter, too, he cannot afford to be conspicuously out of line. The university or college operates within a community ranging from the large city to the country town. Though the city may allow more opportunity for the violation of bourgeois modes, the necessity of meeting a routine of scheduled classes and the pressure from the students and the administration forces him to dress soberly, speak circumspectly and be wary of activities of an ungenteel nature. He therefore finds himself gradually moving into a pattern not of his own making. The conflict engendered by the contradiction between his style of life and his critical attitude toward the prevailing norms may often, in the case of the sensitive individual, take a heavy psychological toll. As a result he either overcompensates by consciously immersing himself in parochial attitudes shared by the folk, or finds that in any action prompted by his critical attitude he is checked by awareness of the ambiguity of his own motives. Often he finds an outlet by contributing to the little magazines where academism is held in scorn. There he indulges in the masochistic pleasure of whipping the sore spots of the academic body social.

This is not to be taken to mean that all academicians fit into the pattern we have described. It is the general outline we have in mind, not particular cases. There are a minority of scholars who, aware of their situation, refuse to accept it and strive to fulfill their role both as transmitters of culture and contributors to knowledge by conscientious adherence to the critical attitude. They maintain their devotion to their calling, though in the process they must suffer for it in terms of diminished rewards and diminished prestige. They are able to leaven the loaf of academic stereotype and to render the continuance of American higher learning not completely futile. Their position, however, is that of marginal men.

The position, function, and role of the group of intellectuals commonly designated as bohemians differs considerably from that of the academy. By bohemians we mean those intellectuals who form the avant-garde in the creation and dissemination of ideas. They are, for the most part, free-lance workers open to the most flexible kind of intellectual exchange. However, their audience is a self-styled elite, very small in number; and the little magazines are the vehicle through which their ideas are made manifest. The minimal size of the audience has as its psychological concomitant the heightening of self-importance, thus compensating to some degree for the group's greater alienation from society as a whole. With respect to the subject matter of these magazines, there is an overlapping with that which the academic minority, mentioned previously, is concerned with—the minority which considers formal academic outlets too narrow, not allowing for that free flow of ideas and the awareness of new intellectual currents which, in the official journals, too often harden into the patterns of sterile, ritualistic epigonism.

The term bohemian should not be considered a derogatory one. Both as a set of intellectual attitudes and as a way of life bohemianism has its roots in the social trends of Western culture since the French Revolution. The breakdown of the patron system has strongly influenced the status and role of the artist-intellectual, who can no longer count, as in the past, on a definite audience, and is therefore insecure both economically and psychologically. In America, of course, the absence of this cultural break—for the patronage system never existed here—has produced a hybrid kind of bohemianism.

Bohemia includes commentators on the arts as well as critics of literature and social critics who write from a broader humanistic standpoint. Formally speaking, the critics remind one of the medieval theologians who concentrated upon highly sophisticated ratiocination of the ineffable religious core in contrast to the mystics who were in communication with the Godhead through direct nonrational means. This distinction, elaborated upon by Rudolf Otto in his *Idea of the Holy*, carries through to the world of art where the artist not given to verbal expression plays a part parallel to that of the medieval mystic. But of course some, like T. S. Eliot, act out both roles.

The avant-garde bohemian intellectual lives in a state of estrangement from the population at large. Deprived of recognition in the social scheme, this type of intellectual, to assure his survival, has tended to drift into defined areas of a few large cities, or has formed communities of his own on the fringes of such cities as New York and San Francisco. Marginal men, the bohemians are paradoxically enough an elite proletariat in the original sense of the word. Outside the minuscule world of their shared values and manner of life they are regarded either with benign philistine amusement or as a threat to faith and morals.

Those of the avant-garde not fortunate enough to possess private means lead a truncated existence. To survive they must at some point compromise by taking a job for some months in the despised commercialized pursuits, but as soon as they accumulate some small savings they abruptly quit to concentrate furiously upon what they consider to be truly creative work. However, the bohemians who "make good" in the accepted monetary sense are faced with a psychological crisis. For if, symbolically speaking, they move from the coldwater flat to the elevator apartment, they are risking surrender to the world they condemn and divorce from the creative source which has given their work substance. Rapid withering of talent, as shown in slick formula novels or plays or "think-pieces" for periodicals, has more often than not been the fate of the intellectual who started out on the periphery and steadily moved toward the center of social power. The career of Clifford Odets illustrates this process. There is constant pressure on the avant-gardist who has won recognition to apply his talents to the construction of easy affirmations and plausible rationalizations of the cultural status quo. The evolution of Van Wyck Brooks is a pertinent example. For a study of the more politically motivated type of backsliding avant-gardist we may refer the reader to Mary McCarthy's probing analysis in "Portrait of the Intellectual as a Yale Man."

The sense of in-groupness of the bohemian intellectual provides a source of psychological security against the isolation which is the fate of the alienated from the larger social structure. The vice of this group cohesion is the stereotyping of what is considered avant-garde without reference to explicitly formulated criteria. The criteria tend to become not a rationally composed set of standards guiding individual expression but rather a merely negative response to the rejected environment. Thus we have the emergence of modish cults and the overestimation of mediocre talents. Psychological dependence being pervasive in this group, there is the inclination to avoid trenchant criticism for fear of forcing the offended member to break away from the group. These factors make for a weakening of discrimination. As a result, we see that a Henry Miller and a Kenneth Patchen receive the adulation more becoming to seers and prophets than to writers of as yet undetermined stature. The warping of judgment to which the bohemian intellectual is subject is due to the distorted role he is compelled to play in a culture which has no defined place for him. Publicists like Dwight Macdonald retreat into a world of fantasy where it becomes easy to ignore the brutal onset of modern power-combinations. This self-created world of infantile regression prohibits an incisive cultural and political criticism informed by a grasp of social realities.

In the early part of the century the French sociologist Durkheim pointed out that as a result of industrialism and the abstract social relations which it brought there is a growing tendency for the individual to suffer from an unrelatedness to the group. He called this condition *anomie*. The intellectuals as a whole are subject to this condition more than other members of society, and among the intellectuals it is the bohemians who are more likely to find themselves without a bulwark of values and hence forced to plot their way through a spiritual wilderness. It is they who most strongly exhibit the characteristics of *anomie*.

The bohemians are, generally speaking, recruited from two social areas. There are those who grew up in metropolitan centers and are for the most part members of minority groups. Because of this background they are able to see more clearly the faults of the existing system, having directly experienced its contradictions. They usually come from proletarian or lower middle class homes and go through a stage of intense political activity in high school or college. If they reject Stalinist ideologists, to whom they are initially drawn, it is often because of an esthetic sensitivity which brings home to them the true meaning of Communism. Manipulation of ideas and of the processes of art for party ends hampers the free flow of intellectual creativity to which the bohemian is committed.

The other major source of bohemian recruitment is from the small towns in the American heartland where native talent, be it genuine or illusory, is stifled by provincialism. Both lower and upper middle class recruits come to bohemia from these towns. In their own class the bourgeois bohemians are a tiny minority. It is a class in which conspicuous leisure and consumption make possible the patronizing of art and the intellect. Social security and established position allow this cursory interest, whereas in the lower strata of the middle class, especially in the smaller cities and towns, ideas and art are suspect because insecurity, both social and economic, enforces rigid conformity to conventional values. In these strata intellectualism immediately takes on revolutionary implications, adding to the already existing anxiety brought on by a problematic status in society.

The upper middle class deviants are given the opportunity for cultivation in their own milieu, but because of the acute realization that in this milieu intellectual and artistic endeavor is at bottom considered to be nonessential and ornamental they are led to cut their social ties and to drift into the centers of bohemia. This divorce from their background, if accompanied by contradictions in their personal life, often breeds neurosis out of which may come significant work, or, as is more general, a pitiful stretching and straining of small gifts. As an example of the former type there is the life and art of Hart Crane, whose anguished existence had the implications of an American tragedy Dreiser never conceived.

The bohemians are the vanguard of the ever-moving cultural frontier. They are the first to feel out the emergent line of sensibility and consciousness; and though often taken in by the spurious or the merely bizarre they nevertheless fulfill the important function of bringing to light new attitudes and interests which portend social and political change.

While the academy is to some extent still in possession of certain standards of criticism drawn from tradition and acquaintance with scientific procedures, the bohemians are in the very nature of their social role deprived of intellectual stability. The defect of their virtue is to be receptive to charlatanism which has the aura of creative originality; all too often they admire the grotesque and the startling regardless of its meaning and content. Thus in the little magazines one finds genuinely valid material together with a mass of undigestible jargon. This stuff is often concocted by people who live on the fringes of the avant-garde and who assimilate the mannerisms of this group for reasons other than a concern with ideas or values—reasons that they themselves are not aware of. They are the parasites of intellectualism, who believe themselves to be possessed of originality and critical acumen merely because they consider themselves to be "different"; their work is no more than a product of their social and psychological maladjustment—a maladjustment not strained through any objectifying process. An inverted snobbishness compensates for their alienation from philistine norms, and their bohemian existence protects them from social pulverization. Actually they are brothers under the skin of their philistine counterparts.

To be distinguished from them are those bohemians whose neurotic patterns are intertwined with the critically and creatively viable. Yet even such people, delimited as they are in role and function by a frustrating social structure, show traces of the deadly blight. To realize fully their potentialities will be impossible for them under conditions of the existing social order. For the present, however, the bohemian intellectuals must continue to live and work as a minority group, subject to the deprivations which are the lot of minorities everywhere.

The distance from the cold-water flats of Greenwich Village to the whited sepulchre of the Time and Life Building off Fifth Avenue is longer than can be gauged from the short subway ride. This does not mean that it cannot be traversed, for the careers of aspiring free-lance intellectuals standing outside the social order all too often testify that it can. Not a few of the intellectuals who begin their careers on the margin of the existing system end up by selling their services to the ingenious molders of public opinion of which the Luce combine is the most typical. (We may again refer the reader to Mary McCarthy's "Portrait of the Intellectual," in which the transition from one world to another is skillfully drawn.) Of course, those who move from the precarious world of the alienated avant-garde to the high-powered organization of the slick disseminators of prefabricated ideas pay a price in loss of creative talent and power of analysis. Frequently, however, the body social of bohemia loses nothing by their desertion, for they mostly belong to the type whose relation to bohemia is parasitical. This parasitism serves as an apprenticeship for their subsequent careers, as it enables them to acquire a glibness of expression which fits in splendidly with their later efforts. Also, their usual origin, as that of the Yale man intellectual portrayed by Mary McCarthy, is in the upper middle class, and thus their shift to the uptown milieu is by way of being a homecoming, a return to that which was only tentatively rejected. This return is not necessarily motivated in a purely economic fashion, as motives of this order are often subordinated to the need for relatedness to the dominant social trends, the compulsion to break away from the desperate sense of isolation which is the lot of those living on the fringes of the social structure.

The ex-expatriates who return to the bourgeois fold are but a minor part of the group which we might describe as the fellow-travelers of the haute bourgeoisie. Not all types of journalists, however, should be included in this category. There are some on the big city dailies who are nothing more than artisans of the phrase, without cultural pretensions. Then there are honest journeymen who divorce their journalistic tasks from their existence as a whole, groping to understand what underlies their obscure conflicts. They nourish a secret desire to write a novel or a muckraking book, but it seems as though the time for such independent writing never arrives. So they drink more than their average fellow-Americans, acquiring a protective layer of cynicism to prevent their really sensitive skins from being continually rubbed the wrong way.

The hard core of the stratum that lives off ideas, of which the Lucites are the most typical representatives, are the graduates of the fashionable Eastern colleges whose social origin is in the upper income-bracket groups. This is no coincidence, of course. Those placed on the policy-making level of the hierarchy favor the employment of this type because of their knowledge of his reliability both in the production of desired copy and in the creation of an *esprit de corps* derived from class and status. Family, which in America means a background of several generations of wealth and identification with approved ethnic groups, is a major criterion of employment. Those who lack the proper qualifications must assimilate the manners, dress, and attitudes of the favored group if they desire to rise in the organization. The fellow-travelers of the haute bourgeoisie often regard themselves as "liberals," that is to say, they have no objections to strategic renovations in the existing social structure provided their position remains secure. In addition to their "liberalism" they have a superficial acquaintance with what has been traditionally considered "intellectual" subject matter. They have Proust and Joyce and Mann prominently placed on their bookshelves and they command a store of epigrammatic erudition gleaned from disparate corners of the intellectual world. This lends them that masterful glibness of sophisticated philistinism in which their copy abounds.

Their way of life follows the pattern of the upper middle class —in dress, manners, and tone. Mating flexibility makes a succession of marriage partners an accepted routine, even though the marriages must be arranged through the proper church channels with florid social embellishment and due notice in the newspapers. Their rhythm of life changes with the quick shifts they are called upon to make in manipulation of ideas which best serve the demands of their employers. On occasion they will confess their distress at these demands. They are doubtful of the quality of the work they turn out, yet they are deprived of an alternative mode of life, being limited by years of doing the proper thing and by an acquaintance no more than casual with the internal rigors of the intellectual process. They have been digesting for short-run purposes of exploitation the work of more scrupulous and imaginative men much too long. These popular journalists make much of the justification that their labors lift the general level of culture among the masses. But the truth is that for the masses they have a lofty contempt.

The stratification in the fellow-travelers of the haute bourgeoisie is more or less identical with that found in the nonintellectual members of the class. It breaks down along the lines of schools attended, affluence, and the ethnic group of the individual. Consequently there operates among them a covert yet pervasive anti-Semitism—a genteel social prejudice not to be equated with the lower class counterpart of this disease. The anti-Semitism of the lower class variety has Hitlerian overtones, whereas the more fashionable sort has its mainsprings in the social life of the upper middle class suburbia. It manifests itself in an overpolite attitude toward Jews, a mixture of unconscious guilt and deliberate condescension. The social lines are not drawn hard and fast, for Jews of the same class are accepted with reservations. Jews of lower class origin, however, must bear the stigma of complete exclusion.

This group's way of life has been well portrayed in the novels of J. P. Marquand, who himself so well typifies its outlook and mannerisms. As writers the members of this group possess a small technical competence, and when working in a wider frame of social reference they have the ingenuity to dress up stale ideas in glittering generalities. Their intellectualism is self-conscious and ornamental. If they suffer a high degree of neurosis it is not because they have had to play the pariah-role of the avant-garde but rather because of the disintegration of family ties in their social milieu. The relationship between their parents is usually devoid of organic quality; the percentage of divorce is high; the children are pampered, it is true, but only in a kind of abstract fashion which

corresponds more to social convention than to integral feeling.
These people are in a sense the historical counterparts of the enlightened aristocrats of pre-revolutionary France. In their case,
however, it is quite unlikely that in the near future they will fall
victim to a political convulsion.

The ideologists are those intellectuals whose ideas and policy
are derived from the Communist Party. We may mark them off
into concentric circles, each circle taking in larger areas of the
American social structure. Obviously not all Communists or fellow-
travelers are to be considered intellectuals; it is nevertheless true
that under the guidance of the party leadership or as convenient
pawns the intellectuals play an important part in the Communist
movement. The dupes or pawns among them make up a group of
totalitarian liberals and other intellectuals who, in escaping bewilderment and painful ambiguity, find their way into the numerous front organizations.

These groups have only one use for ideas—though the attitude
that makes this use possible becomes less marked as it radiates outward from the party core—and that is to manipulate them in such
a way as to further the party's struggle for power. Ideas and values
are thus not considered as ends in themselves but only as weapons for political bludgeoning. In the inner circle of disciplined
Stalinism the instrumentation of ideas is wielded according to the
party version of Marxism—a secular faith to which the comrades
have sworn absolute fealty. For these fervent believers the truth
has been given once and for all, hence to them ideas are either
adaptable to current party ends or to be dismissed as hostile to the
class interests of the "proletariat." There is no need to meet opposing concepts on their own ground, for their logical truth or
falsity is irrelevant by Stalinist standards. The problem is "to
unmask" them, that is to say, to discredit them by exposing their
origin in the class structure. No recognition of the fact that the
truth of ideas is in no sense identical with the explanation of their
origin is allowed to discourage the Stalinists. In the *New Masses*
the job of smearing and discrediting is done on a crude level, while
in a journal like *Science and Society* the job is done with considerably more finesse, as its contributors are drawn from the followers

of Stalinism in the academy. The two magazines share the same general orientation, but in the latter the language and tone are more elevated. Here too, however, ideas are measured by one criterion, and that is whether their role is "reactionary," a protean concept, or "progressive," a concept even more protean.

Both the intellectual who holds a party-card and his brother who, for strategic reasons, holds no such cards, conceive of themselves as missionaries whose function is to soften up those liberal members of the intelligentsia who are peculiarly suceptible to the party creed. Of course, the creed is never presented in an abstract manner; worrisome issues of the day, especially as they refer to international affairs, are used as the basis for persuasion. No group since the early Christians has displayed such dogged devotion to propaganda. They have surely taken St. Augustine's dictum to heart, for they work on the assumption that in order to understand one must believe. And their belief in the rightness of their cause passeth all understanding to those not under the spell.

These fellow-travelers are to be found in every segment of the social structure. The avowed party-member stands self-exposed and is therefore not as effective as the fellow-traveler who operates in an academic outpost or in some liberal journal. The latter understands how to discover the weak spots of the free-floating liberal. He is adept in exploiting the liberal ideologically, for he has steeled himself to iron discipline so as not to betray heat or vindictiveness in argument. Hence he leads a double life. Outwardly his manner conforms to the liberal's standards of decorum and sanity, but he gives himself away when discussing matters not politically relevant; on such occasions his smugness or inquisitorial attitude makes plain what he wishes to conceal. You can tell him by the look of pained patience with which he listens to those liberals who criticize the Soviet fatherland or its doctrines and by his tendency to make use of such epithets as "social democrat" and "fascist" on any and all occasions.

Each of the groups we have considered affects the larger American social pattern and is in turn affected by it. Thus the impact of the contemporary crisis which has forced America into a position of world responsibility for the first time, is likely to alter considerably the role of each of these groups, both as intellectuals and as citizens. Further, the ever-growing politicalization of intellectual life makes more and more difficult a disinterested theoretical approach. The value systems by which the intellectual operates professionally may come into conflict with the values to which he adheres in his personal and social life. If he is to reconcile these conflicting claims, he must at least be conscious of what his extra-intellectual values are. The will to believe usually leads only to elaborate rationalizations.

The Highbrow in American Politics

by Arthur Schlesinger, Jr.

AMID the other perplexities it bequeathed to the American people, the campaign of 1952 has bequeathed a particular perplexity to the philologists. In September of that year, Mr. Stewart Alsop, the well-known syndicated columnist, was traveling through Connecticut with Governor Stevenson. In order to get a Republican estimate of the local situation, he phoned his brother, Mr. John Alsop of Avon, a prominent younger figure in Connecticut politics. In the course of the conversation, Stewart Alsop pointed out that certain intellectuals, who had backed General Eisenhower up to the convention, were now deserting him. This comment somewhat irritated John Alsop; so, dredging a term up from his subconscious, he dismissed these defections as the "egghead" vote.

John Alsop did not invent the term "egghead"; but no one had ever before applied it to the nation's intellectuals. "I suppose if one were to analyze the term," John Alsop wrote later, "one would say that is a visual figure of speech, tending to depict a large, oval head, smooth, faceless, unemotional, but a little bit haughty and condescending." It should be emphasized that for the Alsops, graduates of Yale and anti-anti-intellectuals, "egghead" was still an amiable epithet; and it was in this sense that the word made its debut in the language.

On September 26, after a visit to Springfield, Stewart Alsop used the word publicly in a column, applying it both to those intellectuals who were swinging to Governor Stevenson and to the young men who were active in the Stevenson headquarters in Springfield. At this stage, "egghead" had rather an Ivy League connotation—an A. B. degree, button-down collars, tweeds and flannels, perhaps pipes and crew haircuts, with a lively but amateur interest in the intellectual life and a capacity to read without moving one's lips. Governor Stevenson himself was amused by the word and used it while speaking to an egghead audience at the

University of Wisconsin. In the next weeks the term caught on
with a rapidity which suggested that it filled some precise need in
American discourse or perhaps touched some sensitive nerve in the
social organism.

Certainly there was rough justice in the application. While
Governor Stevenson had no more eggheads about him than Franklin D. Roosevelt used to have, he diluted them less with the professional politicians, the admirals, the old Harvard cronies and
the other non-intellectual types who moved in the Roosevelt en-
tourage. Moreover, while Roosevelt had an active and detailed
interest in issues of public policy, his reactions to art or literature
were perfunctory and conventional. Stevenson, with his literate
and well-stocked mind, his urbane and apt allusions and quotations, gave the impression of being a man of far broader and more
humane culture.

To the intellectuals of the country, he seemed one of their
own; and they responded to him as they had never responded to
Roosevelt. Or, at least, so I have been repeatedly told since the
campaign; and, when I have wondered whether this was simply
the application of the rule that people in love find all their previous affairs tawdry and superficial, I have been told, No—that
there was a sense of kinship and sympathy with Stevenson which
had never been felt with the more remote, abstract, contrived
Roosevelt. As Eudora Welty well stated the Stevenson appeal,
"The voice of the passionate intelligence speaks to the whole
range of the mind—in politics as well as in poetry." And, as she
went on, in a post-election message to Governor Stevenson, "This
writer knows of people here and there like herself, previously political ignoramuses (we now feel a fellowship)—well-intentioned ever,
but not ever in the sense of being personally involved, concerned
deeply by a political campaign until this year. Then, with your appearance on the national scene, we found out how deeply concerned we could be."

Certainly, as the campaign progressed, writers and artists began to discover a wholly unexpected intensity of commitment.
Men like Richard Rodgers and Howard Lindsay, who had been
for Eisenhower in February, found themselves swept away by the
Stevenson movement in October. Others, who had exhausted

themselves through the years in a series of political disappoint-
ments and felt that they could never respond again, found welling
up within new reserves of political emotion and energy. Still
others, who had never before strayed from the strict sectarianism
of third-party politics, now voted with enthusiasm for a major
party candidate.

No doubt, intellectuals being intellectuals, the involvement
took some absurd extremes. One activist of the *Scrutiny* circle
proposed after the election that such people as Leavis, Djuna
Barnes and Cecil Beaton make up a package of their books, appropriately inscribed to the Governor, in order to help relieve in
some amiable way the painful tension of defeat. But this very
gesture from the avant-garde, surely unprecedented in the history
of American presidential politics, reveals the special feeling evoked
by the Stevenson candidacy among even the most attenuated of
the intellectuals.

Writers have been involved in politics enough—perhaps too
much—in the recent past. But the Stevenson involvement was
qualitatively different from the others—from the sordid liaisons
of Popular Front days, for example, or from the heavy propaganda
of the Writers' War Board. Those involvements had primarily
served political ends. The Stevenson involvement, retaining an
innocence, even perhaps a purity, of its own, primarily served humane and artistic ends. The intellectuals desired Stevenson's victory, not to attain public objectives or even to affect public policy,
but to affirm an interior sense of admiration and of belief.

This passion of the intellectuals for Stevenson, while not to
be a major factor in the outcome, could not escape due notice in
the heat of the campaign. The Republicans became considerably
irritated by what appeared to be a closing of the literary and academic ranks behind the Democratic candidate. Anti-intellectualism is always epidemic in the business community; and the campaign of Senator McCarthy and his associates, as well, doubtless,
as past excesses of the intellectuals themselves, had spread the
infection through much of the country. In the last weeks of the
campaign, the Republicans made a calculated effort to rouse and
exploit this accumulating exasperation.

It was in the course of this effort that the word "egghead"

entered a new phase of its evolution. What had started out as an affable and friendly term now began to acquire uglier connotations. Senator McCarthy, while avoiding the word, devoted two nation-wide broadcasts to attacks on the Stevenson advisers, a sinister crew of people which included two Pulitzer Prize historians, one of them a former editor of the *Saturday Review of Literature*, as well as a Bollingen Prize poet and former Librarian of Congress. Others seized with relish on the new word itself. "There has come a wonderful new expression," exulted Louis Bromfield, a McCarthy admirer, on October 26, "to define a certain shady element of our American population. Who conceived the expression, I do not know. . . . It seems to have arisen spontaneously from the people themselves."

Mr. Bromfield went on to offer a voluble and excited definition—"a person of intellectual pretensions, often a professor or the protégé of a professor . . . superficial in approach to any problem . . . feminine . . . supercilious . . . surfeited with conceit . . . a doctrinaire supporter of middle-European socialism . . . a self-conscious prig . . . a bleeding heart"—166 hot words pouring out in a confused stream an interesting collection of Mr. Bromfield's own resentments and rancors. If Stevenson were to be elected, he sternly concluded, "the eggheads will come back into power and off again we will go on the scenic railway of muddled economics, Socialism, Communism, crookedness and psychopathic instability."

It was this approach which set the tone for much of the post-election discussion. The returns were hardly in before *Time* Magazine, recounting the tribulations of the Eisenhower crusade, observed that it had survived "the egghead rebellion, the desertion . . . by scores of intellectuals, journalists, Hollywoodians and other opinion makers." From this fact *Time* drew ominous conclusions. "The final victory discloses an alarming fact, long suspected: there is a wide and unhealthy gap between the American intellectuals and the people."

This theory of the gap instantly commended itself to all those seeking to discipline the intellectuals. It soon received a more comprehensive exposition under formidable religious auspices. In an article late in November in the Protestant weekly the *Christian*

Century, Rev. Dr. Robert A. Fitch, a graduate of Yale, Union Theological Seminary, Columbia and the Sorbonne, a member of the American Philosophical Association, and currently dean of the Pacific School of Religion, addressed himself to the subject of the "Intelligentsia in Defeat."

For the Rev. Dr. Fitch, the election marked, above all, the long-awaited punishment of the American intelligentsia. In Governor Stevenson he saw "the perfect incarnation of the liberal logos." The Democratic candidate, in Dr. Fitch's view, was characterized by his passion for truth; and, while Dr. Fitch made clear that he had nothing against truth, "more vulgar politics might argue that the real objective is not truth but right action; and that, while it should be an ingredient in all right action, truth must mingle with other necessities that determine a course of conduct."

It was no doubt this theory of the limited role of truth in politics which would permit Dr. Fitch to spread his ecclesiastical mantle over Senator McCarthy. The one issue which really concerned the intelligentsia, Dr. Fitch continued, was civil liberties, which, he added disagreeably, was their class issue—much presumably as the wool tariff would be the class issue for the owners of sheep. "With this lofty passion," Dr. Fitch said, in an appropriate vein of sarcasm, "the intelligentsia recognized only one real incarnate devil in the campaign, and that was Senator McCarthy." But was not Senator McCarthy, Dr. Fitch asked, really justified? It is true that the character of the treason of the intellectuals "was not altogether [sic] of a sort that can be recognized in a court of law." It consisted rather "in the gross of a whole tradition of scholarship and of philosophy which dealt in too cavalier a fashion with the irreducible articles of the American faith," Dr. Fitch said, trailing off in a sputter about "positivism . . . nihilism . . . ethical relativism." Seen this way, Dr. Fitch declared, McCarthy was but "the spokesman for the suspicions of inarticulate people that somehow and somewhere in their country a great betrayal was going on." (One hardly knows how to interpret the news that the Union Theological Seminary has recently engaged Dr. Fitch to take the place of Dr. Reinhold Niebuhr during Dr. Niebuhr's current illness; Fitch pinch-hitting for Niebuhr may show the trend of the times.)

Nor was the theory that Senator McCarthy had become the appointed instrument of divine wrath to chastise the intellectuals confined to such emblems of the Protestant clergy as Dr. Fitch. Rabbi Benjamin Schultz, at a luncheon for the Senator at the Hotel Astor in New York, declared that the great tragedy of our times is the "dichotomy between the people and the so-called intellectuals." But do not despair. "Thank God, the people have arisen to protest through the person of Joseph R. McCarthy." And what was intoned by Protestants and Jews had long since received the assent of Catholics.

What these expressions signaled was a rise to climax of the hatred of the intellectuals which had long been stewing and stirring in various sections of American society. The dominant sentiment of the '20s, our last interlude of business rule, it had been driven underground by the depression and the New Deal to find only sporadic vent through the years in congressional investigations and in the gutter press. Now it bursts forth in full violence. By early November the word "egghead" seemed almost to detonate the pent-up ferocity of twenty years of impotence. On November 4 the Republican victory licensed those feelings and, in a sense, established them in power.

The new President, of course, was no particular enemy of the intellectuals. He had himself been a university president, of a sort; and even before his inauguration, he had appointed three other captains of education to key positions in his administration (though, perhaps significantly, no university professors). But other members of his party were less admiring of the life of the mind. A number of Republican senators and congressmen, flushed with political victory, now sought to convert the Democratic defeat into an egghead rout by tracking the intellectual down to his final stronghold, the university.

These men did not underestimate what they described as their courage in thus pressing the hunt. "This will be the most unpopular, the most unpleasant task any one can do," Senator McCarthy bravely explained, "that is, exposing Communists and Communist thinkers—I'd rather use the words 'Communist thinkers' than 'Communists'—in your educational institutions, because the minute you do that all hell breaks loose. From coast to coast you hear the screaming of interference with academic freedom." But, fortified by a series of decorations tardily conferred by the United States Marine Corps, the junior Senator from Wisconsin has announced himself ready to lead the assault—if Congressman Velde and Senator Jenner and the other aspirants for the honor will let him. In any case, the bullies are forming their pack. And, as usual, a few intellectuals who would like to have been bullies are running out in front, snuffling along the ground to uncover the trail, ready to rush back to their new masters, wagging their tails, whenever they find an egghead track. Mr. James Burnham and the *Freeman* (or ex-*Freeman*) set are convenient examples.

Today, as a consequence of the election, the American intellectual finds himself in a situation he has not known for a generation. The *Partisan Review's* symposium in reconciliation, "America and the Intellectuals," celebrated the end, and not the beginning of an epoch. For twenty years, the government of the United States, while often one which the intellectual has found confused or mistaken, has nevertheless been one which has basically understood, respected and protected intellectual purposes. Now business is in power again; and with it will inevitably come the vulgarization which has been the most invariable consequence of business supremacy. American writers have already been denounced for not providing favorable portraits of businessmen in their novels, as Communist writers are berated for not doing justice to the new Soviet man. And, while no modern equivalent of Bruce Barton's *The Man Nobody Knows* has yet been produced, Harry A. Bullis, chairman of the board of General Mills, a director of the National Conference of Christians and Jews, a Legionnaire, a Republican and a Methodist, has already written an article entitled "God is my Senior Partner" (with full immunity from suspicions of blasphemy; think what would happen to an intellectual who wrote an article entitled "God is my Literary Agent"!).

A position of alienation is, of course, normal and essential for an artist. Indeed, no other position is possible; for no society can ever satisfy all the subtle scruples and needs of the individual sensibility. The artist must be a lonely man. (When Simonov writes, "If you ask me what the Soviet system has done for the writer I should answer that, first of all, it has erased from his inner self all sense of loneliness, and given him the feeling of complete and absolute 'belonging' to society," he gives the whole Soviet show away.) But there is a difference between the normal alienation of any artist in society, and the organized official hostility which puts the artist on the run and obsesses him with the necessities of self-defense.

In the '20s, this situation was manageable. The social pressures were heavy, but escape was easy. Satire was an available weapon: Mencken, Lewis, Lardner and their imitators could cope with society by ridiculing it. Or, if this form of intellectual escape was unsatisfying, then physical escape was easily possible, and a literary generation fled to Paris. And, in any case, there was an abundance of outlets; it was possible for persons with modest sums of money to start new publications and, in one way or another, gain circulation for even the most vapid and eccentric writing.

In the generation since, the horizon has closed in. The cold war and the Soviet threat have necessarily narrowed alternatives; and the indulgence of freedom must inevitably take second place in the real world to the harsh requirements of survival. And the intellectuals themselves, in many cases, have forfeited sympathy or respect because of the arrogance and egotism they displayed when they were riding high—an arrogance too often accompanied by political imbecility, if not by political guilt. Yet the demagogues of the right, trying to pluck power out of anxiety, have narrowed the alternatives far beyond the point of necessity. And, though the intellectuals may have deserved much in the way of correction, they did not deserve as the instrument of chastisement a blatant liar whose own awakening to the Communist threat was delayed until February 9, 1950—a date by which time all but the most obtuse intellectuals had long since tumbled to the facts of life.

The new atmosphere is no longer conducive to the old escapes. To satirize the American businessman today, for example, is to invite suspicion and attack; what was once satiric is now (in the business community, at least) subversive. When Robert E. Sherwood presented the most unfamiliar dramatic type of the hardfisted local banker in The Best Years of Our Lives, he was attacked as providing propaganda for the Communists. James Thurber said last summer that it would no longer be possible to write a satiric comedy so "free and exuberant" as *The Male Animal*. And he is clearly right: the businessman who was the comic trustee in 1940 would be the university president today, and hardly a fit subject for humor. The most brilliant and daring of our comic strip cartoonists, Al Capp, finally had to marry off his two leading characters, because, no longer feeling himself free to "kid hell out of everything," he felt he had no choice but to convert knock-about satire into a fairy story. "For the first 14 years [of the strip] I reveled in the freedom to laugh at America. But now America has changed. The humorist feels the change more, perhaps, than anyone. Now there are things about America we can't kid."

And the range of outlets has narrowed drastically too. The cost of entry into the magazine field is almost prohibitive today. For a generation freedom of expression in America has survived in part because one group in the country controlled the government and another group controlled the mass media. Now the same group controls both, and we are confronted with the possibility of a communications monopoly unprecedented in our history. The effect of this potential monopoly will be grave enough in the political field, where the Democratic party and the liberals will be badly handicapped in their attempts to combat the right-wing Republican effort to smear the Democratic party as incurably devoted to disloyalty and treason; but its effect there may well be less grave than its effect on the general level of culture. The mass communications, as Gilbert Seldes has pointed out, are dominated by the concept of the "great audience." By concentrating on the lowest common denominator, they may in time create the very uniform unleavened mass which is already the postulate of their activities.

The intellectual in 1953 thus faces an incalculable but depressing combination of factors. He is dismissed as an "egghead," governed by a party which has little use for him and little understanding of what he is about. He is the natural and obvious scapegoat for the country's new rulers; he caused the Japanese attack on Pearl Harbor, lost China, invented the graduated income tax

and piled up the national debt; anti-intellectualism has long been
the anti-Semitism of the businessman. Escape into satire only
worsens the intellectual's position in the United States. Escape into
foreign lands only deepens his predicament and his melancholy:
after all, Jean-Paul Sartre is both far more irritating and a far
greater enemy of freedom than Herbert Brownell. Publication, in
general, will be far more difficult than ever before; the problem of
the mass media ever more pressing; the attack on cultural diversity
ever more methodical and effective.

This is far deeper than a political problem; but, like all problems in this age, it has a political cast. The intellectual should
take heed from the "egghead" episode. He is on the run today in
American society; and he cannot hope to escape by silence or by
retiring to cultivate his garden or—certainly—by sidling up to his
pursuer and offering his services. In a sense, the Rev. Dr. Fitch was
right; civil liberties are the class issue of the intelligentsia; and
nothing has been more pathetic than the scurrying to cover of
certain intellectuals when called upon to stand up for the freedom
of expression. And this freedom too, in the long run, affords the
only basis on which the problems of mass culture can be answered.
Tocqueville commented a century ago that many people considered equality of conditions as one evil and political freedom as
a second. "When they are obliged to yield to the former, they
strive at least to escape from the latter. But I contend, that in
order to combat the evils which equality may produce, there is
only one effectual remedy—namely, political freedom."

Not all intellectuals may be willing or able to understand the
complexities of the dollar gap or the price-support program. But
they should at least, like the trade unionist or the cattleman or the
oil magnate, be willing to understand their own class interests.
Most of them rightly recognized that one candidate in the 1952
campaign spoke with wisdom and courage and understanding on
the issue of the free mind, while the other showed only a blank
indifference. Defeat does not foreclose the issue: the blankness of
Republican victory may yet be inscribed by Senator McCarthy—
or, perhaps, by James B. Conant. The fight continues and must
command our best efforts.

Much as the highbrow in his present mood may dislike politics, he cannot escape or reject it. We hear that the new intellectual is entering into a phase of contemplation and withdrawal. But, if he decides to flee it all and become a Yogi, he will have no one else to blame if Senator McCarthy becomes the Commissar.

"American-type" Painting

by Clement Greenberg

THE latest abstract painting offends many people who accept the abstract in art in principle. New painting (sculpture is a different question) provokes scandal when little that is new in literature or even music appears to do so any longer. This can be explained in part by the very slowness of painting's evolution as a modernist art. Though it started on its "modernization" earlier perhaps than the other arts, it has turned out to have a greater number of *expendable* conventions imbedded in it, or these at least have proven harder to isolate and detach. As long as such conventions survive and can be isolated they continue to be attacked, in all the arts that intend to maintain their vitality in modern society. This process has come to a stop in literature because literature has fewer conventions to expend before it begins to deny its own essence, which lies in the communication of conceptual meanings. The expendable conventions in music, on the other hand, would seem to have been isolated much sooner, which is why the process of modernization has slowed down, if not stopped, there. (I simplify drastically. And it is understood, I hope, that tradition is not dismantled by the avant-garde for sheer revolutionary effect, but in order to maintain the level and vitality of art under the steadily changing circumstances of the last hundred years—and that the dismantling has its own continuity and tradition.)

That is, the avant-garde continues in painting because painting has not yet reached the point of modernization where its discarding of inherited convention must stop lest it cease to be viable as art. Nowhere do these conventions seem to go on being attacked as they are today in this country. The commotion about a certain kind of American abstract art is a sign of that. It is practiced by a group of painters who came to notice in New York about a dozen years ago, and have since become known as the "abstract expressionists," or less widely, as "action" painters. (I think Robert Coates of the *New Yorker* coined the first term, which is not altogether accurate. Harold Rosenberg, in *Art News*, concocted the second, but restricted it by implication to but three or four of the artists the public knows under the first term. In London, I heard the kind of art in question referred to as "American-type painting.") Abstract expressionism is the first phenomenon in American art to draw a standing protest, and the first to be deplored seriously, and frequently, abroad. But it is also the first on its scale to win the serious attention, then the respect, and finally the emulation of a considerable section of the Parisian avant-garde, which admires in abstract expressionism precisely what causes it to be deplored elsewhere. Paris, whatever else it may have lost, is still quick to sense the genuinely "advanced"—though most of the abstract expressionists did not set out to be "advanced"; they set out to paint good pictures, and they "advance" in pursuit of qualities analogous to those they admire in the art of the past.

Their paintings startle because, to the uninitiated eye, they appear to rely so much on accident, whim, and haphazard effect. An ungoverned spontaneity seems to be at play, intent only on registering immediate impulse, and the result to be nothing more than a welter of blurs, blotches, and scrawls—"oleaginous" and "amorphous," as one British critic described it. All this is seeming. There is good and bad in abstract expressionism, and once one can tell the difference he discovers that the good owes its realization to a severer discipline than can be found elsewhere in contemporary painting; only it makes factors explicit that previous disciplines left implicit, and leaves implicit many that they did not.

To produce important art it is necessary as a rule to digest the major art of the preceding period, or periods. This is as true today as ever. One great advantage the American abstract expressionists enjoyed in the beginning was that they had already digested Klee and Miró—this, ten years before either master became a serious influence in Paris. Another was that the example of Matisse was kept alive in New York by Hans Hofmann and Milton Avery at a time when young painters abroad tended to overlook him. Picasso, Léger, and Mondrian were much in the foreground then, especially Picasso, but they did not block either the way or the view. Of particular importance was the fact that a large number of Kandinsky's early abstract paintings could be seen in New York in what is now the Solomon Guggenheim Museum. As a result of all this, a generation of American artists could start their careers fully abreast of their times and with an artistic culture that was not provincial. Perhaps it was the first time that this happened.

But I doubt whether it would have been possible without the opportunities for unconstrained work that the WPA Art Project gave most of them in the late '30s. Nor do I think any one of them could have gotten off the ground as well as he did without the small but relatively sophisticated audience for adventurous art provided by the students of Hans Hofmann. What turned out to be another advantage was this country's distance from the war and, as immediately important as anything else, the presence in it during the war years of European artists like Mondrian, Masson, Léger, Chagall, Ernst, and Lipchitz, along with a number of European critics, dealers, and collectors. Their proximity and attention gave the young abstract-expressionist painters self-confidence and a sense of being near the center of art. And in New York they could measure themselves against Europe with more benefit to themselves than they ever could have done as expatriates in Paris.

The justification for the term, "abstract expressionist," lies in the fact that most of the painters covered by it took their lead from German, Russian, or Jewish expressionism in breaking away from late Cubist abstract art. But they all started from French painting, got their fundamental sense of style from it, and still maintain some sort of continuity with it. Not least of all, they got from it their most vivid notion of an ambitious, major art, and of the general direction in which it had to go in their time.

Picasso was very much on their minds, especially the Picasso of the early and middle '30s, and the first problem they had to face, if they were going to say what they had to say, was how to loosen up the rather strictly demarcated illusion of shallow depth he had been working within, in his more ambitious pictures, since he closed his "synthetic" Cubist period. With this went that canon of draw-

ing in faired, more or less simple lines and curves that Cubism imposed and which had dominated almost all abstract art since 1920.
They had to free themselves from this too. Such problems were
not attacked by program (there has been very little that is program-
matic about abstract expressionism) but rather run up against
simultaneously by a number of young painters most of whom had
their first shows at Peggy Guggenheim's gallery in 1943 or 1944.
The Picasso of the '30s—whom they followed in reproduction in
the *Cahiers d'Art* even more than in flesh-and-blood examples—
challenged and incited as well as taught them. Not fully abstract
itself, his art in that period suggested to them new possibilities of
expression for abstract and quasi-abstract painting as nothing else
did, not even Klee's enormously inventive and fertile but equally
unrealized 1930-1940 phase. I say equally unrealized, because Picasso
caught so few of the hares he started in the '30s—which may have
served, however, to make his effect on certain younger artists even
more stimulating.

To break away from an overpowering precedent, the young
artist usually looks for an alternative one. The late Arshile Gorky
submitted himself to Miró in order to break free of Picasso, and in
the process did a number of pictures we now see have independent
virtues, although at the time—the late '30s—they seemed too derivative. But the 1910-1918 Kandinsky was even more of a lib-
erator and during the first war years stimulated Gorky to a greater
originality. A short while later André Breton's personal encouragement began to inspire him with a confidence he had hitherto
lacked, but again he submitted his art to an influence, this time
that of Matta y Echaurren, a Chilean painter much younger than
himself. Matta was, and perhaps still is, an inventive draughtsman,
and in some ways a daring painter, but an inveterately flashy and
superficial one. It took Gorky's more solid craft, profounder culture
as a painter, and more selfless devotion to art to make many of
Matta's ideas look substantial. In the last four or five years of his
life he so transmuted these ideas, and discovered so much more
in himself in the way of feeling to add to them, that their deriva-
tion became conspicuously beside the point. Gorky found his own
way to ease the pressure of Picassoid space, and learned to float

flat shapes on a melting, indeterminate ground with a difficult stability quite unlike anything in Miró. Yet he remained a late Cubist to the end, a votary of French taste, an orthodox easel painter, a virtuoso of line, and a tinter, not a colorist. He is, I think, one of the greatest artists we have had in this country. His art went largely unappreciated in his lifetime, but a few years after his tragic death in 1948, at the age of forty-four, it was invoked and imitated by younger painters in New York who wanted to save elegance and traditional draughtsmanship for abstract painting. However, Gorky finished rather than began something, and finished it so well that anybody who follows him is condemned to academicism.

Willem de Kooning was a mature artist long before his first show in 1948. His culture is similar to Gorky's (to whom he was close) and he, too, is a draughtsman before anything else, perhaps an even more gifted one than Gorky and certainly more inventive. Ambition is as much a problem for him as it was for his dead friend, but in the inverse sense, for he has both the advantages and the liabilities—which may be greater—of an aspiration larger and more sophisticated, up to a certain point, than that of any other living artist I know of except Picasso. On the face of it, de Kooning proposes a synthesis of modernism and tradition, and a larger control over the means of abstract painting that would render it capable of statements in a grand style equivalent to that of the past. The disembodied contours of Michelangelo's and Rubens's nude figure compositions haunt his abstract pictures, yet the dragged off-whites, grays, and blacks by which they are inserted in a shallow illusion of depth—which de Kooning, no more than any other painter of the time, can deepen without risk of second-hand effect—bring the Picasso of the early '30s persistently to mind. There are even more essential resemblances, though they have little to do with imitation on de Kooning's part. He, too, hankers after *terribilità*, prompted by a similar kind of culture and by a similar nostalgia for tradition. Just as little as Picasso, can he tear himself away from the human figure, and from the modeling of it for which his gifts for line and shading so richly equip him. And it would seem that there was even more Luciferian pride behind de Kooning's ambition: were he to realize it, all other ambitious painting would have to stop for a while because he would have set its forward as well as backward limits for a generation to come.

If de Kooning's art has found a readier acceptance than most other forms of abstract expressionism, it is because his need to include the past as well as forestall the future reassures most of us. And in any case, he remains a late Cubist. Then there is his powerful, sinuous Ingresque line. When he left outright abstraction several years ago to attack the female form with a fury greater than Picasso's in the late '30s and the '40s, the results baffled and shocked collectors, yet the methods by which these savage dissections were carried out were patently Cubist. De Kooning is, in fact, the only painter I am aware of at this moment who continues Cubism without repeating it. In certain of his latest "Women," which are smaller than the preceding ones, the brilliance of the success achieved demonstrates what resources that tradition has left when used by an artist of genius. But de Kooning has still to spread the full measure of that genius on canvas.

Hans Hofmann is the most remarkable phenomenon in the abstract expressionist "school" (it is not really a school) and one of its few members who can already be referred to as a "master." Known as a teacher here and abroad, he did not begin showing until 1943, when he was in his early sixties, and only shortly after his painting had become definitely abstract. Since then he has developed as one of a group whose next oldest member is at least twenty years younger. It was only natural that he should have been the maturist from the start. But his prematureness rather than matureness has obscured the fact that by 1947 he stated and won successful pictures from ideas whose later and more single-minded exploitation by others was to constitute their main claim to originality. When I myself not so long ago complained in print that Hofmann was failing to realize his true potentialities, it was because I had not caught up with him. Renewed acquaintance with some of his earlier work and his own increasing frequency and sureness of success have enlightened me as to that.

Hofmann's pictures in many instances strain to pass beyond the easel convention as they cling to it, doing many things which that convention resists. By tradition, convention, and habit we expect pictorial structure to be presented in contrasts of dark and light, or *value*. Hofmann, who started from Matisse, the Fauves, and Kandinsky as much as from Picasso, will juxtapose high, shrill colors whose uniform warmth and brightness do not so much obscure value contrasts as render them dissonant. Or when they are made more obvious, it will be by jarring color contrasts that are equally dissonant. It is much the same with his design and drawing: a sudden razor-edged line will upset all our notions of the permissible, or else thick gobs of paint, without support of edge or shape, will cry out against pictorial sense. When Hofmann fails it is either by forcing such things, or by striving for too obvious and pat a unity, as if to reassure the spectator. Like Klee, he works in a variety of manners without seeming to consolidate his art in any one of them. He is willing, moreover, to accept his bad pictures in order to get in position for the good ones, which speaks for his self-confidence. Many people are put off by the difficulty of his art—especially museum directors and curators— without realizing it is the difficulty of it that puts them off, not what they think is its bad taste. The difficult in art usually announces itself with less sprightliness. Looked at longer, however, the sprightliness gives way to calm and to a noble and impassive intensity. Hofmann's art is very much easel painting in the end, with the concentration and the relative abundance of incident and relation that belong classically to that genre.

Adolph Gottlieb and Robert Motherwell have likewise gotten less appreciation than they deserve. Not at all alike in their painting, I couple them for the moment because they both stay closer to late Cubism, without belonging to it, than the painters yet to be discussed. Though one might think that all the abstract expressionists start off from inspired impulse, Motherwell stands out among them by reason of his dependence on it, and by his lack of real facility. Although he paints in terms of the simplified, quasi-geometric design sponsored by Picasso and Matisse and prefers, though not always, clear, simple color contrasts within a rather restricted gamut, he is less of a late Cubist than de Kooning. Motherwell has a promising kind of chaos in him but, again, it is not the kind popularly ascribed to abstract expressionism. His early collages, in a kind of explosive Cubism analogous to de

Kooning's, have with time acquired a profound and original unity, and between 1947 and 1951 or so he painted several fairly large pictures that I think are among the masterpieces of abstract expressionism: some of these, in broad vertical stripes, with ocher played off against flat blacks and whites, bear witness to how well decoration can transcend itself in the easel painting of our day. But Motherwell has also painted some of the feeblest pictures done by a leading abstract expressionist, and an accumulation of these over the last three or four years has hurt his reputation.

Gottlieb is likewise a very uneven artist, but a much more solid and accomplished one than is generally supposed. He seems to me to be capable of a greater range of controlled effects than any other abstract expressionist, and it is only owing to some lack of nerve or necessary presumptuousness that he has not made this clearer to the public, which accuses him of staying too close to the grid plans of Klee or Torrès-Garcia, the Uruguayan painter. Over the years Gottlieb has, in his sober, pedestrian way, become one of the surest craftsmen in contemporary painting, one who can place a flat, jagged silhouette, that most difficult of all things to adjust to the rectangle, with a rightness beyond the capacity of ostensibly stronger painters. Some of his best work, like the "landscapes" and "seascapes" he showed in 1953, tends to be too difficult for eyes trained on late Cubism. On the other hand, his 1954 pictures, the first in which he let himself be tempted to a display of virtuosity and which stayed within late Cubism, were liked better by the public than anything he had shown before. The zigzags of Gottlieb's course in recent years, which saw him become a colorist and a painterly painter (if anything, too much of one) between his departures from and returns to Cubism, have made his development a very interesting one to watch. Right now he seems one of the least tired of all the abstract expressionists.

Jackson Pollock was at first almost as much a late Cubist and a hard and fast easel-painter as any of the abstract expressionists I have mentioned. He compounded hints from Picasso's calligraphy in the early '30s with suggestions from Hofmann, Masson, and Mexican painting, especially Siqueiros, and began with a kind of picture in murky, sulphurous colors that startled people less by the novelty of its means than by force and originality of the feel-

ing behind it. Within a notion of shallow space generalized from
the practice of Miró and Masson as well as Picasso, and with some
guidance from the early Kandinsky, he devised a language of
baroque shapes and calligraphy that twisted this space to its own
measure and vehemence. Pollock remained close to Cubism until
at least 1946, and the early greatness of his art can be taken as a
fulfilment of things that Picasso had not brought beyond a state
of promise in his 1932-1940 period. Though he cannot build with
color, Pollock has an instinct for bold oppositions of dark and
light, and a signal capacity to assert the shape of the rectangle as
a single and whole image concentrating into one the several images
distributed over it. Going further in this direction, he went far
beyond late Cubism.

   Mark Tobey is credited, especially in Paris, with being the
first painter to arrive at "all-over" design, covering the picture
surface with an even, largely undifferentiated system of uniform
motifs that cause the result to look as though it could be continued
indefinitely beyond the frame like a wallpaper pattern. Tobey
had shown the first examples of his "white writing" in New York
in 1944, but Pollock had not seen any of these, even in reproduction, when in the summer of 1946 he did a series of "all-over"
paintings executed with dabs of buttery paint. Several of these
were masterpieces of clarity. A short while later he began working
with skeins of enamel paint and blotches that he opened up and
laced, interlaced, and unlaced with a breadth and power remote
from anything suggested by Tobey's rather limited cabinet art.
One of the unconscious motives for Pollock's "all-over" departure was the desire to achieve a more immediate, denser, and more
decorative impact than his late Cubist manner had permitted.
At the same time, however, he wanted to control the oscillation
between an emphatic physical surface and the suggestion of depth
beneath it as lucidly and tensely and evenly as Picasso and Braque
had controlled a somewhat similar movement with the open facets
and pointillist flecks of color of their 1909-1913 Cubist pictures.
("Analytical" Cubism is always somewhere in the back of Pollock's mind.) Having achieved this kind of control, he found
himself straddled between the easel picture and something else

hard to define, and in the last two or three years he has pulled back.

Tobey's "all-over" pictures never aroused the protest that Pollock's did. Along with Barnett Newman's paintings, they are still considered the *reductio ad absurdum* of abstract expressionism and modern art in general. Though Pollock is a famous name now, his art has not been fundamentally accepted where one would expect it to be. Few of his fellow artists can yet tell the difference between his good and his bad work—or at least not in New York. His most recent show, in 1954, was the first to contain pictures that were forced, pumped, dressed up, but it got more acceptance than any of his previous exhibitions had—for one thing, because it made clear what an accomplished craftsman he had become, and how pleasingly he could use color now that he was not sure of what he wanted to say with it. (Even so, there were still two or three remarkable paintings present.) His 1951 exhibition, on the other hand, which included four or five huge canvases of monumental perfection and remains the peak of his achievement so far, was the one received most coldly of all.

Many of the abstract expressionists have at times drained the color from their pictures and worked in black, white, and gray alone. Gorky was the first of them to do so, in paintings like "The Diary of a Seducer" of 1945—which happens to be, in my opinion, his masterpiece. But it was left to Franz Kline, whose first show was in 1951, to work with black and white exclusively in a succession of canvases with blank white grounds bearing a single large calligraphic image in black. That these pictures were big was no cause for surprise: the abstract expressionists were being compelled to do huge canvases by the fact that they had increasingly renounced an illusion of depth within which they could develop pictorial incident without crowding; the flattening surfaces of their canvases compelled them to move along the picture plane laterally and seek in its sheer physical size the space necessary for the telling of their kind of pictorial story.

However, Kline's unmistakable allusions to Chinese and Japanese calligraphy encouraged the cant, already started by Tobey's example, about a general Oriental influence on American abstract painting. It is as though this country's possession of a Pacific coast offered a handy received idea with which to account for the otherwise inexplicable fact that it is now producing a body of art that some people regard as original. Yet none of the leading abstract expressionists except Kline has shown more than a cursory interest in Oriental art, and it is easy to demonstrate that the roots of their art lie almost entirely within Western tradition. Tobey himself owes far more to Klee than to the Orient. The fact that Far Eastern calligraphy is stripped and abstract—because it involves writing—does not suffice to make the resemblances to it in abstract expressionism more than a case of convergence.

The abstract-expressionist emphasis on black and white has to do in any event with something more crucial to Western than Oriental pictorial art. It represents one of those exaggerations or apotheoses which betray a fear for their objects. Value contrast, the opposition and modulation of dark and light, has been the basis of Western pictorial art, its chief means, much more important than perspective, to a convincing illusion of depth and volume; and it has also been its chief agent of structure and unity. This is why the old masters almost always laid in their darks and lights—their shading—first. The eye automatically orients itself by the value contrasts in dealing with an object that is presented to it as a picture, and in the absence of such contrasts it tends to feel almost, if not quite as much, at loss as in the absence of a recognizable image. Impressionism's muffling of dark and light contrasts in response to the effect of the glare of the sky caused it to be criticized for that lack of "form" and "structure" which Cézanne tried to supply with his substitute contrasts of warm and cool color (these remained nonetheless contrasts of dark and light, as we can see from monochrome photographs of his paintings). Black and white is the extreme statement of value contrast, and to harp on it as many of the abstract expressionists do—and not only abstract expressionists—seems to me to be an attempt to preserve by extreme measures a technical resource whose capacity to yield convincing form and unity is felt to be nearing exhaustion.

The American abstract expressionists have been given good

cause for this feeling by a development in their own midst. It is, I think, the most radical of all tendencies in the painting of the last two decades, and has no counterpart in Paris (unless in Fautrier and the late work of Masson and Tal Coat), as so many other things in American abstract expressionism have had since 1944. This development involves a more consistent and radical suppression of value contrasts than seen so far in abstract art. We can realize now, from this point of view, how conservative Cubism was in its resumption of Cézanne's effort to save the convention of dark and light. By their parody of the way the old masters shaded, the Cubists may have discredited value contrast as a means to an illusion of depth and volume, but they rescued it from the Impressionists, Gauguin, Van Gogh, and the Fauves as a means to structure and form. Mondrian, a Cubist at heart, remained as dependent on contrasts of dark and light as any academic painter until his very last paintings, "Broadway Boogie" and "Victory Boogie"—which happen to be failures. Until quite recently the convention was taken for granted in even the most doctrinaire abstract art, and the later Kandinsky, though he helped ruin his pictures by his insensitivity to the effects of value contrast, never questioned it in principle. Malevich's prophetic venture in "white on white" was looked on as an experimental quirk (it was very much an *experiment* and, like almost all experiments in art, it failed aesthetically). The late Monet, whose suppression of values had been the most consistently radical to be seen in painting until a short while ago was pointed to as a warning, and the *fin-de-siècle* muffling of contrasts in much of Bonnard's and Vuillard's art caused it to be deprecated by the avant-garde for many years. The same factor even had a part in the under-rating of Pissarro.

Recently, however, some of the late Monets began to assume a unity and power they had never had before. This expansion of sensibility has coincided with the emergence of Clyfford Still as one of the most important and original painters of our time—perhaps the most original of all painters under fifty-five, if not the best. As the Cubists resumed Cézanne, Still has resumed Monet. His paintings were the first abstract pictures I ever saw that contained almost no allusion to Cubism. (Kandinsky's relations with it from first to last became very apparent by contrast). Still's first show, at Peggy Guggenheim's in 1944, was made up predominantly of pictures in the vein of an abstract symbolism with certain "primitive" and Surrealist overtones that were in the air at that time, and of which Gottlieb's "pictographs" represented one version. I was put off by slack, willful silhouettes that seemed to disregard every consideration of plane or frame. Still's second show, in 1948, was in a different manner, that of his maturity, but I was still put off, and even outraged, by what I took to be a profound lack of sensitivity and discipline. The few large vertically divided areas that made up his typical picture seemed arbitrary in shape and edge, and the color too hot and dry, stifled by the lack of value contrasts. It was only two years ago, when I first saw a 1948 painting of Still's in isolation, that I got a first intimation of pleasure from his art; subsequently, as I was able to see still others in isolation, that intimation grew more definite. (Until one became familiar with them his pictures fought each other when side by side.) I was impressed as never before by how estranging and upsetting genuine originality in art can be, and how the greater its pressure on taste, the more stubbornly taste will resist adjusting to it.

Turner was actually the first painter to break with the European tradition of value painting. In the atmospheric pictures of his last phase he bunched value intervals together at the lighter end of the color scale for effects more picturesque than anything else. For the sake of these, the public soon forgave him his dissolution of form—besides, clouds and steam, mist, water, and light were not expected to have definite shape or form as long as they retained depth, which they did in Turner's pictures; what we today take for a daring abstractness on Turner's part was accepted then as another feat of naturalism. That Monet's close-valued painting won a similar acceptance strikes me as not being accidental. Of course, iridescent colors appeal to popular taste, which is often willing to take them in exchange for verisimilitude, but those of Monet's pictures in which he muddied—and flattened—form with dark color, as in some of his "Lily Pads," were almost as popular. Can it be suggested that the public's appetite for close-valued painting as manifested in both Turner's and Monet's cases, and in that of late Impressionism in general, meant the emergence of a new kind of taste which, running counter to the high traditions of our art and possessed by people with little grasp of these, expressed a genuine underground change in European sensibility? If so, it would clear up the paradox that lies in the fact that an art like the late Monet's, which in its time pleased banal taste and still makes most of the avant-garde shudder, should suddenly stand forth as more advanced in some respects than Cubism.

I don't know how much conscious attention Still has paid to Monet or Impressionism, but his independent and uncompromising art likewise has an affiliation with popular taste, though not by any means enough to make it acceptable to it. Still's is the first really Whitmanesque kind of painting we have had, not only because it makes large, loose gestures, or because it breaks the hold of value contrast as Whitman's verse line broke the equally traditional hold of meter; but just as much because, as Whitman's poetry assimilated, with varying success, large quantities of stale journalistic and oratorical prose, so Still's painting is infused with that stale, prosaic kind of painting to which Barnett Newman has given the name of "buckeye." Though little attention has been paid to it in print, "buckeye" is probably the most widely practiced and homogeneous kind of painting seen in the Western world today. I seem to detect its beginnings in Old Crome's oils, the Barbizon School, and even in Boecklin, but it has spread only since the popularization of Impressionism. "Buckeye" painting is not "primitive," nor is it the same thing as "Sunday painting." Its practitioners can draw with a certain amount of academic correctness, but their command of shading, and of dark and light values in general, is not sufficient to control their color—either because they are simply inept in this department, or because they are naively intent on a more vivid naturalism of color than the studio-born principles of value contrast will allow. "Buckeye" painters, as far as I am aware, do landscapes exclusively and work more or less directly from nature (though I suspect that many of them paint from colored photographs). By piling dry paint—but not exactly in impasto—they try to capture the brilliance of daylight, and the process of painting becomes a race between hot shadows and hot lights whose invariable outcome is a livid, dry, sour picture with a warm, brittle surface that intensifies the acid

fire of the generally predominating reds, browns, greens, and
yellows. "Buckeye" landscapes can be seen in Greenwich Village
restaurants (Eddie's Aurora on West Fourth Street used to col-
lect them), Sixth Avenue picture stores (there is one near Eighth
Street) and in the Washington Square outdoor shows. I understand that they are produced abundantly in Europe too. Though
I can see why it is easy to stumble into "buckeye" effects, I cannot understand fully why they should be so universal and so uniform, or the kind of painting culture behind them.

Still, at any rate, is the first to have put "buckeye" effects into
serious art. These are visible in the frayed dead-leaf edges that
wander down the margins or across the middle of so many of his
canvases, in the uniformly dark heat of his color, and in a dry,
crusty paint surface (like any "buckeye" painter, Still seems to have
no faith in diluted or thin pigments). Such things can spoil his
pictures, or make them weird in an unrefreshing way, but when
he is able to succeed with, or in spite of them, it represents the
conquest by high art of one more area of experience, and its liberation from *Kitsch*.

Still's art has a special importance at this time because it
shows abstract painting a way out of its own academicism. An
indirect sign of this importance is the fact that he is almost the
only abstract expressionist to "make" a school; by this I mean
that a few of the many artists he has stimulated or influenced have
not been condemned by that to imitate him, but have been able
to establish strong and independent styles of their own.

Barnett Newman, who is one of these artists, has replaced
Pollock as the *enfant terrible* of abstract expressionism. He rules
vertical bands of dimly contrasting color or value on warm flat
backgrounds—and that's all. But he is not in the least related to
Mondrian or anyone else in the geometrical abstract school.
Though Still led the way in opening the picture down the middle
and in bringing large, uninterrupted areas of uniform color into
subtle and yet spectacular opposition, Newman studied late Impressionism for himself, and has drawn its consequences more
radically. The powers of color he employs to make a picture are
conceived with an ultimate strictness: color is to function as hue

and nothing else, and contrasts are to be sought with the least possible help of differences in value, saturation, or warmth.

The easel picture will hardly survive such an approach, and Newman's huge, calmly and evenly burning canvases amount to the most direct attack upon it so far. And it is all the more effective an attack because the art behind it is deep and honest, and carries a feeling for color without its like in recent painting. Mark Rothko's art is a little less aggressive in this respect. He was likewise stimulated by Still's example. The three or four massive, horizontal strata of flat color that compose his typical picture allow the spectator to think of landscape—which may be why his decorative simplicity seems to meet less resistance. Within a range predominantly warm like Newman's and Still's, he too is a brilliant, original colorist; like Newman, he soaks his pigment into the canvas, getting a dyer's effect, and does not apply it as a discrete covering layer in Still's manner. Of the three painters—all of whom started, incidentally, as "symbolists"—Rothko is the only one who seems to relate to any part of French art since Impressionism, and his ability to insinuate contrasts of value and warmth into oppositions of pure color makes me think of Matisse, who held on to value contrasts in something of the same way. This, too, may account for the public's readier acceptance of his art, but takes nothing away from it. Rothko's big vertical pictures, with their incandescent color and their bold and simple sensuousness— or rather their *firm* sensuousness—are among the largest gems of abstract expressionism.

A concomitant of the fact that Still, Newman, and Rothko suppress value contrasts and favor warm hues is the more emphatic flatness of their paintings. Because it is not broken by sharp differences of value or by more than a few incidents of drawing or design, color breathes from the canvas with an enveloping effect, intensified by the largeness itself of the picture. The spectator tends to react to this more in terms of décor or environment than in those usually associated with a picture hung upon a wall. The crucial issue raised by the work of these three artists is where the pictorial stops and decoration begins. In effect, their art asserts decorative elements and ideas in a pictorial context. (Whether this has anything to do with the artiness that afflicts all three of them at times, I don't know. But artiness is the great liability of the Still school.)

Rothko and especially Newman are more exposed than Still to the charge of being decorators by their preference for rectilinear drawing. This sets them apart from Still in another way, too. By liberating abstract painting from value contrasts, Still also liberated it, as Pollock had not, from the quasi-geometrical, faired drawing which Cubism had found to be the surest way to prevent the edges of forms from breaking through a picture surface that had been tautened, and therefore made exceedingly sensitive, by the shrinking of the illusion of depth underneath it. As Cézanne was the first to discover, the safest way to proceed in the face of this liability was to echo the rectangular shape of the surface itself with vertical and horizontal lines and with curves whose chords were definitely vertical or horizontal. After the Cubists, and Klee, Mondrian, and Miró, and others had exploited this insight it became a cliché, however, and led to the kind of late Cubist academicism that used to fill the exhibitions of the American Abstract Artists group, and which can still be seen in much of recent French abstract painting. Still's service was to show us how the contours of a shape could be made less conspicuous, and therefore less dangerous to the "integrity" of the flat surface, by narrowing the value contrast its color made with that of the shapes or areas adjacent to it. Not only does this keep colors from "jumping," as the old masters well knew, but it gives the artist greater liberty in drawing—liberty almost to the point of insensitivity, as in Still's own case. The early Kandinsky was the one abstract painter before Still to have some glimpse of this, but it was only a glimpse. Pollock has had more of a glimpse, independently of Still or Kandinsky, but has not set his course by it. In some of the huge "sprinkled" pictures he did in 1950 and showed in 1951, value contrasts are pulverized as it were, spread over the canvas like dusty vapor (the result was two of the best pictures he ever painted); but the next year, as if in violent repentance, he did a set of paintings in black line alone on unprimed canvas.

It is such insights that help explain why a relatively unpopular painter like Still has so many followers today, both in New York and California (where he has taught); and why William Scott, the English painter, could say that Still's was the only completely and originally American art he had yet seen. This was not necessarily a compliment—Pollock, who may be less "American," and Hofmann, who is German-born, both have a wider range of power than Still—but Scott meant it as one.

The abstract expressionists started out in the '40s with a diffidence they could not help feeling as American artists. They were very much aware of the provincial fate around them. This country had good painters in the past, but none with enough sustained originality or power to enter the mainstream of Western art. The aims of the abstract expressionists were diverse within a certain range, and they did not feel, and still do not feel, that they constitute a school or movement with enough unity to be covered by a single term—like "abstract expressionist," for instance. But aside from their culture as painters and the fact that their art was all more or less abstract, what they had in common from the first was an ambition—or rather the will to it—to break out of provinciality. I think most of them have done so by now, whether in success or failure. If they should all miss—which I do not think at all likely, since some of them have already conclusively arrived!—it will be at least with more resonance than that with which such eminent predecessors of theirs as Marin, Maurer, Hartley, Dove, and Demuth did not miss. And by comparison with such of their present competitors for the attention of the American art public as Shahn, Graves, Bloom, Stuart Davis (a good painter), Levine, Wyeth, etc., etc., their success as well as their resonance and "centrality" is assured.

If I say that such a galaxy of powerfully talented and original painters as the abstract expressionists form has not been seen since the days of Cubism, I shall be accused of chauvinist exaggeration, not to mention a lack of a sense of proportion. But can I suggest it? I do not make allowances for American art that I do not make for any other kind. At the Biennale in Venice this year, I saw how de Kooning's exhibition put to shame, not only that of his neighbor in the American pavilion, Ben Shahn, but that of every other painter present in his generation or under. The general impression still is that an art of high distinction has as much chance of coming out of America as a great wine. Literature—yes: we now know that we have produced some great writing because the English and French have told us so. They have even exaggerated, at least about Whitman and Poe. What I hope for is a just appreciation abroad, not an exaggeration, of the merits of "American-type" painting. Only then, I suspect, will American collectors begin to take it seriously. In the meantime they will go on buying the French equivalent of it they find in the art of Riopelle, De Stael, Soulages, and their like. The imported article is handsomer, no doubt, but the handsomeness is too obvious to have staying power. . . .

"Advanced" art—which is the same thing as ambitious art today—persists insofar as it tests society's capacity for high art. This it does by exploring the limits of the inherited forms and genres, and of the medium itself, and it is what the Impressionists, the post-Impressionists, the Fauves, the Cubists, and Mondrian did in their time. If the testing seems more radical in the case of the new American abstract painting, it is because it comes at a later stage. The limits of the easel picture are in greater danger of being destroyed because several generations of great artists have already worked to expand them. But if they are destroyed this will not necessarily mean the extinction of pictorial art as such. Painting may be on its way toward a new kind of genre, but perhaps not an unprecedented one—since we are now able to look at, and enjoy, Persian carpets as pictures—and what we now consider to be merely decorative may become capable of holding our eyes and moving us much as the easel picture does.

Meanwhile there is no such thing as an aberration in art: there is just the good and the bad, the realized and the unrealized. Often there is but a hair's breadth between the two—at first glance. And sometimes there seems—at first glance—to be no more distance than that between a great work of art and one which is not art at all. This is one of the points made by modern art.

New Innocents Abroad

by William Barrett

THE American's inevitable fate abroad, from Henry James to Henry Miller, seems to be chiefly to bear witness to his own countrymen. In the summer of 1949, the greatest tourist season Europe had yet known, even the American most determined to forget his own baffling nationality could hardly have escaped this fate. For his countrymen were everywhere: the casual acquaintances of shipboard would turn up in remote villages on the Continent, on the road in the same railway compartment or bus, at the returning boat or plane, so that you always seemed to be running into the same people, as if all were traveling together in one great family from which you couldn't have escaped even if you tried. The War had closed the door on Europe, after which in the first uncertain years of the peace the misery of the Black Market and living conditions on the Continent had discouraged travel; but by '49 the Marshall Plan had at last restored a tiny economic stability, the rates of exchange were practicable to travelers of modest means, and the war scare had subsided. So the restraining dykes were unlocked, and the pent-up flood burst forth over the Continent that has known so many migrations and invasions. "The American invasion of colonial Europe," the Communist press sneered, ". . . you are lucky if you can hear French spoken in the streets of Paris." The jibe had its small grain of truth, for the flood of tourists at times seemed to push the natives into the background.

All roads still lead to Paris, at least for the tourist, since there the holiday atmosphere he carries with him can become explosive. Its reputation as a city of sin still provides Paris with one of its minor industries. This aspect of the city was discovered for Americans by their troops after the first World War in the era of *hinky-dinky parly-voo, Lulu,* and *M'mselle Fifi,* and its glorified image lingered through all the high literate days of the twenties. In the mind of the average tourist Paris is still mainly a montage of the

cancan, naked breasts at the *Folies*, filthy postcards sold on the
streets, the whores plying their brisk trade near the Madeleine and
Opéra, and formerly the tour through the brothels that was as
much a tourist's "must" as a visit to Notre Dame. Though the
brothels have been publicly closed, Paris is still an immense shop-
window displaying all the wares of sensuality. One could see the
release going on all around one. There were the college boys
whispering with the pimps of Pigalle to arrange an "exhibition";
there was the blonde post-deb from Philadelphia who used to
play the hard-boiled teaser late into the night at the cafés, but
who this time had overstepped herself, and suddenly broke down,
cowering in a corner, as the two whores undressed in the bath-
room before coming out to go through their postures; and, in a
quieter vein, there were the two middle-aged business men fum-
bling with guilty glee under the counter at Brentano's for the
forbidden copies of Henry Miller, furtive and giggling, more like
boys out of school than grown men. All around one, the Americans on their sexual vacation abroad seemed to be marked by
just this quality of a pawing, gawkish, excitable adolescence.

Under the influence of this atmosphere I decided to look into
Henry Miller again. Re-read in an attic on the Left Bank, the
Tropic of Cancer rang bells. I realized I had considerably under-
estimated Miller: the book had still all the faults that had palled
in previous reading, but I felt in it now the rude vitality that makes
it monumental, and, as I could see from the Americans erupting
around me, a document in the history of the American's attempt
at self-liberation. You couldn't, of course, take Miller at his own
estimate of himself: he is really a prime example of the American
adolescent raucously erupting into sex, trying violently to release
himself into some kind of mature freedom. But this may be part
of his value for us, establishing him as the archetype of the American adolescent struggling against the national heritage of Puritanism. And Miller has the energy typical of his race: he goes at sex
with the cool fury with which Americans turn their bulldozers
loose on a problem of engineering.

But times have changed, and it did not take long to see that
the young men on the Left Bank were seeking in this city something else beside the seamy image of the twenties. After all, this

was Europe, Paris, the roof was off, and they need not worry about
that oppressive contempt which America, in fear of its own shadow
side, turns on the homosexual. Their explosiveness had got to the
point where it was scandalizing the French. The French may make
a minor religion of love and sex, or at least of the talk of sex and
love, but they insist that these things be pursued with the usual
French sense of discretion, *mesure* or proportion, which is at bottom merely the terrifying habit of calculation that haunts the
Frenchman in everything he does. Now, the youthful and innocent violence of the Americans was upsetting the French when
it was happening in their own home—like a host alarmed when
the guest whom he has invited to be completely at home takes
him at his word and begins smashing the furniture. The French
reacted as if they had not meant quite what they had said, as if all
their talk about love had only been talk after all. The police
staged a series of raids on the homosexual joints where the young
Americans hung out, carting the boys away in paddy wagons to
the Préfecture, where they drew up dossiers for them, asking
whether or not the young men were inverts and duly recording the
answer. That was all; since homosexuality is no crime under
French law, the police could go no further; they only wanted to
give the boys a scare, and so perhaps break up the gangs, or at
least keep them from carrying on so brazenly in public. Perhaps
no public disturbance was being created, but the effect was not
always pleasant: in one of the raided cafés, from the sidewalk
you could see the boys standing around the bar and pawing each
other, and some people formed the habit of a detour to avoid
the place. Rumors of the American antics were being fed to the
general public, which in this moment of French history seems to
want reasons for its resentments toward wealthy America: nearly
every issue of *Samedi Soir*, the lurid weekly of Paris, carried some
report on "the wave of immorality from the new world," the reporter ridiculously leering over the more salubrious items. "The
Scandal of the Latin Quarter" would be a title that usually announced some new American exploit. This general uneasiness
among the French finally reached André Gide himself, perhaps
the remote choregos of it all: when one of the young American
literati made his pilgrimage to the Master, the old Protestant

presented him with a copy of *Corydon* (which promulgates another and much more Spartan kind of homosexuality), and waved a solemn admonitory finger in the young man's face: *"Je ne suis pas tapette, Monsieur, je suis pédéraste."*

By an entirely consistent stroke of luck I had descended upon a small hotel on the Left Bank where I was surrounded by the gay boys. My room was just under the roof, where far into the night their whispers drifted up to me from below. I never heard a girl's voice at night all the time I was in that hotel. In daylight, mostly in the afternoon, I used to run into them as they came gowned from the bath, trailing a thick cloud of perfume behind them all the length of the hallway, pausing to rake me with the classic stare of the tailor threading the eye of his needle. It wasn't all fun for them, though: a few months before, one of them, the vein in his wrist cut, had been fished out of the bathtub by the *patron* and sent off to an asylum outside Paris; he had been released after a month or so and was now back at the hotel; the *patron* did not mind, for the young man had paid his rent regularly, and the attempted suicide had made no *scandale*—there had only been the trouble of washing the bathtub. The incident gave the hotel something of a macabre legend for me as I lay awake at night listening to the whispers. I was uneasy enough anyway: it seemed to me I had strayed into the wrong place, a close-knit family in which I was bound to feel myself a stranger, and inevitably with the stranger's uneasy feeling that there is something wrong with him when he does not fit in.

The great advantage of travel is that it scrambles everything. In the compartments of trains, busses, the smoking-rooms of ships, you rub elbows with all the inconceivable types that you normally do not meet back home. New York is a megalopolis divided and subdivided again into thousands of isolated communities among which the homosexual has established his own city of night. You catch enough glimpses of it, but you are never living *in* it, because your own groove holds you so snugly that you forget the enormously different human worlds that surround you. But travel scrambles everything, and here, three thousand miles from home, I was immersed in their city of night through all the accidents of voyage that make the traveler unable to select the precise orbit of his wandering.

Though this city of night was very much of a daylight affair in Paris, in the general confusion you could not always be sure of the person you were talking to. Some future edition of Baedeker, I imagine, will have to deal with this new problem of travel conversation: What kind of conversation is appropriate among homosexuals, heterosexuals, or among mixed company, while *en voyage*? When do you transgress the bounds of propriety by a remark that presupposes your own sex or the sex of your interlocutor? I saw one boy wince at a casual reference to a woman, and by now many travelers must know the embarrassment of the isolated heterosexual in the midst of homosexual chatter. Such confusions of identity, of course, are all part of the familiar and traditional game of recognition that the invert is compelled to play out of self-defense. But travel provides an opportunity for a still richer confusion of roles, varieties, and nuances, in the course of which the traveler may even permit himself to be pleasantly confused about his own identity. Two of these varieties that flourish in remarkable forms abroad are the homosexual mother and the homosexual virgin.

In her most noticeable social version, the homosexual mother is the girl who plays the reigning queen for a whole circle of the boys. She helps supply the feminine atmosphere that they desire, and in return she may preen her ego as the center of attention. Usually she gets out of this an excessive but bogus femininity, a certain glittering ability for chatter, wisecracks, flash; but the ambiguity of her position is also more than likely to make her go bitchy, hard, and brittle because, though her reason for being in the group is that she is a woman, she is not in the end treated as such by any of the men. Wherever a colony forms abroad, some such mother is bound to appear. But the traveler no longer leaves this merely to chance, he makes his mother part of his travel preparations. Walking one day along the Rue Rivoli, opposite the Tuileries, I was hailed by a former friend, Louis X—whom I had not seen in ten years. (This kind of chance encounter was typical of a summer in which everyone was on the move, so that you were as likely as not to run into anybody anywhere.) Louis had grown a bit bald and had filled out, but looked just as I should have expected: a bright and aggressive young businessman in his early thirties, who had been so successful in establishing a firm of his own that he was now able to take several months off for the grand tour of Europe. Being in a hurry to an appointment, he asked me to come along for a drink and to meet his "traveling companion," who turned out, to my astonishment, to be a woman almost twice his age. Frances, twice married and twice divorced, had preserved at sixty all her chic, elegance, and tremendous appetite for men. The arrangement they had worked out suited them perfectly: she always had an escort for the low dive where Louis could pick up his sailor and she hers. As mother and infant son, they insisted on sharing a double room in their travels, charming each other by the rustle and perfume of a male-female atmosphere, which never descended however to the raw contact with the heterosexual flesh that he could not abide, for they drew a line at the double bed. In all this Louis was not in the least a bohemian type, simply a young businessman making the grand tour in his own grand manner. Later in the summer I heard about their stopping at a small town in Italy, where they found that the only room available in the hotel contained a double bed: for an hour Louis argued with the proprietor until the latter finally dug up a cot from somewhere and put it in the room. Since then I have lost track of them; for all I know they may still be on their travels together, and perhaps they have now overcome even this last barrier, and at this moment may be sharing blissfully, but chastely, a double bed somewhere on the Continent.

On the swank Avenue Bosquet, not far from the Eiffel Tower, Dick and Arthur shared a very luxurious but strangely virginal apartment. Dick was a middle-aged lawyer, a beaten-down but very kindly little man, who had established an office in Paris because he preferred to be away from America. Arthur, his guest for the summer, was a graduate student in French literature at one of our big universities, a young bookish monster from whom I came away feeling that I had not encountered a human being but a kind of animated edition of a literary review given over entirely to the new criticism. Arthur had fluffy tow-colored hair (that always looked freshly washed), a perpetual gesture of two fingers smoothing a curl at his forehead, and a skin that naturally looked as if it wore powder; moreover, he talked incessantly and with a rich lisp. Nevertheless he still had doubts about his own sex. He used to discuss the problem with the others in the circle as elaborately and dispassionately as if he were making an *explication de texte* in his university seminar back home. "Arthur doesn't know yet whether he's straight or not," one of the circle reported to me. "He's still a virgin, you see. So how can he know? He won't know, he says, until he has lost his virginity." My informant was grinning from ear to ear. Nobody in the circle had any doubts which side of the fence Arthur was on, but they were all immensely amused to watch the debate go on until the fine day when Arthur woke up and found out. But it was something of a torture for Dick. He had known the family since Arthur was a boy, and Arthur's mother (the father was long since dead) had written that she felt safe about her boy's being in Europe so long as he was with Dick, who was practically an uncle to him. Back in Chicago she could never imagine those weird nights that passed in the apartment where Arthur debated platonically the question of his sex and Dick, self-effacing in his gentleness, hovered over the youth, waiting. I thought of two chaste Victorian souls sleeping with a sword between them, devouring each other in the spiritual purity of their union.

By this time I had strayed so far into the jungle of confused identities that I began to have the nightmarish feeling that I was really living *inside* Proust's novel—especially toward the end of it where anything might happen and any character discover a secret and unexpected sex. The last time I had read him, it had seemed to me that Proust's human obsessions had violated the artist in him so that he had loaded his dice too heavily, constructing a world too distorted to be credible. Now, however, I was not so sure. It looked rather as if Proust had really got hold of an essential theme in modern experience. The invert had been his *means* of portraying the death at the heart of the modern world. In a world where the primitive simplicities of life have been lost the search for love must take the twisted and condemned shapes

of the Proustian grotesques. At any rate, this seemed to be Proust's
world, the one in which I was actually existing: a sexually un-
stable universe where anything might happen. But had I myself
perhaps constructed a distorted picture out of a few accumulated
accidents of experience? I decided, out of caution, that I had
better check these impressions with a few friends.

When I begin to ask Kaplan about these things, he nods
assent but immediately launches into a general lament on the
neighborhood of St. Germain des Près and its degradation since
Life magazine wrote an article that brought the flood of American tourists there. Kaplan says "mon Paris" like an old Parisian
speaking of the avenues and costumes of the 1890's. *His* Paris is
the Paris of the Liberation in 1945, when, to be sure, the American army was there, but no tourists, and the French were ready to
receive certain intelligent young Americans with curiosity and joy.
There are almost tears in Kaplan's eyes as he speaks of those by-
gone days and quiet quarters. Nor can I get very much out of
Abel these days, for he seems to be obsessed lately with only one
theme, that Being and Nothing are the same in Heidegger, and
that this is Heidegger's real secret, and he repeats this so often
that I can no longer believe I have heard incorrectly.

Tonight, more than ever, it is difficult to ask the questions I
want to, for I arrive at the restaurant a little late and the two of
them are already plunged into their own conversation, and when
these two get into a conversation, it is not easy to interrupt them.
I listen, thinking that one of these conversations ought to be
staged in an auditorium before a large crowd, for here surely are
two of the most remarkable performers of our time. They bring
out each other because they are so different. Abel, the charming
old-world bohemian from Eighth Street, and Kaplan, flamboyantly
dressed, looking like an impresario of the arts or a young diplomat
in a relaxed moment. Looking at Kaplan, I think of the world of
high diplomacy and—Hollywood. With his green tweed jacket and
yellow silk shirt open at the neck, he looks vaguely like one of film-
dom's more brilliant young directors; and for a moment I have the
fantasy that if there were a megaphone on that empty chair beside him, we and this conversation would be immediately trans-
ported to Hollywood. Tonight Kaplan has elected to step im-

mediately into Abel's world, and such is his mastery of any area of existence that he moves here too completely at home.

They are at it hammer and tongs, talking about Michel Leiris' *L'Age d'homme,* which I haven't read, so that I am automatically excluded from the conversation. This book is an autobiography in which Leiris has chosen to break with the usual rules of literature and tell everything. Naturally, therefore, it is something of an unpleasant book, with Leiris telling all kinds of disquieting things about himself, including the disappointing size of his penis. While Abel dislikes the book, Kaplan defends it. "You mustn't look at Leiris' book as a piece of 'literature,' in the old sense," he says. "This is a new conception of literature altogether—one on which, if I may say so, I've been working myself for some time: Literature as a Scandal." The theme is launched, and in a moment both of them are carrying literary criticism into the stratosphere of abstraction. This is Abel's usual atmosphere, where he draws his life's breath, but tonight Kaplan goes soaring with him into the blue, out of that grave suave courtesy of his, and a little too with that same *disponibilité* with which he goes slumming in the Arab hashish joints in Paris.

The word "scandal" sticks unaccountably in my mind, as, shut out from the conversation, I let my eyes wander around the restaurant and catch a glimpse of two American youths across the room, one of whom had been pointed out to me a few days earlier as the original love-object and hero of a lush novel that created a mild stir in America a year or so ago. The couple are "married," the degree of their domestic intimacy is a standing joke among some people on the Left Bank, and now the two of them, sitting side by side against the wall, have the demure and courting air of a man with his date. The word "scandal" suddenly comes to life, and I snap my ear back on the conversation at our table.

Kaplan and Abel are higher up in the stratosphere than ever, talking about the problem of communication and silence, authenticity and banality. "All of modern art," Kaplan says, "is an immense effort to escape from the museum—if you wish, even to destroy the museum. Literature offers us something comparable in the idea of the scandal—a destruction of literature in the usual belletristic sense. For Leiris, literature is like a bullfight, in which the writer risks himself in the arena before the eyes of the crowd. He chooses to tell things that used to be passed over in silence. He may even incriminate himself."

Suddenly I realize that here, precisely in Leiris' sense, there is a scandal across the room, though Kaplan does not see it, the same scandal that has been all around me since I arrived, and that perhaps I ought to put pen to paper, against my own wishes, to deal with it, incriminating myself if necessary. The idea is as yet only dimly present, but it stirs already a faint anxiety, for I am aware I know very little about the subject. Nevertheless it is something to have an idea, any idea, working in one, so that now I return cheerfully to this conversation in which I have already given up any hope of being able to raise my questions.

But with Bellow I am able to raise these questions about the "scandal," which now in our conversation acquires for me a sharp and sudden focus. Having already been in Europe for more than a year, and having seen many more Americans than I, Bellow is still disquieted by the same observations: "That was the way I had begun to feel too," he says to my opening question, "that America's chief export to Europe had become its homosexuals." Suddenly I am at home in this conversation in a way I have not been since I left America, for all the time that Bellow is tenaciously sifting the European experience he still seems to have his feet firmly planted back in Chicago. With his big sensitive eyes he strikes me as half Hebrew dreamer, the other half being a solid Jewish business man, and yet the whole person is also the midwestern American who tells me that every moment more he exists in Europe the more American he feels. When he opines that "the American writer's great opportunity may be just to escape from culture," I am delighted, for he has formulated for me something that had been floating around in my own mind since I have been in this French atmosphere heavy with its closed tradition, where I've even come to understand the attraction for the French of certain kinds of American fiction that I had too easily despised back home. Now Bellow confirms me also in the uneasy feeling of being an alien among the American inverts abroad. A deeper uneasiness comes to the surface as our talk brings up an instinctive prejudice that we cannot disguise. Our language has already acquired a certain edge of hostility, certain derisive and even vulgar words have appeared; and now we are a little ashamed and depressed for we have almost forgotten the barbarism with which the third sex is still pursued in America. We are in the embarrassing conflict of a man who discovers in himself a prejudice that publicly he must denounce. In the relation with certain friends this aversion does not appear, but now it cannot be repressed when we confront the fact *en masse*, and so we are guilty about something it would be unnatural not to feel. Woe unto him from whom the scandal cometh! But in this case who really brings, and who really suffers, the scandal? I leave Bellow with the very sombre feeling that this is a real *scandal* into which I have wandered, not as a mere journalistic sensation, but in the universal human sense that it implicates all alike in a single guilt.

II

In Italy everything became a little clearer. It is characteristic of that beautiful peninsula, with its clear light and warm colors, that the very outlines of human life seem to become simpler in its atmosphere. To go overnight from Paris to Florence was for me to confirm again all of Stendhal's perceptions about the difference between France and Italy: the world of Italian "energy" is no abstraction, you seem to breathe a biologic vitality in the air around you, and the stir of men and women walking in the street of the southern city surrounds you with a different rhythm and life of the senses that immediately takes you into itself. The rapidity of modern travel makes it easier to catch this first shock of recognition: later, for example, returning just as abruptly from Italy to France, I was overwhelmed by the homeliness of the French after the handsome race south of the Alps. In Italy too the relation between the sexes has a simpler outline. Italian women do not have the glaze or chic, the sexual *esprit* or wit, that you see in the prettier Parisiennes. Of a much more stoic and enduring race, they are slow, solid, and gentle in their movements; and with their rich warm color they suggest inevitably that hackneyed image—which however does not seem at all hackneyed while you watch them—of some ripe sunwarmed fruit of the earth. I used to tease the Francophile Abel by telling him, "To prefer the French-woman to the Italian woman is already the first step toward homo-sexuality." But I was serious too, for the separation of the woman from the earth, the bearing of fruit and the bearing of children, may be the first step toward transforming sex into sensation, a matter of *cuisine* and elegance, from which point on the invert appears only as another sauce, another variety, for taste. After the homosexual bohemia of Paris, Italy was like a bracing air, reviving one's faith in the beautiful possibilities of heterosexuality.

Against this Italian background the foreigners also show up more clearly in their true colors—or pigmentation. The English, with their straw hair and blanched color, stick out like sore thumbs —all elbows, haunched shoulders, and bad teeth. One senses the difference between races with color and without it—a connection possibly between pigmentation and passion. At any rate, the rich color of the Italians seems to be the visible emblem of their particular eroticism. And the Americans?

Away from the bohemians of Paris, I could scrutinize more carefully the face of the *ordinary* American traveler. I told myself that after all I had seen a rather special group in Paris; that they were Americans who had perhaps come abroad for just this reason, and therefore could hardly be taken as typical; that, moreover, most of these people were connected in some way with the arts, where a greater percentage of inverts is always found; etc. etc. I might thus have dismissed Paris altogether as the antics of a few adolescents except that now the face of middle-class America, against a foreign background, seemed to tell its own story. Nearly always a soft youthful face, it grows old by sagging, without ever seeming to show the harsh masculine lines of cheekbone and jawline: older Americans abroad look like the aged boys in comparison with their European contemporaries. Even the American Negro's face shows the same soft contours in comparison with the sculptural mask of the French Senegalese. Americans, it has been observed, are a race given over to soft drink and soft food: the greatest drinkers of milk, Mother's food, in the world, eaters of soft white doughy bread, ice cream, pie, and doughnuts. Soft foods and soft faces—perhaps it is this diet that shows in the facial contours. To be sure, it is nearly always an engaging face, but when you see it surrounded by the faces of other nations and look for the erotic line in it, it looks always a little boyish, therefore less masculine, and so slightly effeminate, and, one step further, pansy. The face of Alan Ladd, supposed to be the cold tight face of a ruthless killer, is a good example of this American face that can also be the pretty face of Mama's boy.

Physiognomy can be wrong, and sexual physiognomy particularly, but still one has to ask what it is that enables one to spot an American face so easily abroad. I remember spending three-quarters of an hour in an excursion train on just this question while examining a face that was just visible to me over the wooden bench in front, so that it was not by his clothes that I knew him as an American; and neither by his gestures nor speech, for he was alone. A good face, this old man's face, with its thatch of white hair, and with the decency and kindness in it that is also so American. But again it was the American boy-man, with old age displaying itself as the withered face of an adolescent. But there was also something else visible beneath the well-fed contours: the grey bleak Protestant lines that Grant Wood has painted in his "American Gothic." The American Gothic may belong for the most part to our past, but the residue of this past still seems to lie beneath the smooth middle-class features of the elderly American travelers, and even the Helen Hokinson lady, if she is not too fat, will show these pinched lines, at least when you see her against the background of Italy.

Nothing was more startling among the great flood of tourists than the number of grown young men traveling with their mothers, apparently content to pass nearly every waking moment in Mother's company, even while meeting the adventure of Europe. A typical pair were Gene and his mother, whom I met in a bus traveling through Tuscany. The bus itself was a slice of the respectable American middle class: mothers, daughters, sons, and maiden aunts; and it was with something of a shock that I heard this mincing voice from the back of the car saying, "I'll sit with Mother," as he offered his seat to a lady; and with the thought, "Well, here we go again," I turned around to see a nice-looking young man, with the soft American face, probably in his early thirties, and beside him his mother, a lady with the prim and tidy

lines of the American Gothic. When the bus stopped at an inn for
lunch, Gene and I were put at the same table, and we struck up a
conversation. He talked very readily, with the incessant flow of
trivialities that is supposed to characterize woman's chatter, and
before the trip was over I felt I knew nearly every detail in the
daily round of his life back home. Siena, Pisa, Lucca; the dusty
and beautiful landscape of Tuscany rolled by outside the window
while Gene's talk unrolled the cinema of his life in Schenectady,
N.Y., where he was surrounded by the middle-aged ladies, Mother's
friends, who came for tea or bridge. Mother and Mother's friends
—that seemed to be his life. Where was Father in all this? Father
must be dead, or the emotional equivalent. I wanted to ask but
checked myself, for it seemed almost unpleasant to suggest that
there had ever been a father. The son had long since taken the
place of the husband, and shared a common life with his mother
more intensely than most husbands do with their wives. When
one looked at Gene's mother, one could read in her bleak face the
need to convert the child into a husband to take the place of the
real husband with whom there had never been the satisfactions
of adult love. From time to time the bus would stop on the road,
and Gene would pop out to shoot something with his camera; it
gave me a funny feeling to see him standing there against the
Italian earth, as he manoeuvred for a shot, while a few peasants
might stop work to gawk gravely. I looked at Gene, raffish in his
seersucker jacket, flannel slacks, and white shoes, and then at the
grave and coppery peasants, and I thought, "Here is one of the
young virile race, conquerors of these ancient peoples," but I could
not think of him in any relation to that dunged and dry earth.
Then Gene would pop back into the American world of the bus,
which rolled on, and begin his chatter about how he developed his
own pictures at home, or what lovely concerts they had in Schenectady, and the musical club Mother belonged to that met once a
month at their house. I found myself suddenly thinking of those
ladies in Schenectady. How did they see Gene? In what terms did
they describe him to themselves? Probably they said no more than,
"Gene is not the marrying kind," accepting the fact, which must
remain unexplored for them, with the fatality of euphemism, and
perhaps adding with a pleasant coo, "He is so devoted to his

mother!" Would they ever dream of connecting a nice young man
like Gene with the bohemians of the Left Bank, if somehow these
ladies of Schenectady were able to catch a glimpse of the private life of the latter? The connection, nevertheless, exists, and
Americans will be compelled to make it more often as time goes
on.

I saw hundreds of Genes abroad, and have known many more
in this country, but he sticks in my mind for those few moments,
which seem to contain all his paradox, when he stood, a very
exotic plant indeed, against the Tuscan earth. Though the Italian
scene brings out details like this more clearly, it would be a mistake
to think that the Italian situation itself, the result of centuries of
adjustment, is not changing under the impact of modern life.
There are other traces of American penetration beside the Coca-
Cola signs that now dot the whole length of the Lido at Venice. An
American might think it a trivial matter that Italian women now
walk about publicly in slacks, but the ordinary Italian is alarmed
at this violation of a tradition, and as suspicious as an American
would be at a man wearing skirts in the streets of New York. Several Italians told me that there has been an enormous increase in
homosexuality throughout Italy. The Americanization of the globe,
it seems, is proceeding even on this front. Perhaps fastest of all
among the fashionable and chichi circles in Italy, who in fear of
the provinciality of Italian life have always sedulously aped the
reigning international set, which used to be the French and the
English, but now, with the Hollywood movie crowd all over Italy,
is definitely the Americans, and particularly the Americans of a
certain sex. It is depressing to think that a people might be willing
to give up one of its most attractive qualities for a fashion that
looks more glittering, modern, and cosmopolitan.

It is ironical too (something to make old Stendhal turn over
in his grave) that the American inverts show a special predilection
for Italy and that their colonies now dot the peninsula from the
Riviera down to Capri, where they have taken over. For me the
final and parting irony was that in Italy, of all places, I should become most aware of the internationally organized network of the
inverts' world. On my last evening in Venice I had dinner with
two young Americans, one of whom was flying back to America

the next day. Before the evening was out the two of them went into diligent consultation on the other side of the table from me, digging notebooks out of their pockets. I could catch only parts of what they said, but it was clear that the older of the two, a tall blond painter from Boston, was giving the other, a graduate student at Yale, some addresses in New York that the latter ought to look up when he got back. The blond explained that for these addresses it was worth making the brief trip from New Haven since he himself had found it worthwhile to come down from Boston for them. The young man from New Haven copied out a few addresses, turned a few more pages, then exclaimed: "But all these are positives! If you're positive, how is it you know only positives?" The blond cocked his head and let a broad grin play over his face: "Ah-ha, that's just it: it's the positives who know where all the negatives in the neighborhood are." Then pointing to the notebook: "Now these people really have their territories organized." At this moment he happened to catch my eye as I eavesdropped across the table, but his reaction seemed to be that I must feel neglected by all this attention to the other, for a little while later he came around the table to inquire solicitously where I was headed for tomorrow. When I told him I was returning to Paris, he advised me to look up a certain bar off the Champs Elysées. What would I find there, I wondered, and he told me that this bar kept a big book listing all the "gay" spots on the Continent. Anyone returning to Paris from a trip on which he has found a new "gay" café or bar writes it down in this book, with whatever comments will be useful to other travelers who intend to go to that part of the world. I was suddenly reminded of the Big Book at the various outposts of the American Express, where the travelers inscribe their names, addresses, and destinations, still maintaining all the threads of the tourist's social life while *en route*. Apparently, the fraternity of the gay is a network as carefully organized as the American Express, and, like the latter, now takes in the whole of Europe as its territory.

III

Back in Paris, the end of the summer seems already to have passed me by as I stare out mournfully at the grey weather that

enshrouds the city. It has been a grim season of drought for all of
Europe, and this is the first good rain I have encountered for
months, but I salute it dolefully for, as luck would have it, I lost
my raincoat moving around Europe and have just had a drenching.
I have to sit waiting by the window, damp in body, trying to dry
myself out with a blanket over my shoulders, and damp in soul
too, for though this weather brings out at first all the grey elegance
of Paris, its continuing murk begins to eat into one's mood like a
spiritual cancer. When Paris is grey, an Italian had warned me before I left Italy, it can drive one to madness. Beyond the block of
grey houses at which I am staring is another just like it, and beyond that and again beyond that a little house on the Ile St. Louis
with a plaque announcing that Charles Baudelaire once lived
there, and right now I feel just how he must have sat day after day,
trying to roll away the heavy stone of his *acedia*, staring out on
just such a grey Paris as this. When I try to review my summer, it
seems like a flickering of images that has passed me by while I
have really been sitting all the while in this room.

Actually I have been imprisoned here for only a day and a
half, waiting for the rain to stop, but that has been enough to
produce the illusion that the whole summer has stood still. Earlier
this evening there had been a break, but one which only intensified
this unreal feeling that amid the flux of travelers everything has
really stayed just where it was all summer. For this was dinner with
Kaplan and Abel again, and when I arrived, I found them in the
midst of the very same conversation: Literature as a scandal. A
summer has passed, they are still *hocking* the same *tcheinuk*, and
Michel Leiris' penis has not got any longer! I look around the
restaurant for the "married" couple that I had observed the last
time we were here, as if by the inexorable law that fixes all things
to their place they too should be sitting in exactly the same spot,
casting the same fond glances at each other and eating the same
dishes. But it turns out some things have changed, for Kaplan,
cheerful and expansive after his own vacation, breaks off the conversation with Abel, and begins to ask me about my own travels,
where have I been and what have I seen. When I tell him my
dominant impression, this time he becomes really interested.
"Somebody ought to say something about all this," he announces

decisively; then, after a moment of thought, looking at me: "Maybe you. You might write it up." I forgot to tell him that he has already given me the idea some time ago. I nod, "Perhaps. But if the subject were really done as it ought to be, the title should be 'The Botched Sexes.'"

On the way back from dinner, which broke up early, I got caught in another downpour, and having to strip, rub myself down, and dry out near this window, I begin to feel that I have not left this chair all day. Luckily I have stumbled upon a bottle of cognac that I had left here and forgotten about before my departure, and this begins to crawl warmly in my stomach now and drive away the dampness. The fog outside turns from grey to chocolate, and one by one the panes of light come on in the houses opposite, but I prefer my own darkness and do not switch on the light. Thanks to the cognac I am now quite warm; the heavy stone begins to roll away and my thoughts pick up a little life. But as soon as I begin to think it is not at all of Paris that I am thinking, nor even of the summer, but strangely of New York, and as vividly as if the silhouette of its skyline were projected against the wall of my darkened room.

I am neither a psychiatrist nor a sociologist, and I know that on a subject like this I am not even entitled to anything like a "theory"; but I have to put my ideas together if only to make a picture that will connect together my summer, Louis and Gene, Dick and Arthur, mothers and virgins, and connect them too with that brooding image of New York that I cannot now get out of my mind. It is only as such a picture, a moment of experience in a dark room at the end of a summer, worth whatever it may be, that I offer these ideas. Besides, as ideas they are not really new: the idea had often come to me when I stared up at the tall cliffs of apartment houses in Manhattan and thought of the fate of modern marriage in the metropolis, with all those couples locked up in their boxlike apartments, that America was in fact a vast human laboratory where the relations between the sexes were slowly being transformed for the rest of humanity. "America is a great experiment," Sigmund Freud said after his one visit to the United States, "but I do not think it will succeed." Success or not, the point is that, even more than an adventure in technology, America represents a vast sexual experiment, in the course of which it may have become an advance outpost in the evolution of the species.

No other society has ever pushed the struggle between the sexes so clearly into the open. You need only think how much of a staple the theme has become in the pages of *The New Yorker*, where urbanity usually forbids reference to the uglier realities, in order to realize the degree to which this struggle has already permeated the American mind. This is the one subject too on which *The New Yorker* (as in the cartoons of Thurber) has permitted its humor to be savage rather than gentle. And with good reason, I think, for nowhere else have I heard such bitter resentment toward women expressed by men as in New York, and none of them inverts; and nowhere else, either, so many complaints from the other sex that American men are unable to make their women happy.

Some years ago Thurber at last gave his theme a name in a series of cartoons actually entitled, "The War Between the Sexes," but at the conclusion he had the women rather surprisingly surrendering at Appomattox—perhaps because their victory would be still too shocking to most readers. The concensus, however, of nearly all his other cartoons, and of nearly all other witnesses, is that woman is really winning the war. Women already own seventy percent of the wealth and direct ninety percent of the purchasing power of America. And she has already won a more decisive victory in that crucial battle sector: the family. Since Mother has the leisure to attend lectures and read books, she appears as the font of wisdom at home, while Father is so absorbed in making a living for the family that he can only cut a ridiculous figure as a crude ignoramus. The young boy growing up in this atmosphere can nourish his natural Oedipal feelings with a generous dose of contempt. So he is given another great push to identify with Mother and to find her feminine role more interesting, attractive, and powerful. A few years later the young boy becomes a young man in a world where women are (just like his mother, but unfortunately not his mother) open and aggressive competitors. Already staggering under the burden of an excessive attachment to Mother, he is supposed to approach sexually these other females who compete with him in every field, and to play a masculine role toward them. The dénouement may be left to the reader's imagination.

Great waves of homosexuality have come and gone in the past, sometimes coinciding with exceptional levels of civilization, as in Greece, Florence, Elizabethan England; what is novel in the American situation is that the present wave has come in a culture where woman has been accorded an unprecedented status of equality, on the basis of which she has already moved ahead to secure dominance. We seem to be in transition to a matriarchy, and the present period may be only the temporary interregnum of maladjustment. Already in an enormous number of ways women in America have become more like men, and consequently men more like women—so that in certain circles of a metropolis like New York one can now see evolving before one's eyes a society of neuters, where men and women are, respectively, less masculine and less feminine in comparison with the couples of other nations and cultures.

The great experiment may fail, as Freud gloomily prophesied, but in the meantime one can still admire the American race in this new domain of its adventuring abroad. A nation of pragmatists, once possessed by Puritanism, has discovered the life of the senses, into which it flings itself with all of its traditional practical energies. Thus the American invert abroad hardly resembles his lukewarm British cousin. Having spent some time during the War with British Army officers, I gave up after a while the game of guessing who was and was not an invert, for the final difference did not seem to be very great after all. The American in his energetic naiveté seems to know, what the jaded Briton ignores, that when the attraction to the other sex is so tepid, the game is not worth the candle, and one might as well "switch" and have fun. The Paris police may well be alarmed, for these young Americans in all the innocent pragmatism of their race are determined to take ancient Sodom by storm.

Here is a new chapter in the history of the traditionally corrupt image that Europe has always represented for the American. In Henry James' *The Ambassadors* the dreadful thing—too awful for James to come out and state it flatly—that chains young Newsome to Europe is an affair with a European woman. The wheel has turned, even if it has not yet come full circle. The American mother who fears that her son, drifting about in Europe on the

G.I. Bill, may be seduced by some European hussy, is no longer up-to-date. Mother, that boy of yours loitering along the European dockside at evening, gazing out at the water and apparently lost in reflection, has his eye peeled, not for the poor drab who winks vainly at him from the quay, but for the pretty young sailor boy of his dreams who just at this moment may be descending from the boat out there in the twilit harbor.

Contributors

MANNY FARBER was for many years movie critic for *The Nation*.

MILTON KLONSKY is a young poet and critic. His work has appeared in *Hudson Review* and *Partisan Review*, among other places.

SEYMOUR KRIM has published fiction and criticism in various literary magazines. He is the editor of two short-story anthologies.

DON J. HAGER is Research Director for the American Jewish Congress.

BERNARD WOLFE is the author with Mezz Mezzrow of *Really the Blues*, and two novels, *Limbo* and *The Late Risers*.

HEINZ POLITZER teaches at Bryn Mawr College.

NORMAN PODHORETZ is a graduate of Columbia University. His criticism has appeared frequently in *Commentary*.

ELIZABETH HARDWICK writes fiction and criticism for the literary magazines, and is the author of the novel *The Ghostly Lover*.

ANATOLE BROYARD is an advertising executive.

LIONEL TRILLING's latest book is *The Opposing Self*.

HARVEY SWADOS is the author of the novel *Out Went the Candle*.

MARSHALL MC LUHAN teaches at the University of Toronto.

ARNOLD W. GREEN teaches sociology at Pennsylvania State University.

DAVID T. BAZELON taught at Bard College for a while and also published reviews and criticism in the *New Republic* and *Partisan Review*. He is now a lawyer.

ROBERT WARSHOW was working on a book about the movies when he died.

REUEL DENNY teaches sociology at The University of Chicago. He worked for *Time* and *Fortune* for several years.

WILLIAM S. POSTER formerly was an editor on *The American Mercury*. His criticism and poetry have appeared in several magazines.

HAROLD ROSENBERG works for the Advertising Council in New York.

WELDON KEES is a poet, painter, and musician.

The late MR. WOLPERT taught at the University of Buffalo.

ARTHUR SCHLESINGER, Jr., is the author of *The Age of Jackson*. His latest book, written with Quincy Howe, is *Guide to Poetics*.

CLEMENT GREENBERG is an associate editor on *Commentary*. He was art critic of *The Nation* for a long time and is also the author of a book on Miró.

WILLIAM BARRETT is an editor of *Partisan Review*, and also teaches philosophy at New York University.

Date Due